OF SPEECH AND TIME
Temporal Speech Patterns in Interpersonal Contexts

Edited by
ARON W. SIEGMAN
STANLEY FELDSTEIN
UNIVERSITY OF MARYLAND BALTIMORE COUNTY

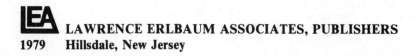 LAWRENCE ERLBAUM ASSOCIATES, PUBLISHERS
1979   Hillsdale, New Jersey

DISTRIBUTED BY THE HALSTED PRESS DIVISION OF
JOHN WILEY & SONS
New York   Toronto   London   Sydney

106650

Copyright© 1979 by Lawrence Erlbaum Associates, Inc.
All rights reserved. No part of this book may be reproduced in
any form, by photostat, microform, retrieval system, or any other
means, without the prior written permission of the publisher.

Lawrence Erlbaum Associates, Inc., Publishers
365 Broadway
Hillsdale, New Jersey 07642

Distributed solely by Halsted Press Division
John Wiley & Sons, Inc., New York

Library of Congress Cataloging in Publication Data

Main entry under title:
Of speech and time.

Contains the papers presented at a symposium held at
the University of Louisville, in May of 1976.
Includes bibliographies and indexes.
1. Psycholinguistics—Congresses. 2. Time—
Congresses. 3. Language acquisition—Congresses.
4. Interpersonal communication—Congresses.
I. Siegman, Aron Wolfe. II. Feldstein, Stanley,
1930-
P37.035   401'.9   79-17403
ISBN 0-470-26831-X

Printed in the United States of America

To Our Parents,
Wives, and Children

106650

100630

Contents

Preface

The Lord God formed man from the dust of the earth,
and He blew into his nostrils the breath of life,
and man became a living being.
—(Genesis 2:7)

Targum Onkelos, an ancient Aramaic translation of the Bible,
renders "the breath of life" as the "power of speech."

In May of 1976, an interdisciplinary conference called "Perspectives on Language" was held at the University of Louisville (Louisville, Kentucky). Part of the conference was a symposium ("Temporal Aspects of Speech and Conversation") concerned with the temporal patterning of speech, mostly—although not entirely—within the context of interpersonal exchanges. The purpose of the symposium was to present a cross section of the research then being conducted in the area, and its contributions ranged from theoretical notions about the origin of language to the time patterns that characterize the development of speech and to relationships between the pacing of adult conversations and self-reported personality attributes. Indeed, it seemed to us that the contributions were sufficiently important and provocative to warrant their publication in the form of a monograph.

This book, then, contains the papers presented at the symposium. However, in order to broaden its sampling of the research even further, we invited a number of other scholars to contribute reports of their own research to the collection. They are Drs. Beebe, Stern, Beattie, Brotherton, Butterworth, and Goldman-Eisler, the authors of Chapters 1, 6, 8, and 9, respectively. We are indebted to them for accepting our invitation.

Yet in spite of its breadth, the book cannot claim to provide a comprehensive survey of current theories and findings about temporal speech patterns. Although those researchers who have a programmatic interest in the investigation of such patterns form a relatively small group, their number seems to be increasing steadily. We believe, however, that the chapters represent major directions that research in the area has taken.

The book is intended as a reader for all those who are intrigued by the possibility that time as a dimension of speech reflects many of the important processes that occur during the production of speech. In addition, it can very well serve as a supplementary text in courses on psycholinguistics and human (particularly nonverbal and paralinguistic) communication. Finally, we hope that the contents of the book will spur even further explorations of the chronography of speech.

Although it is apparently *de rigueur* to refrain from acknowledging the helpfulness of one's publisher, we should like to note with much gratitude the constructive patience, suggestions, and support of Ms. Judith Abrams of Lawrence Erlbaum Associates throughout the publication process of the book. We are also grateful to Ms. Madelon Kellough, whose secretarial skills helped us through many drafts.

ARON W. SIEGMAN
STANLEY FELDSTEIN

Introduction

The notion that time is an integral dimension of speech is not especially new or surprising. Speech is emitted in linear strings, or sequences, of sounds and silences. Each "sound" is not necessarily a word; it may be a vocal segregate ("mm-hmm"), or it may in fact be part of a word. More commonly, a sound will comprise several words that are not separated by any silence that can be detected by the human ear. In any case, each sound follows a silence and each silence a sound, and it is this succession of events that, in part, allows for a perception of the sequence as "occupying" or "taking up" time (Fraisse, 1963). Moreover, each sound and each silence, as well as the entire sequence, has a certain measurable duration, which is the amount of time it "takes up."

What is perhaps surprising is that the durations of these events, particularly (although not only) the silences and particularly within the context of a two-person exchange, seem to be related systematically to a number of interesting psychological states and processes. Some silences, of course, are a consequence of the structure of the organs used for speech production and of the type of language spoken. For example, since in occidental languages the inspiration of air is not used for the production of sounds, some of the silences can be shown to be breathing pauses. Other silences are related at least in part to the syntactic structure of the language. However, part of these silences and certainly other nonsyntactic silences are thought to reflect cognitive processes and/or affective states of the speaker. Moreover, the durations of the silences, as well as of the sounds and combinations of the two events, appear to be associated with certain personality characteristics attributed to speakers by listeners and by the speakers themselves.

1

Most research concerned with the temporal dimension of speech has looked at factors that influence the durations and frequencies of speech sounds and silences. Increasing efforts are being made, however, to determine whether such factors as well as others also affect the *patterning* of the sound–silence sequences and possibly the locations of the silences with respect to the syntactic and semantic dimensions of the speech.

The chapters of this book address themselves to a variety of issues that are relevant to the timing of speech in monologues and dialogues. Some of the issues are familiar; others involve newly emerging concerns such as the developmental progression of the temporal patterns and the possibility that the mere occurrence of a conversational interaction is partly under biorhythmical control. All the issues are potentially important contributors to the current attempt to integrate the temporal dimension of speech within the framework of a more general psychological heuristic.

The book is divided into three parts. The first one consists of three chapters that have to do with the biology and development of the time patterns of speech. At first blush, the chapter by Beebe, Stern, and Jaffe entitled, "The Kinesic Rhythms of Mother–Infant Interactions," may seem to be an inappropriate inclusion. It is based, however, upon the intriguing notion that "the distinction between vocal and kinesic acts is less compelling in infancy than later in development [p. 23]." The study is clearly exploratory. Indeed, it is a frame-by-frame analysis of 2,880 frames of a continuous interaction of only one mother and her 4-month-old infant. And the 2,880 frames last only 2 minutes of real time!

Within the 2 minutes of their sample, the authors examined the patterning of two kinds of events. One is called a "coactive episode," a period during which the mother and infant are simultaneously engaged in kinesic behavior. The other type is a "noncoactive episode," during which the behaviors of the mother and infant do not overlap. Two other events that are important to the analysis of mother–infant interaction are "behavioral pauses" and "onset-to-onset times." A behavioral pause is an interval of time during which no kinesic behavior occurs that is codable within the authors' system. Onset-to-onset time begins with the initiation of behavior by the mother and ends with the initiation of behavior by the infant ("infant onset time"), or it begins with the initiation of the infant's behavior and ends with the initiation of the mother's behavior ("maternal onset time").

These parameters that are used to describe the temporal patterning of the mother–infant interaction are similar, topologically at least, to some of those Jaffe and Feldstein (1970) propose to describe the temporal patterning of conversation (see also Chapter 4 of this book). A behavioral silence or pause is comparable to a speech pause, an onset time is similar to a speaking turn, and a coactive episode is similar to simultaneous speech. In fact, the authors discovered that their temporal analysis of the kinesic behavior of the mother–infant pair yielded patterns that are quite similar to the temporal patterns of the vocal interactions of mothers and infants (Stern, Jaffe, Beebe, & Bennett, 1977). They also found that in noncoactive episodes, the mother and infant tended to match the durations of their kinesic rhythms, a phenomenon similar to the achievement of congruence in adult conversations (Feldstein & Welkowitz, 1978). Thus, the authors suggest that both the coactive and noncoactive vocal and kinesic patterns can be seen as the temporal precursors of later adult conversational patterns, that indeed the patterns might be considered "protoconversation."

The issue that concerns Beebe and her associates is viewed in more fundamental terms by Jaffe and Anderson in their Prescript to Chapter 1. They consider briefly the role of gesture in the evolution of language and, more specifically, the gestural-communicative hypothesis of speech origins. In discussing evidence relevant to the hypothesis, they especially note the importance of *"the capacity for rhythmic entrainment in social communication* [p. 20, original italics]" and speculate that "human communication is based on an evolved capacity for the acquisition, use, and elaboration of rhythmically structured gestural systems [p. 21]." To a great extent, their discussion provides the theoretical justification for including Chapter 1 in a book about speech.

The second chapter in this section is by Sabin, Clemmer, O'Connell, and Kowal, who have been studying pausing behavior in their laboratory at St. Louis University. The chapter is concerned with developmental changes in speech rate (computed in syllables per sec) and duration of silent or unfilled pauses and their frequency. The developmental picture presented is based on a series of 12 studies conducted over 8 years by the same investigators using the same procedures. This integration of many studies makes it possible to present data from 880 subjects representing a wide range of ages (6 to 49 years) and educational levels (kindergarten to college professors). It is important to specify the tests that were used in these studies, since it has been repeatedly established by these and other investigators that the nature of the task influences pausing patterns. The descriptive data presented in this paper are based on three main types of speech tasks: (a) readings of prose poetry; (b) retellings of prose readings; and (c) spontaneous narratives based on a sequence of cartoon pictures. Significant successive increases in speech rate were found between kindergarten and second grade, between second and fourth grade, and between sixth and eighth grade. However, a decrease in speech rate was noted between high school seniors and college seniors. "The general developmental pattern of increasing speech rate from early childhood to a peak rate in adolescence documents the greater fluency evident in the speech of preadolescents and adolescents. The decline in speech rate following adolescence can be interpreted as the gradual development of reflective and rhetorical dimensions of adult speech [p. 40]." Essentially, similar findings were obtained with the other two indices, duration and frequency of pauses, except that the rate of change seemed to vary as a function of the hesitation index and the task. Thus, the *frequency* of silent pauses dropped dramatically between childhood and preadolescence for the reading task and much less so for the narrative task, but no such discrepancy occurred in relation to the duration of silent pauses. On the basis of this and other findings, the authors suggest that: "In the most general sense, the length of unfilled pauses is related to cognition and frequency of unfilled pauses to linguistic skill [p. 51]." This is of interest, because in his studies on the effects of cognition on hesitation phenomena (Chapter 7), Siegman repeatedly found that the duration of silent pauses is a much more sensitive index of cognition than their frequency: in some studies, he actually dropped the latter measure from the array of pausing indices on the assumption that it is not very sensitive to experimental manipulations. This is obviously not the case, and the sensitivity of the different pausing indices may very well depend on the nature of the experimental manipulation. The authors, however, quite prudently point out that "since the category of frequency subsumes location, the specific locations of unfilled pauses and vocal hesitations should receive additional attention in future research [p. 51]." For example, the increase in pausing that seems to occur between adolescence and adulthood, and which the authors attribute to "increased levels of expressive interpretation" on the part of the adults, may not be indiscriminately distributed. In fact, in reporting that literary scholars used a greater number of unfilled pauses when reading poetry than do other adults, the authors point out that "they locate more of them between rather than within syntactic units or words." It is becoming increasingly clear that increases or decreases in pausing can assume a different meaning depending on their location. A detailed analysis of pause location is the major focus of Dr. Brotherton's chapter later in the book.

An interesting feature of the chapter is the "built-in" cross-validation studies. Similar developmental curves were obtained for both German- and American-speaking groups. Moreover, within adult groups, variations in pausing as a function of proficiency level in a foreign language are analogous to the developmental pausing curve.

The authors indicate that these various findings are most parsimoniously accounted for within a cognitive framework. "The writings of Goldman-Eisler (1968) have provided the fundamental hypothesis that temporal aspects of speech behavior systematically reflect underlying cognitive processes. More specifically, pause and rate phenomena reflect processes involved in the generation of information [p. 36]."

Chapter 3 by Hayes and Cobb reports a unique effort to explore the possibility that the conversations of a pair of individuals recur in relatively predictable cycles throughout the waking day. The hypothesis of the study is that the length of the cycles is in part determined by an endogenous timing mechanism, that the cycles represent a biorhythmic activity similar to the REM cycles of sleep and the larger sleep–wakefulness cycle. Indeed, the authors suggest that all of these rhythms may be related, that "there is one latent biorhythm underlying all of these manifestations [p. 58]."

The notion that the rhythms of social interactions may be biological in nature was proposed earlier by Chapple (1970), who views such rhythms as part of a larger biological pattern of action and nonaction cycles. He believes that biological rhythms are the critical regulators of human functioning, "From the individual cell and its metabolic processes, . . . to a man as the total organism." He asserted (1970) that "Their significance lies in the fact that they provide what might be called the engines which drive behavior and its physiological components; they are the source of the spontaneity which the need to respond to the external environment may tend to conceal [p. 10]."

The data obtained by Hayes and Cobb seem to reveal three conversational cycles of 46, 91, and 183 minutes. They also suggest that the cycles are apt to be easily perturbed—as are other biorhythms—by a host of environmental events and demands as well as by some cognitive states of the participants. The authors discuss the possibility that even the perturbations of the circadian sleep–wakefulness cycle revealed by their data may contribute indirectly to the destabilization of the conversational cycle.

The authors are properly cautious about interpreting the data as firm proof of the existence of a conversational cycle. The data are, however, more than suggestive. Indeed, the existence of such a cycle is also intimated by independent findings. Martin (1972) has provided evidence for a model of the rhythmic structure of monologues. Support for the rhythmic patterning of dialogues has been offered by Jaffe and Feldstein (1970), although—unlike the proposal of Hayes and Cobb—the patterning occurs at a microlevel within dialogues. Thus, the notion that there is an underlying periodicity to the recurrence of dialogues seems quite reasonable. Although Hayes and Cobb do not discuss directly the implications of their results, one important implication concerns the meaning of conversation. It is usually assumed that the raison d'être of a conversation is its function as an information-exchange process. The finding of conversational periodicity, however, strongly suggests that simply the occurrence of conversation, whatever its content may be, satisfies a biological need.

Part II of the book examines some of the ways in which the temporal patterning of speech is affected by personality characteristics and interpersonal or, more broadly, social interaction. Chapter 4, the first chapter of the section, is concerned with personality attributes. In it, Feldstein, Alberti, and BenDebba explore the "possibility that the timing of an individual's participation in a dialogue may be related to those characteristics he or she attributes to him- or herself [p. 73]." Moreover, they explore the possibility that such timing may also be related to the self-attributed characteristics of their conversational partners. The characteristics are those measured by the *Sixteen Personality Factor Questionnaire* (Cattell, Eber, & Tatsuoka, 1970).The timing is measured not simply in terms of pauses but in terms of all (but one) of those parameters that comprise the temporal structure of dialogues, i.e., *pauses, switching pauses, vocalizations,* and *speaking turns.* Thus, the data are derived from the relatively "natural" conversations in which the participants in the study engaged.

The results seem reasonably in line with what might be intuitively expected. For example, speakers who were "reserved, cold, suspicious, insecure, and tense" were apt to have the longer pauses. Longer vocalizations, on the other hand, tended to be produced by persons whose description of themselves could be characterized by such terms as "warmhearted, outgoing, assertive," etc. Perhaps most interesting is the finding that the relation between the speaker's personality characteristics and the temporal parameters decreased from vocalizations to pauses to switching pauses to speaking turns; the average duration of speaking turns was related only to the characteristics of the listener.

The authors note that all their participants were women and, therefore, that the relationships they uncovered may be different for men.

The second chapter in this section, "The Voice of Attraction: Vocal Correlates of Interpersonal Attraction in the Interview" by Siegman, is probably more directly pertinent than any other chapter in the book to the social psychology of pausing behavior. It examines the assumption that different social relations are associated with different pausing patterns. Bernstein's (1964) theory that different temporal patterns characterize middle-class speech as opposed to lower-class speech attracted wide attention during the early sixties, not only among sociologists and linguists but also among educators. Considerable excitement was generated by Bernstein's claim that these differences reflect fundamental class differences in the speech-encoding process, with the middle class relying largely on elaborated codes and the lower class on restricted codes. This hypothesis is examined by Brotherton in a later chapter. Her data led her to conclude that social class differences do not reflect different linguistic competencies.

To return to Siegman's chapter, he reports a series of studies, all conducted within the context of the initial interview, that suggest that the conversations of people who like each other and who are attracted to each other are characterized by shorter pauses than the conversations of people who do not share such positive feelings. According to Siegman, this relationship is cognitively mediated: "Interviewees who do not like their interviewer are likely to be more guarded in what they say, and to engage in more self-monitoring than those who feel at ease with their interviewer [p. 110]." Interestingly enough, this interpretation suggests that where attraction produces an increase in self-monitoring—for example, intense attraction in opposite-gender dyads—it is likely to be associated with an increase rather than a decrease in pausing. The same would be true wherever interpersonal attraction is likely to be threatening or anxiety provoking.

The strong inverse link between interpersonal attraction and the duration of within-response silent pauses leads Siegman to advocate the use of pausing indices as dependent variables in attraction studies. It is pointed out that the advantage of pausing indices as measures of interpersonal attraction is not only their unobtrusive nature but also that they allow for the monitoring of changes in attraction levels over time.

Although the participants in the three experiments described by Beattie in Chapter 6 all engage in monologues, Beattie's ultimate concern is with the influence of social interaction on the temporal patterning of speech. "The most striking implication of these studies is that in conversation, when listeners attend to what is said, and signal their continued attention and interest therein, they may, unwittingly, and unbeknown to the speaker, be determining the temporal organization of the spoken message [p. 144]."

This concern with the modifiability of temporal structure is translated into an investigation of the pauses within speech. Beattie takes issue with the notion that *all* unfilled pauses are used for the cognitive planning involved in lexical selection, clause construction, and ideational content. To this deliberately strong cognitive hypothesis, he poses the possibility that there is an as yet undetermined proportion of unfilled pauses that represents a class of "socially conditioned" silences that reflect other processes. To test this possibility, he uses an operant conditioning paradigm with the expectation that if the possibility is viable, changes in the rate and distribution of pauses ought not to affect adversely the semantic content of speech in which they are embedded.

The results of the first experiment do not support the notion of a class of noncognitive pauses, although they do demonstrate that rate of pausing can be changed. The second study compared a storytelling task with a story-retelling task in terms of the modifiability of their temporal structure. The findings of that study indicate that the pause rate involved in the retelling of a story is significantly more susceptible to systematic, external influence than that involved in the composition of a story.

It is in the third study that Beattie most closely approaches the question of whether the temporal structure of speech can be affected within the context of a natural speaking situation. However, the greater "naturalness" of the situation in the third study simply means that the appropriate reinforcement is delivered by a person rather than by a machine. In addition, auditory ("good") and visual (head nods) reinforcers are used in order to evaluate their relative efficacy. The results suggest that a visual reinforcer may be more effective than an auditory one in influencing pause rate.

Taken together, the findings of the three studies indicate that the pause rates and distributions of at least certain types of speech can indeed be modified by reward and punishment, whether mechanical or social. They do not, however, provide any clear information about whether all pauses serve cognitive functions or whether some of them reflect noncognitive processes. On the other hand, the strong cognitive hypothesis to which Beattie takes exception is probably more useful as a foil than as a serious expectation unless the definition of cognitive processes is made exceedingly broad.

The three chapters constituting the final section of this book ("Hesitation, Cognition, and Speech Production") deal in a general way with silent pauses and other hesitation phenomena in speech as indicators of cognition and information processing that take place at the time of the pausing or the hesitation and, more specifically, with pauses and hesitations as clues to the process of speech production.

As pointed out by Siegman in Chapter 7, it was Goldman-Eisler's programmatic research on pausing that produced a "new look in pausing research. Prior to that work, silent pauses, and certainly filled pauses, were perceived as similar to the speech disturbances studied by Mahl (1956), as "extralinguistic" phenomena that disrupt the normal flow of speech. Typically, such pauses were attributed to some affective process that was believed to interfere with the speech-encoding task, and to some extent this approach is not totally absent even in Goldman-Eisler's early publications. However, as a result of her two classical experiments, the one on the predictability of words following silent pauses and the one that used the *New Yorker* cartoons, a cognitive heuristic slowly but unmistakably began replacing the earlier motivational framework, not only in her own work but also in that of others. It should be pointed out that Maclay and Osgood's (1959) now classical paper concerned with hesitation phenomena in speech appeared at about the same time, and it, too, undoubtedly contributed to this new cognitive approach to pausing research. The important change that occurred as a result of these studies is that silent pauses were no longer considered extraneous intrusions but were viewed as intrinsic to the speech production process and thus as a necessary consideration in any conceptual model of that process.

The findings obtained by Goldman-Eisler in her cartoon study as well as the data obtained in her earlier experiments on the predictability of words following silent pauses in the speaker provided her with the basic elements for a model of speech production, the process in which our "intention of saying a thing" becomes transformed or encoded in words. In her cartoon study, she distinguishes between an initial pause—which is the silent pause before the subject begins the description of the interpretation of a cartoon—and a within-sentence pause—the latter being somewhat of a misnomer since the word *sentence* in the name apparently refers to an individual's complete response whether it involves part of a grammatical sentence or several of them. At any rate, on the basis of earlier findings that silent pauses precede words of low predictability, the within-sentence pauses are attributed to lexical decision making. On the other hand, the initial pauses are attributed primarily to the general planning of content. A very similar model is presumed for all spontaneous speech: Relatively long initial pauses are devoted primarily to semantic planning, whereas subsequent within-sentence pauses reflect lexical choices.

Each of the chapters in this section focuses on some aspect of Goldman-Eisler's theory about the role of silent pauses and other hesitation phenomena in the speech production process.

Siegman's chapter, "Cognition and Hesitation in Speech," summarizes three separate studies: One replication of Goldman-Eisler's cartoon study and two extensions or conceptual replications of Goldman-Eisler's findings. The results of the replication study provide a striking confirmation of Goldman-Eisler's original findings. They are striking in that the actual pausing values for cartoon descriptions versus interpretations in this most recent study closely approximate those reported by Goldman-Eisler, despite the quite disparate subject populations and the different procedures that were used to obtain the pausing values.

The findings of the remaining two studies reported in this chapter, which were designed to test the generality of the results obtained in the cartoon studies—a most crucial question if the results of the latter are to serve as a model of the speech production process—were somewhat more ambiguous with regard to Goldman-Eisler's position than were the results of the cartoon study. The second study compared the participants' descriptions and stories of TAT cards. The stories were associated with significantly longer initial delays than the descriptions, but there was no significant difference between the two tasks in relation to within-response silent pauses. These findings present no particular difficulty to Goldman-Eisler's position if we are willing to make the not unreasonable assumption that the two tasks differed primarily in complexity of semantic planning but not in lexical decision making.

The third study looked at the effects of asking subjects to formulate their thoughts as concisely and economically as possible on their pausing behavior—in this particular situation, within the context of formulating the moral or meaning of *New Yorker* cartoons. In this study, the additional constraint on the participants' information-processing load increased their within-response pauses but not their initial pauses. Again, these findings present no particular difficulty for Goldman-Eisler's position if we are willing to make the assumption that the additional cognitive load consisted primarily of lexical decision making rather than semantic planning. By and large, then, the results of all three studies reported by Siegman are consistent with Goldman-Eisler's position on the role of silent pauses in the speech production process.

If there is a challenge in these data to Goldman–Eisler's position, it is the finding that some subjects who were instructed to speak concisely and economically did so without any evidence of increased pausing over and above their normal pausing patterns. True, in this study, the investigators did not look at other hesitation indices besides silent pauses, some of which may have been affected by the experimental manipulation. Alternatively, perhaps it is after all possible to engage in cognitive activity while simultaneously generating new speech sequences, albeit within certain limits, namely, relatively brief utterances. Precisely such a hypothesis is also suggested by Brotherton in the next chapter.

Brotherton examines Goldman-Eisler's model of speech production in light of data obtained in an interview study. An important feature of this study is that the silent pauses are identified in terms of their location: at the beginning of an utterance (which is defined as the interviewee's response to the interviewer's question), at clause boundaries, and within clause boundaries. Some of these silences are linked to a single lexical item, whereas others could conceivably involve planning at a level lower than the clause but higher than the single word. Another important feature of this chapter is that the author did not limit herself to an analysis of silent pauses but performed an analogous analysis for filled pauses, such as "ahs," "ums," and similar expressions; it should be pointed out, however, that these were completely separate analyses, i.e., the author did not treat the filled and unfilled pauses as alternate forms of hesitation. Finally, in each analysis the data are presented separately for middle-class and lower-class respondents. This part of the analysis, however, should be viewed with some caution, since only five persons participated in each socio-economic group.

The author reports that a number of complete utterances were found to have no measured pauses of any kind, filled or unfilled, before or after them. Nevertheless, the author concludes that: "It would be premature to draw the conclusion that unfilled pauses are not, after all, a systematic accompaniment of speech, for there were only five instances of complete utterances consisting of three or more clauses in length, and where no pauses of any kind were present. This strongly suggests that there is some limit to the number of clauses which can be produced as a complete utterance without benefit of pauses [p. 191]." Considering the brevity of these utterances, it is of course possible that some planning occurred in the short silent pauses that did not meet the 250-sec criterion cutoff point. Alternatively, and contrary to Goldman-Eisler, cognitive planning, even of a complex nature, may not always require the suspension of speech. The two may occur simultaneously within the limits of a relatively brief speech sequence.

Perhaps the greatest challenge in Brotherton's data to the Goldman-Eisler model of speech production is the finding that individuals frequently launched into sustained passages of speech without initial pausing. In fact, this was the case in about one-fourth of all long utterances. The author concludes that "the suspension of speech is not a *necessary* condition for the planning of speech sequences in the way envisaged by Goldman-Eisler." One wonders, however, whether there were any filled pauses associated with these speech sequences in the initial pause position. If there were, they may have served the planning function otherwise served by silent pauses. Brotherton, however, takes the position that initial delays are not necessary for speech production. Nevertheless, although long utterances can be commenced without an initial response pause, they cannot be sustained without clause-boundary pauses, which then serve a planning function related to the semantic intention of the speaker.

Brotherton also rejects Boomer's (1965, 1978) position that the clause is the basic unit of the encoding process, partly because 68% of all clause transitions were fluent. Brotherton, therefore, rejects the suggestion of isomorphism between the clause and the pause; "far too many within-clause pauses and far too many clauses without detectable pauses are found for this to be a sensible construction [p. 194]." Instead, the data suggest that unfilled pauses generally represent semantic planning points. Although the representation of meaning may be realized in segments that are shorter than the clause, they are most often realized in segments that are longer. This view, like that of Goldman-Eisler (1968), could be said to place the major planning focus in speech production on "ideas" and the associated time required for their formulation.

The third and final chapter in this section is by Butterworth and Goldman-Eisler and provides empirical evidence in support of the revised version of Goldman-Eisler's original speech production model. The original version, which is the version that has been examined thus far, is based on the assumption that unfilled pauses reflect information processing that takes place at the time of the hesitation and involves the immediately following verbal output or, in Boomer's (1970) terms, proximal decisions.

As has been pointed out earlier in these introductory remarks, the existence of fluent runs free from silent pauses (and presumably other hesitations) presents an embarrassment to the proximal planning model if one assumes, as Goldman-Eisler does, that the generation of new speech must take place in real time and requires the suspension of ongoing speech. In order to cope with this challenge and on the basis of the observation that spontaneous speech frequently consists of alternating periods of hesitant and fluent speech, Goldman-Eisler proposes a two-phased speech production process consisting of a planning phase and an execution phase (Goldman-Eisler, 1968). According to this model, the pauses during the hesitant phase reflect not only "proximal" decision making—semantic and lexical choices for local concurrent speech—but also "distal" decision making—semantic choices for the succeeding fluent utterance (Goldman-Eisler, 1968, p. 82). As pointed out by Rochester (1973), this view of linguistic planning is appealing for at least two reasons:

> On the one hand, it suggests units of speech production which are functional rather than structural in nature, i.e., units based on cognitive activity rather than on linguistic analysis which may or may not be relevant to encoding

processes. On the other hand, it suggests a possible series of hierarchies of decisions which might go into the composition of these large, functional units. Where the units themselves may reflect semantic decisions, they might include several smaller units of structural and lexical choices [p. 62].

That spontaneous speech consists of cycles of hesitant speech followed by fluent speech was first proposed in a paper by Henderson, Goldman-Eisler, and Skarbek (1966) and in a follow-up paper by Goldman-Eisler (1967). In "eye-balling" cumulative graphs of periods of vocalizations and silent pauses, they seemed to observe that periods of long pauses and short vocalizations alternate with periods of long vocalizations and little pausing. They proceeded to fit straight lines to these phases in order to demonstrate the alternating pattern of steep "hesitant" slopes with shallow "fluent" slopes. Jaffe and his associates, however, have questioned the existence of such patterns. They argue that in any sequence of random events, "runs" will occur, and by arbitrary inspection we can always find subsequences, which will give the appearance of a definite pattern. In support of their claim, they have shown that random sequences of sound–silence durations generated by computer show the same pattern postulated by Henderson et al. (1966). According to Jaffe and his associates, then, the cycle of hesitant speech followed by fluent speech as postulated by Goldman-Eisler may very well be no more than an artifact (Jaffe, Breskin, & Gerstman, 1972; Schwartz & Jaffe, 1968).

It is to this issue that the chapter by Butterworth and Goldman-Eisler addresses itself. They reject the artifact hypothesis on the grounds that the hypothesized phases can be shown to have empirical correlates. They cite previous data and the results of three new studies in support of their claim that these phases represent psycholinguistically meaningful units.

In the first of the three new studies, they analyze the locations of silent pauses in the hesitant or planning phases versus the fluent or execution phases. They identify three classes of silent pauses: (a) at clause boundaries, (b) before unpredictable words, and (c) "other" pauses. It turns out that the duration of "other" pauses is longer and constitutes half of the pause time in the planning phases, whereas in execution phases, three-quarters of the pause time is located at clause boundaries or before unpredictable words. It is argued that these findings are consistent with the claim that in execution phases, pauses have essentially a local function—to make word choices or to mark clause boundaries—but that in planning phases, both local and forward planning is carried out.

In the second study, further evidence is derived from a study of speech-focused movements. A subclass of SFMs—gestures—are differently distributed in planning and execution phases. In the former, they are less frequent and their onset tends to coincide with the onset of phonation: in the latter, their onset tends to coincide with pauses and thus to precede the words they are associated with. The authors infer that gestures reflect the making of lexical choices, and in the execution phase a semantic specification of the word required is available before the word itself.

In the final study, the relationship between gaze and planning is investigated. Planning should leave less time and processing capacity available for other functions (for example, monitoring the behavior of the listener). It turns out that looking at the listener relatively frequently during planning phases interferes with the organization of the speech.

Elsewhere, Boomer (1970) has taken Goldman-Eisler to task for introducing the distal model of speech production without making explicit that it represents a major shift from, if not an outright contradiction to, the earlier proximal model. However, perhaps the two can be reconciled if we keep in mind Goldman-Eisler's distinction between semantic planning and lexical decisions. Semantic planning, which according to Goldman-Eisler takes place during initial delays and perhaps also at clause boundaries and between major surface-structure phrase boundaries as suggested by Brotherton, may very well involve proximal as well as distal planning. On the other hand, lexical decision making is likely to be proximal in nature. After all, the major support for a proximal model comes from Goldman-Eisler's studies on the predictability of *words* following silent pauses, that is to say, decisions involving lexical choices.

REFERENCES

Bernstein, B. Elaborated and restricted codes. Their social origins and some consequences. *American Anthropologist,* 1964, *66* (Part II), 55–64.

Boomer, D. S. Hesitation and grammatical encoding. *Language and Speech,* 1965, *8,* 148–158.

Boomer, D. S. Review of F. Goldman–Eisler, Psycholinguistics: Experiments in spontaneous speech. *Lingua,* 1970, *25,* 152–164.

Boomer, D. S. The phonemic clause: Speech unit in human communication. In A. W. Siegman & S. Feldstein (Eds.), *Nonverbal behavior and communication.* Hillsdale, N.J.: Lawrence Erlbaum Associates, 1978.

Cattell, R. B., Eber, H. W., & Tatsuoka, M. M. *Handbook for the Sixteen Personality Factor Questionnaire.* Champaign, Ill.: Institute for Personality and Ability Testing, 1970.

Chapple, E. D. *Culture and biological man.* New York: Holt, Rinehart & Winston, 1970.

Feldstein, S., & Welkowitz, J. A chronography of conversation. In A. W. Siegman & S. Feldstein (Eds.), *Nonverbal behavior and communication.* Hillsdale, N.J.: Lawrence Erlbaum Associates, 1978.

Fraisse, P. *The psychology of time.* New York: Harper & Row, 1963.

Goldman-Eisler, F. Sequential temporal patterns and cognitive processes in speech. *Language and Speech,* 1967, *10,* 122–132.

Goldman-Eisler, F. *Psycholinguistics: Experiments in spontaneous speech.* New York: Academic Press, 1968.

Henderson, A., Goldman-Eisler, F., & Skarbek, A. Sequential temporal patterns in spontaneous speech. *Language and Speech,* 1966, *9,* 207-216.

Jaffe, J., Breskin, S., & Gerstman, L. J. Random generation of apparent speech rhythms. *Language and Speech,* 1972, *15,* 68-71.

Jaffe, J., & Feldstein, S. *Rhythms of dialogue.* New York: Academic Press, 1970.

Maclay, H., & Osgood, C. E. Hesitation phenomena in spontaneous English speech. *Word,* 1959, *15,* 19-44.

Mahl, G. F. Disturbances and silences in the patient's speech in psychotherapy. *Journal of Abnormal and Social Psychology,* 1956, *53,* 1-15.

Martin, J. G. Rhythmic (hierarchical) versus serial structure in speech and other behavior. *Psychological Review,* 1972, *79,* 487-509.

Rochester, S. R. The significance of pauses in spontaneous speech. *Journal of Psycholinguistic Research,* 1973, *2,* 51-80.

Schwartz, J., & Jaffe, J. Markovian prediction of sequential temporal patterns in spontaneous speech. *Language and Speech,* 1968, *11,* 27-30.

Stern, D., Jaffe, J., Beebe, B., & Bennett, S. The infant's stimulus world during social interaction: A study of caregiver behaviors with particular reference to repetition and timing. In H. R. Schaffer (Ed.), *Studies in mother-infant interaction.* New York: Academic Press, 1977.

BIOLOGICAL AND
DEVELOPMENTAL
PERSPECTIVES

Communication Rhythms and the Evolution of Language

Joseph Jaffe
Samuel W. Anderson
College of Physicians and Surgeons,
Columbia University
   and
New York State Psychiatric Institute

The claim that speech is an example of gesture is an old one. It is at least as venerable as Paget's observation that speaking is in fact a series of precise gestural positionings of the tongue and the other articulators (1930). This fact has all too often been discounted, perhaps because articulatory gestures are largely invisible and are transmitted between speaker and hearer over an *acoustic* channel; they seem to take on greater reality as sounds rather than as movements.

The gestural basis of speaking has also been overshadowed by a preoccupation, both on the part of scientists and everyone else, with the remarkable capacity of human listeners to quickly extract the significance of an utterance, the meaning of which will remain with them long after the exact words, and hence the gestures, are forgotten. In contrast, visible gesture seems limited to the immediate communication of simple signals with which we usually associate the concept. Hence, the historical dichotomy between linguistics and kinesics.

But it is not our present purpose to recapitulate the argument that the vocal tract is a device for encoding movement into sound, nor the fact that gestural systems such as American Sign Language can convey messages of abstract and universal significance. Rather, we attempt to support the claim from a third point of view: the startling similarities between the immediate time patterns of gestural events studied by kinesics and the temporal course of articulatory actions and hesitations that occur during speech.

Our view of language origins is in terms of social-emotional communication, conveyed by paralinguistic properties of dialogue, with their major locus in prelinguistic mother–infant interaction. Specifically, we suggest that skill

17

in interpersonal matching of communication rhythms (variously designated as congruence, convergence, synchrony, conversational coupling, etc.): (a) was an important principle in the evolution of language; (b) is still operative in the phenomena of interpersonal attraction and assortative mating; and (c) provides a potent method for predictive studies in behavior genetics.

The question of speech origins has preoccupied people for thousands of years. Yet the state of the art in neurolinguistics, anthropology, and genetics may still be such as to render the question premature. A recent major conference (Harnad, Steklis, & Lancaster, 1976) on the evolution of language amply documents the degree of controversy as well as the multiple new methods that are being brought to bear upon it (Marschak, 1976). At the worst, major speculations have been humorously dismissed with appellations such as "divine origin," "ding-dong," "bow-wow," and "yo-heave-ho" theories (Brain, 1965; Eisenson 1938). More seriously, Wundt (1928), Bloomfield (1933), and Paget (1930) display a progressively developing argument that implicates paralinguistic and nonverbal behaviors to explain *how* speech began at its evolutionary dawn. Also, de Laguna (1927) invoked emotional-social communication to explain *why* speech evolved, and more recently Searle (1970) has placed communication philosophically at the center of linguistic inquiry.

The constellation of arguments can be characterized as a gestural-communicative hypothesis of speech origin. In one extreme version, gesture is seen as a second-rate substitute for speech—at a distance, when the mouth is full, or in deaf or aphasic communicators. In another radical version, gesture was said to have preceded speech historically, only to be preempted by the manual demands of developing technology ("the hands had their mouths full, so people had to speak"). These are idle speculations that might seem inappropriate in this volume but for three recent lines of evidence:

1. The resurgence of interest in human and simian nonverbal linguistics;

2. The suggestion (Beebe, Stern, & Jaffe, Chapter 1, this volume; Jaffe, 1977a, 1977b; Stern, Beebe, Jaffe, & Bennett, 1977; Stern, Jaffe, Beebe, & Bennett, 1975) that the modality of stimulation (acoustic, visual, tactual, kinesthetic) may prove a less crucial feature of maternal behavior for an infant than the temporal patterning of that stimulation;

3. The finding that pairs of field-dependent women, notoriously skillful conversationalists, are particularly adept at modifying their endogenously generated speech rhythms to match those of their dialogic partners.[1] Furthermore, the degree of this rhythmic entrainment to an exogenous speech source is associated with positive social evaluation and interpersonal

---

[1]The analogous experiment has not been performed for males, but since females are regularly found to be more field dependent than males, this experimental finding *within* a group of normal females is a particularly compelling demonstration of the functional significance of rhythmic entrainment.

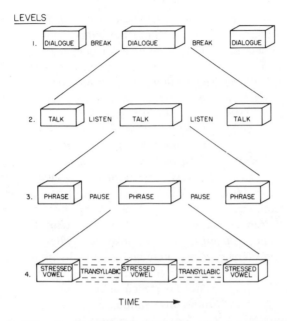

FIG. 1. Hierarchy of conversational rhythms. Level 1 represents the recurrence of dialogue in a relationship; Level 2, the "turn taking" of one of the participants; Level 3, the phrase–pause rhythm of one participant during a turn (while holding the floor); Level 4, the rhythm of stressed (accented) syllables within a phrase. Each level is a two-state system, and rate increases from the top to the bottom of the hierarchy. Each of the levels is a finer-grained analysis of the marked state in the level above. (From Jaffe, Anderson, & Stern, in press.)[2]

attraction (Marcus, Welkowitz, Feldstein, & Jaffe, 1970). Such a social skill has not, to our knowledge, been included in the extensive catalogue of variables known to operate in human assortative mating. Gray and Buffery (1971) have, however, noted the biological advantage of superior linguistic ability for the child-rearing role. It is the paralinguistic aspect of this ability that we wish to invoke as part of the gestural-communicative hypothesis of speech origins. The rationale is the "biogenetic law," that ontogeny recapitulates phylogeny.

We first reinterpret a well-documented research finding (Jaffe & Feldstein, 1970) in terms of interpersonal rhythmic entrainment of verbal communication. Figure 1 depicts a nested hierarchy of two-state conversational rhythms with each lower level being a decomposition of one of the states at the next higher level. Focusing on Level 3, we have documented a powerful tendency for speakers to match *pause durations* within conversations ("pause congruence"). It is notable that *phrase durations* at Level 3 do not exhibit this

---

[2]For purposes of this publication, the words "phrase" and "vocalization" are synonymous.

phenomenon; they are rather idiosyncratic endogeneous constants, relatively resistant to exogenous influence. Since the phrase–pause cycle at Level 3 consists of a relatively stable component (phrase) and a highly malleable component (pause), we may conclude that pause congruence is actually an aspect of *phrase rhythm entrainment* between conversationalists. This specific hypothesis has been confirmed and its psychopharmacological relevance demonstrated (Natale, Dahlberg, & Jaffe, in press).

The point that can be distilled from these various findings and speculations is: *The capacity for rhythmic entrainment in social communication, both verbal and nonverbal, may have been and may still be an important principle in human assortative mating, and consequently in the evolution of language.* The evidence from adults' verbal interaction has already been mentioned, and there is now confirmatory evidence relating entrainment to socialization in preschool children (Welkowitz, Cariffe, & Feldstein, 1976). Additional evidence from the *prelinguistic* period is provided by Beebe et al. (Chapter 1, this volume), who show precise matching of kinesic rhythmic periods between a mother and her 4-month-old infant during noncoactive "responsive" behavioral sequences. It is not farfetched to consider this kinesic rhythmic matching an aspect of "proto-conversation."

In fact, Marschak (1976) feels that vocal-call systems in primates may "affect mark" elements of hand-gestural or symbol-sign systems and that humans could learn them. Rhythmic aspects of this affect-call system could then be studied, as are human conversations in our own laboratory, in spite of the ape's lack of hominid laryngeal development. Cross-modal synchronization of acoustic affect-call systems with visual-gestural signing systems would implicate a common rhythmic pacemaker or "biological clock." Marschak also believes that the further evolution of these systems in the hominids was more likely acquired during child development rather than during the hunt (a point alluded to previously).

Finally, there are intriguing recent psychopathological lines of evidence that are relevant to the gestural-rhythmic-communicative hypothesis. Specifically, selective mating has been documented by Dunner, Fleiss, Addonizio, & Fieve (1976) in the case of manic-depressive psychosis. Since these matings were consummated *prior to the first illness* of both partners, some phenotypic (perhaps behavioral) characteristic may have been critical. Natural selective breeding for a type of mental illness may at first blush seem biologically contradictory. However, the disease is intermittent, and these patients are often socially charming extroverts during their normal and hypomanic mood phases. Thus, the apparent contradiction may be spurious.

The notion that conversation grows ontogenetically out of rhythmic coaction between a mother and her baby supplies us with developmental hypotheses about rhythmic interaction between two persons, both gestural and vocal, that can be tested against a large body of evidence already available

106650

from studies of adult conversation. Extrapolating from Stern et al. (1975, 1977), one is led to the speculation that human communication is based on an evolved capacity for the acquisition, use, and elaboration of rhythmically structured gestural systems.

These systems include, but are not limited to: chanting, singing, reciting poetry, pantomime, kinesic cueing, using sign language, and speaking. This view is not inconsistent with the findings of Lomax and Berkowitz (1972), who have classified ethnic patterns of song and dance forms among many of the world's cultures. These patterns appear to show about the same amount of diversity as do the prosodic timing patterns of the world's languages, which are based on tones, stresses, syllables, or *morae*. He finds that the song and dance patterns are correlated with the predominant work activities engaged in by members of the culture.

So our "rhythmic-gestural-communicative" hypothesis can be construed as an updated version of the "yo-heave-ho" hypothesis of language origins, a humble origin indeed for the evolution of the capacity for language.

ACKNOWLEDGMENTS

Supported in part by a Biomedical Research Support Grant to the Research Foundation for Mental Hygiene, Inc., and by the New York State Department of Mental Hygiene.

REFERENCES

Bloomfield, L. *Language.* Holt, D.C.: 1933.

Brain, Lord. *Speech disorders.* Washington, D.C.: Butterworth, 1965.

de Laguna, G. A. *Speech: Its function and development.* New Haven, Conn.: Yale University Press, 1927.

Dunner, D. L., Fleiss, J. L., Addonizio, G., & Fieve, R. R. Assortative mating in primary affective disorders. *Biological Psychiatry,* 1976, *11*, 43.

Eisenson, J. *The psychology of speech.* New York: F. S. Crofts, 1938.

Gray, J. A., & Buffery, A. W. H. Sex differences in emotional and cognitive behaviour in mammals including man: adaptive and neural bases. *Acta Psychologica,* 1971, *35*, 89.

Jaffe, J. The biological significance of Markovian communication rhythms. In S. Rosenberg (Ed.), *Sentence production: Developments in research and theory.* Hillsdale, N.J.: Lawrence Erlbaum Associates, 1977. (a)

Jaffe, J. Markovian communication rhythms: Their biological significance. In M. Lewis & L. A. Rosenblum (Eds.), *Interaction, conversation, and the development of language.* New York: 1977. (b)

Jaffe, J., Anderson, S. W., & Stern, D. N. Conversational rhythms. In D. Aaronson & R. W. Rieber (Eds.), *Psycholinguistics research: Implications and applications.* Hillsdale, N.J.: Lawrence Erlbaum Associates, in press.

Jaffe, J., & Feldstein, S. *Rhythms of dialogue.* New York: Academic Press, 1970.

Lomax, A., & Berkowitz, N. The evolutionary taxonomy of culture. *Science*, 1972, *117*, 228–239.

Marcus, E., Welkowitz, J., Feldstein, S., & Jaffe, J. *Psychological differentiation and the congruence of temporal speech patterns*. Presented at Eastern Psychological Association meeting, April 1970.

Marschak, A. Some implications of the paleolithic symbolic evidence for the origin of language. In S. R. Harnad, H. D. Steklis, & J. Lancaster (Eds.), *Annals of the New York Academy of Sciences*, 1976, *280*.

Natale, M., Dahlberg, C. C., & Jaffe, J. The effect of LSD and dextroamphetamine on therapist–patient matching of speech "rhythms." *Journal of Communication Disorders*, in press.

Paget, R. A. *Human speech*. Harcourt Brace, 1930.

Searle, J. *Speech acts*. Cambridge University Press, 1970.

Stern, D. N., Beebe, B., Jaffe, J., & Bennett, S. L. The infant's stimulus world during social interaction: A study of caregiver behaviors with particular reference to repetition and timing. In H. R. Schaffer (Ed.), *Studies in mother–infant interaction*. London: Academic Press, 1977.

Stern, D. N., Jaffe, J., Beebe, B., & Bennett, S. L. Vocalizing in unison and in alternation: Two modes of communication within the mother–infant dyad. In D. R. Aaronson & R. W. Rieber (Eds.), *Annals of the New York Academy of Sciences*, 1975, *263*, 89–100.

Welkowitz, J., Cariffe, G., & Feldstein, S. Conversational congruence as a criterion of socialization in children. *Child Development*, 1976, *47*, 269–272.

Wundt, W. *Völkerpsychologie*. New York: Macmillan, 1928.

1 The Kinesic Rhythm of Mother–Infant Interactions

Beatrice Beebe
Yeshiva University

Daniel Stern
New York Hospital
and
Cornell University
Medical Center

Joseph Jaffe
College of Physicians and Surgeons,
Columbia University
and
New York State Psychiatric Institute

Temporal aspects of mother–infant interaction have been relatively neglected in recent literature (Ashton, 1976). Important exceptions are the work of Condon (1977) and Fogel (1977). In the authors' laboratory, too, the significance of temporal factors in early mother–infant interaction has become increasingly prominent. Subtleties of communicational exchanges are seen to be highly dependent on timing, and temporal organization may be the fundamental principle underlying the earliest social integrations. That is, "... the modality of stimulation may prove a less crucial feature of human behavior for an infant than the temporal patterning of that stimulation" (Stern, Beebe, Jaffe, & Bennett, 1977, p. 192).

Our previous work (Stern et al., 1977; Stern, Jaffe, Beebe, & Bennett, 1975) suggested that the distinction between vocal and kinesic acts is less compelling in infancy than later in development, when vocal and kinesic acts can be dissociated. At this age, when vocalization does occur, it tends to occur as a cohesive constellation with other kinesic behaviors. The results indicated that with 3- to 4-month-old infants in play sessions with their mothers, there was unexpected simultaneity in vocalization—unexpected to the degree that antiphonal adult conversation served as the model (Jaffe & Feldstein, 1970). In Stern et al. (1975), the statistic used to quantify speech showed that in mother–infant speech, simultaneity occurred at an order of magnitude 40 times greater than that found in polite adult conversation. One factor that contributed to this surprising degree of simultaneous vocalization in mother–infant pairs was the prolongation of maternal speech when the infant began to simultaneously vocalize; again the opposite of the expected adult pattern where simultaneous speech leads to mutual cessation. A further interesting finding, to which we refer later, was that this simultaneous mother–infant vocalization occurred preferentially at heightened states of affectively positive arousal.

The simultaneity shown for vocalization is common in kinesic communications such as mutual gaze and posture sharing (Stern, 1971). It has not been clear, however, to what degree more extensive kinesic interactions (other than gaze and posture sharing) might share similar temporal structures with vocalization. This issue was the focus of the current investigation.

With respect to temporal organization in the kinesic realm, one of the most salient findings has been that in the period of 3 to 4 months, infant and mother both literally live in a "split-second world" where the average behaviors of each last approximately 1/3 second (Beebe, 1973; Stern, 1971). Further, this is a world of "microreactivity" in which each is extraordinarily sensitive to the movements of the other, each potentially "responding" to the other within less than ½ second (Beebe & Stern, 1977).

Although it is difficult not to conceptualize mother and infant as "responding" to each other, there is a question as to what to consider a "response" and to what extent "stimulus–response" formulations are helpful. When, for example, the "latencies" (however defined) begin to approach or even become smaller than some minimal reaction time, the concepts of both "latency" and "response" become increasingly questionable, and the problem of the location of the functional stimulus becomes more difficult. We have accordingly decided to omit the term *latency*, which assumes a "response," and to talk instead in the more neutral terms of onset–to–onset times in a single case study of mother–infant kinesic interaction to see what set of temporal patterns it covers.

METHOD

The method was frame–by–frame analysis of a film of one mother–infant pair. The infant was 4 months, of normal development. Two cameras monitored the interaction, one on the infant's face and one on the mother's face, with a resulting split-screen composite for analysis.

The films were 16mm, with 24 frames per second. Consecutive numbers were printed on each frame of the film. The films were viewed on a hand-crank Craig Projecto-Editor movie viewer, which allowed the experimenter to go back and forth over any number of frames, in slow motion, to determine the exact frames in which a movement started and stopped. Units of behavior were defined as movements in process of transformation, from the beginning to the end of ongoing action. The behavior was defined as having ceased when a steady posture was held. Thus, for example, the process of the head moving up was defined as a unit of behavior, its boundaries delimited by the exact beginning and end of the movement to the nearest 1/24 second. Once the head was held in a steady "up position," it was not scored as a behavior; the steady state was conceived as a "behavioral silence."

For the current analysis, the following kinesic behaviors of mother and infant were scored: (1) head movements in the directions of vertical (up–down), sagittal (forward–back), and horizontal (side–to–side); (2) body movements in the horizontal and sagittal directions; (3) hand and arm movements; (4) facial movements of mouth opening–closing, mouth widening–narrowing, grimace, frown. In addition, the "mock-surprise" (Stern, 1971) expression of the mother was scored, as was maternal repositioning of the infant by picking him up and putting him down on her lap.

The analysis was made of 2 minutes, or 2,880 frames, of continuous interaction. This sample was chosen on the basis of its being the first 2 minutes of the interaction. On the basis of previous (Beebe & Stern, 1977) frame–by–frame analysis, certain one-step sequences of mother behavior followed by infant behavior, and infant behavior followed by mother behavior, were demonstrated to have functional significance in this specific interaction (Table 1.1). In this previous analysis, it was established that the chief features of the interaction was a "chase-and-dodge" sequence in which

TABLE 1.1
Summary of Significant Interactions

		Preceding Event		Following Event
1.	*Dodging:*			
	a.	Mother loom (head-forward-and down-and-lean-in	·	Infant (head back) head away $X^2 = 17.7, p < .001 \ N = 249$
	b.	Infant dodge (head away head through	→	Mother chase (pull, follow with head or body) $X^2 = 8.6, p < .01 \ N = 108$
	c.	Mother chase (pull, follow, tickle)	→	Infant dodge (head away, head through body back or side-away) $X^2 = 19.8, p < .001 \ N = 214$
	d. & e.	"refusing a re-orientation"; Mother pick up	→	Infant head center, eyes closed $X^2 = 26.3, p < .001 \ N = 346$
		and put on lap	→	Infant head away $X^2 = 33.1, p < .001 \ N = 346$

Note: A "following event" occurs within the range of up to 1 second after the initiation of the preceding event. (From Beebe & Stern, 1977.)

the mother "chased" the infant primarily with her head, torso, and hand- or arm-pulls and the infant "dodged" the mother with an impressive repertoire, in which to every maternal overture, the infant could duck, move back, turn away, or pull away. It is important to note that the "chase and dodge" interaction on which this analysis is based conveyed an aversive rather than playful quality, on the basis of the infant's extensive negative facial behavior and repeated attempts to avoid the mother posturally and visually. The infant rarely looked at mother with foveal gaze but rather monitored mother through peripheral vision.

The present study examines in more detail the temporal characteristics of these reciprocal mother–infant one-step sequences in the first 2 minutes of the previous analysis. (Although the study could be described as an examination of latency and duration, due to considerations described earlier, the term *latency* has been dropped, and the term *onset-to-onset time* has been substituted.) Two seconds was arbitrarily chosen as the cutoff point with which to examine onset–to–onset times in any one-step sequence. To avoid repeating onset–to–onset time, we will refer to "onset time" with the following conventions. Infant onset time refers to the situation where the mother precedes, and it is a measurement from the initiation of the mother's behavior to the initiation of the infant's behavior. Maternal onset time refers to the situation where the infant precedes, and it is a measurement from the initiation of the infant's behavior to the initiation of the mother's behavior.

RESULTS

The total frequency distribution of mother and infant onset–to–onset times is shown in Figs. 1.1a and 1.1b. One hundred seventy one-step sequences in the 2 minutes were examined: 79 infant onset times in sequences initiated by the mother and 91 maternal onset times in sequences initiated by the infant. Although 2 seconds was chosen as an arbitrary cutoff point for maximum onset–to–onset time, for neither mother nor infant did the onset time exceed 1 second in these one-step sequences. The two distributions of maternal and infant onset times have quite similar means (7.25 and 7.70 frames, respectively), variances (4.95 and 4.66 frames, respectively) and frequencies. A comparison of the means yielded a nonsignificant t of 0.61.

It is clear from the total frequency distributions of the onset–to–onset times that for both mother and infant, many are of extremely short duration. Since the average behavior of each (approximately 1/3 second: Beebe, 1973; Beebe & Stern, 1977; Stern, 1971) lasts longer than these very short onset–to–onset times, there almost always occurs an overlap in the latter, with a period in which both mother and infant are behaving simultaneously, which is defined as *coaction*.

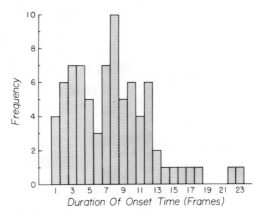

FIG. 1.1a. Frequency distribution of infant onset times measured from initiation of maternal behavior to initiation of infant behavior. Twenty-four frames equals 1 second.

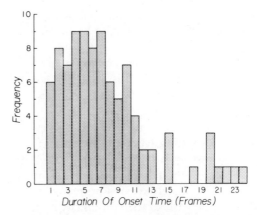

FIG. 1.1b. Frequency distribution of maternal onset times measured from initiation of infant behavior to initiation of maternal behavior. Twenty-four frames equals 1 second.

We arbitrarily adopted ¼ second to partition onset–to–onset times into long and short events. When the shorter onset times were investigated for both mother and infant, it was found that they were all coactive for the infant (32/32) and virtually all coactive for the mother (43/47). By comparison, for onset times greater than ¼ of a second, coaction was as likely to occur as noncoaction (24/47 vs. 23/47, respectively). For the mother, for onset times greater than ¼ of a second, approximately ¼ are coactive and ¾ are noncoactive; i.e., noncoactive onset times are somewhat more probable. Furthermore, the entire short segment of the distribution of ¼ second or less is accounted for by coaction.

The Temporal Pattern of Coaction

Of the total 170 one-step sequences, there were found to be 110 coactive events—56 initiated by the mother (56 infant coactive onset times) and 54 initiated by the infant (54 maternal coactive onset times). The respective mean

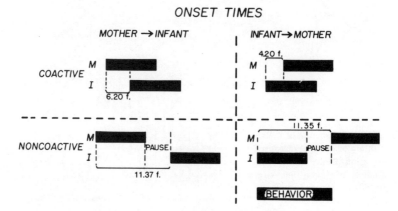

FIG. 1.2. Coactive and noncoactive onset times for mother and infant.
M = Mother; I = Infant; f = Frame; 24 frames = 1 second.

onset times of mother and infant in these coactive events were 4.2 frames and 6.2 frames (Fig. 1.2). The mother's coactive onset times are significantly shorter than the infant's, with comparison yielding a t of 2.63 ($p < 0.01$ for 108 df).

If not for the mother (adult motor reaction times to stimulus onset in the laboratory setting average ¼ second), at least for the infant, these onset times are too fast for a stimulus–response system with reference to this one-step sequence. Although the infant may be responding in stimulus–response fashion to a maternal event prior to this one-step sequence, it is conceivable that on the basis of the rhythmicity of prior maternal events, the infant has built up sufficient expectation of when the mother will behave that he is in a predictive system with her during these coactive episodes. Stern (1971) has speculated that short runs of synchronous or semisynchronous events may be based on the capacity of each to predict the timing of the other's next behavior. He has additionally shown that the timing of the mother's behavior is repetitive with minor variations and thus ideally suited to create such temporal expectancies in the infant.

The Temporal Pattern of Noncoaction

In an attempt to further understand the meaning of these very short onset times that were concentrated in the coactive episodes, those of the noncoactive onset times in Figs. 1.1a and 1.1b were examined. The definition of *noncoactive* was the absence of any overlap of action. The mean onset times for these noncoactive episodes were 11.37 frames or ½ second for the infant and 11.35 frames or ½ second for the mother (Fig. 1.2). These onset

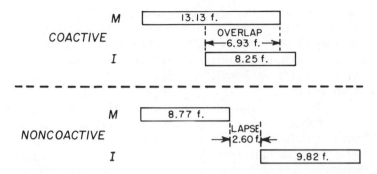

FIG. 1.3. Durations of maternal and infant behaviors and the overlap and lapse, comparing coactive and noncoactive episodes, respectively, in mother-initiated sequences. M = Mother; I = Infant; f = Frame; 24 frames = 1 second.

times in the ½-second range are well within the reaction-time capabilities of mother and infant. The noncoactive onset times are not significantly different for mother and infant.[1] By contrast with onset time in coactive episodes, which by definition contain no behavioral pauses, onset time in the noncoactive episodes is composed of two parts: a behavioral event and a behavioral silence or pause (Fig. 1.2). Repetitions of such a cycle of event plus pause define a rhythm. It is the mean duration of this rhythmic two-part cycle that is exquisitely matched in noncoactive episodes (Fig. 1.2).

In comparing the incidence of coactive versus noncoactive episodes in the mother-initiated sequences, coactive episodes were found to be more than twice as frequent (56 vs. 23, respectively). This result is consistent with our previous finding for vocalization (Stern et al., 1975). Thus, it appears that in selected kinesic interactions as well as in vocal interactions, the 3- to 4-month infant lives in a predominantly coactive world.

The Mother's and the Infant's Contribution to Coaction in Mother-Initiated Sequences[2]

An additional interesting finding was that the duration of maternal behavior was significantly ($t = 3.63$, $df = 77$, $p < 0.001$) prolonged during coactive episodes ($\bar{X} = 13.13$) as compared to noncoactive ($\bar{X} = 8.77$) episodes (Fig. 1.3). This finding suggests that once the mother begins a behavior, the infant's coactive "participation" may be sufficiently reinforcing, facilitating, or

---

[1]The noncoactive onset times for the mother are, however, significantly different from her coactive onset times ($t = 8.89$, $df = 89$, $p < .001$). The same is true for the infant ($t = 5.15$, $df = 77$, $p < .001$). Both types of onset times are graphically presented in Fig. 1.2.

[2]The corresponding data for infant-initiated coactive sequences are not currently available.

arousing for the mother that she prolongs her behavior, thus sustaining the average period of coaction. This finding for coactive kinesic behavior is a direct analogy to our previous finding with coactive vocalization, that the mother tends to continue vocalizing while the infant is vocalizing (Stern et al., 1975). In other words, mother prolongs the duration of her vocalization when vocal coaction occurs.

A comparison of the durations of infant behavior during coactive vs. noncoactive episodes (which the mother initiated) revealed no significant difference (Fig. 1.3). It is interesting to note that the infant can dramatically shorten his onset time to mother in coactive episodes, whereas his duration of activity remains constant, suggesting an endogenous timing mechanism for the latter. It is not surprising that the mother is more flexible in that both onset time and duration are significantly altered during coactive episodes, with onset time significantly shorter and duration significantly longer, as just demonstrated. Thus, both onset time and duration are subject to exogenous influence for the mother.

If the transition from noncoactive to coactive in mother-initiated sequences is considered, an examination of both the mother's and infant's contribution to coaction reveals that the mother contributes by decreasing onset time and prolonging duration, whereas the infant contributes solely by shortening onset time. The average overlap of action during coactive episodes is 6.93 frames ($\frac{1}{4}$ second), as shown in Fig. 1.3. If only the infant shortened his onset time from 11.37 to 6.20 frames and the mother's duration remained the same as during noncoactive (8.77 frames), there would be an average overlap of only 2.57 frames. Conversely, if only the mother increased her duration from 8.77 frames (noncoactive) to 13.13 frames (coactive) and the infant's onset time remained the same as in noncoactive (11.37 frames), there would be only a 1.76-frame overlap. Neither mother nor infant changing alone could account for the average 6.93-frame or $\frac{1}{4}$-second overlap during coactive episodes. Clearly, it is an interactive system, and both contribute to the creation of coactive episodes.

In summary, during all *noncoactive* episodes, mother and infant "match" duration of behavior–pause cycles (Fig. 1.2); i.e., there are no significant differences between mother and infant mean onset times, and in mother-initiated episodes at least, the mother matches the duration of the infant's behavior as well. The noncoactive kinesic pattern thus exhibits rhythmic matching. By contrast, in *coactive* episodes, there is a more literal synchronization of onset times. Although the infant does not seem capable of changing his duration of behavior, he is quite capable of significantly altering his onset time. The mother significantly alters both duration and onset time. This documents some of the differences of temporal patterning in coactive versus noncoactive sequences.

DISCUSSION

The study demonstrates the occurrence of mother–infant coactive and noncoactive temporal patterns in kinesic behavior (other than gaze), as was previously demonstrated for vocalization (Stern et al., 1975). Both the coactive and noncoactive vocal and kinesic patterns can be seen as the temporal precursors of later adult conversational patterns, with different functions and levels of arousal. It has been suggested (Stern et al., 1975) that noncoactive vocal patterns may transform into antiphonal, dialogic exchanges, whereas coactive vocal patterns may transform into more "emotional" exchanges at heightened levels of arousal, such as choral speaking, cheering, or lovemaking. The finding that temporal patterns in the kinesic realm share the same coactive–noncoactive distinction found previously for vocalization lends additional credence to the hypothesis of the similar nature of vocal and kinesic behavior in "proto-conversation."

It has also been suggested (Stern et al., 1975) that one function of coaction may be dyadic (or even group) bonding, prevailing at moments of heightened positive arousal. The previous finding was that in at least one mother–infant pair, vocal coaction especially predominated at high levels of "positive" affective arousal, at moments of infant "gape-smiles" (Beebe, 1973). Mutual gaze is a system of coaction that has similarly been suggested to operate at heightened levels of positive excitement.

The presence of coactive episodes found in the present case was based on an interaction in which mother and infant were locked into sequences of mother "chasing" and infant "dodging," which seemed affectively aversive on the basis of the infant's extensive "negative" facial expressive behaviors of sobering, frowning, and grimacing in the context of extensive turning away and on the basis of "negative" maternal facial expressivity (sobering, frowning, grimacing, jutting out jaw; thin, tight lips). "Chase and dodge" seems to be a state of heightened aversive arousal for the infant and mother. Thus, coaction may encompass heightened states of either positive or aversive arousal.

In demonstrating that coaction occurs in kinesic behaviors (other than gaze), further evidence is accrued for the notion that the modality of stimulation may be less crucial than the temporal patterning. Whether it is mutual vocalization, mutual "gape-smiles," mutual gaze, or mother-"chase," infant-"dodge," the same principle of coaction potentially applies across behaviors at this age.

Furthermore, as kinesic coaction occurs, the mother behaves longer, which ends up as a tendency toward coaction, because of the way in which the mother treats the infant. This same tendency toward coaction was found for vocal behaviors as well (Stern et al., 1975). Thus, a major part of the

mother–infant world occurs in the realm of overlapping or coactive behavior.
Discussions of "reciprocity" in the infant literature primarily use a conversational or antiphonal model, similar to adult speech. Brazelton, Koslowski, and Main (1974) describe reciprocity as each waiting for the other to respond, and Sander (1962) defines reciprocal interaction as stimulus–response alternation, back-and-forth exchange. Both these discussions follow primarily an alternating model and thus may limit conceptualizations of reciprocity. Simultaneity or coaction is an equally important model (see also Condon & Sander, 1974).

The conclusion suggested from the above detailed analysis of mother–infant one-step sequences in a single case study at four months is that a different kind of temporal organization obtains during coactive than during noncoactive episodes in the kinesic realm (other than gaze). In noncoactive sequences both mother and infant elongate their onset times, staying within the realm of half-second, and they match their onset times perfectly (Fig.1.2). In addition, the mother also matches the durations of the infant's behavior. In noncoactive episodes, onset times are composed of repetitive "behavior-pause" cycles, in which mother and infant match their kinesic rhythms. This finding parallels the rhythmic matching of phrase-pause cycles in adult conversation (Jaffe, Anderson, & Stern, in press).

Welkowitz, Cariffe, and Feldstein (1976) showed a progressively more extensive pause matching in vocal rhythms as a developmental phenomenon in peer conversations from ages 5 to 7. One could speculate that the matching of both duration and latency in noncoactive kinesic episodes described earlier is a nonverbal precursor of this later vocal conversational matching ability. Furthermore, the kinesic latencies investigated in the noncoactive sequences are an analogue to "switching pauses" in adult conversation. This "interpersonal" pause is the first to be matched in child–to–child conversation ages 5 to 7 (Welkowitz et al., 1976) and is here matched between mother and child at 4 months.

In coactive sequences, by contrast, both mother and infant onset times are significantly shortened to ¼ second or less, durations of mother and infant onset times are significantly different, and mother's average duration of behavior is prolonged.

Despite the differences in temporal organization in the two modes of coactive and noncoactive, it seems reasonable to assume that in both modes each partner is acting on the basis of previously established rhythmic expectancies. Within each one-step sequence, in neither mode does a traditional stimulus–response paradigm fit. In the coactive sequences, the initiations of the behaviors of mother and infant seem synchronously entrained to each other, and the reaction time is too rapid (at least for the infant) to be based on the immediately preceding (maternal) behavior; the infant seems to be predicting maternal initiations of behavior. In noncoactive episodes, rhythmic matching also suggests a system based on temporal expectancies, in which there is an alternating as opposed to a synchronous entrainment.

The extremely rapid onset times of infant movement following maternal movement in the coactive sequences are an analogue in the purely kinesic realm of Condon's (1977) finding of neonatal infant kinesic "tracking" or "entrainment" as "a mode of temporal processing which occurs well below the level postulated by the traditional stimulus–response model [p. 163]."

To summarize, we have investigated the temporal patterning of kinesic interactions at 4 months. Temporal structures of selected kinesic interactions with demonstrated functional significance were found in this case study to be consistent with those previously demonstrated for vocal interactions at this age. For both vocal and kinesic modalities, (a) coaction between mother and infant is the dominant pattern; and (b) the mother contributes to the coactive pattern by prolonging the duration of her behavior. Furthermore, the less frequent, noncoactive kinesic pattern revealed a rhythmic matching that presages the matching found in adult vocal conversation. These parallelisms are common temporal structures that are at the basis of our notion of "proto-conversation."

ACKNOWLEDGMENTS

This research has been supported in part by: Department of Psychology, Ferkauf Graduate School, Yeshiva University; The Jane Hilder Harris Foundation; The Grant Foundation; Biomedical Research Support Grant from The Research Foundation for Mental Hygiene, New York State Psychiatric Institute.

REFERENCES

Ashton, R. Aspects of timing in child development. *Child Development,* 1976, *47,* 622–626.

Beebe, B. *Ontogeny of positive affect in the third and fourth month of the life of one infant.* Unpublished doctoral dissertation, Columbia University, 1973.

Beebe, B., & Stern, D. Engagement–disengagement and early object experiences. In N. Freedman & S. Grand (Eds.), *Communicative structures and psychic structures.* New York: Plenum, 1977.

Brazelton, T. B., Koslowski, B., & Main, M. Origins of reciprocity: The early mother–infant interaction. In M. Lewis & L. Rosenblum (Eds.), *The effect of the infant on its caregiver.* New York: Wiley, 1974.

Condon, W. A primary phase in the organization of infant responding. In H. R. Schaffer (Ed.), *Studies in mother–infant interaction.* New York: Academic Press, 1977.

Condon, W., & Sander, L. Neonate movement is synchonized with adult speech: Interactional participation and language acquisition. *Science,* 1974, *183,* 99–101.

Fogel, S. Temporal organization in mother–infant face-to-face interaction. In H. R. Schaffer (Ed.), *Studies in mother–infant interaction.* New York: Academic Press, 1977.

Jaffe, J., Anderson, S. W., & Stern, D. N. Conversational rhythms. In D. Aaronson, & R. W. Rieber (Eds.), *Psycholinguistic research: Implications and applications.* Hillsdale, N.J.: Lawrence Erlbaum Associates, in press.

Jaffe, J., & Feldstein, S. *Rhythms of dialogue.* New York: Academic Press, 1970.

Sander, L. Issues in early mother–infant interaction. *Journal of the American Academy of Child Psychiatry,* 1962, *1,* 141–166.

Stern, D. A microanalysis of mother–infant interaction. *Journal of the American Academy of Child Psychiatry*, 1971, *10*, No. 3, 501–517.

Stern, D., Beebe, B., Jaffe, J., & Bennett, S. The infant's stimulus world during social interaction: A study of caregiver behaviors with particular reference to repetition and timing. In H. R. Schaffer (Ed.), *Studies in mother–infant interaction.* New York: Academic Press, 1977.

Stern, D. Jaffe, J., Beebe, B., & Bennett, S. Vocalizing in unison and alternation. *Transactions: New York Academy of Sciences,* 1975, *263,* 89–101.

Welkowitz, J., Cariffe, G., & Feldstein, S. Conversational congruence as a criterion of socialization in children. *Child Development,* 1976, *47,* 269–272.

2 A Pausological Approach to Speech Development

Edward J. Sabin
Edward J. Clemmer
Daniel C. O'Connell
Sabine Kowal
Saint Louis University

> *When I was a child, I used to talk like a child, and think like a child, and argue like a child, but now I am a man, all childish ways are put behind me.*
> (Saint Paul's First Letter to the Corinthians; 13:11)

The research reported here is based on the conviction that the temporal and hesitation properties of reading aloud and speaking yield lawful results that are essential to a viable psycholinguistic explanation of speech behavior. The focus of the present research is observable, measurable, real-time aspects of speech behavior. The ultimate goal of our program of research is to explain the complex, dynamic interaction of language and thought in the speech act by investigating the moment of speech production.

Generically, our research tradition began with consideration of the work of Maclay and Osgood (1959), especially in terms of their specification of various types of hesitation variables: unfilled pauses, filled pauses, repeats, and false starts (cf. Kowal, O'Connell, & Sabin, 1975). The writings of Goldman-Eisler (1968) have provided the fundamental hypothesis that temporal aspects of speech behavior systematically reflect underlying cognitive processes. More specifically, pause and rate phenomena reflect processes involved in the generation of information. Therefore, our program of research has adopted a cognitive orientation in which the planning, formulation, and execution of successive speech events in real time are of central importance.

Our hypothesis that measures of pause and rate phenomena are sensitive indicators of central processes was supported by our first pausological research (O'Connell, Kowal, & Hörmann, 1969), which addressed the semantic determinants of speech behavior. These and subsequent results (Clemmer, 1976; Kowal, O'Connell, O'Brien, & Bryant, 1975, Experiment 1; O'Connell & Kowal, 1972) confirmed the significant effects due to semantic or presuppositional variation in reading and retelling a short passage.

Since our first study, several independent variables have been investigated. They include *structural variables*: stimulus format, punctuation, and syntactic complexity; *cognitive variables*: semantic variation, speech task, bilingualism, schizophrenic speech, and glossolalia; *social variables*: cross-language effects, social-situational context, and socioeconomic status; *developmental variables*: age and educational level, and proficiency in a second language; and the *sex variable*. The genuine complexity of speech has been reflected in the multiple determination of pausological variables. However, the focus of the present discussion is directed to the overriding developmental trends evidenced throughout the research.

The developmental aspects of pause and rate phenomena have been specifically selected for consideration here for several reasons. First, a knowledge of developmental aspects can provide a basis for moving beyond the present prototheoretical position of pausology and can afford substantial guidance for heuristic research. However, we have yet to integrate a variety of findings and develop a comprehensive theory of language development. Second, we provide normative data on speech behavior, in terms of pause and rate phenomena, based on an objective, systematic methodology.

Existing studies report conflicting results typically based on small numbers of subjects, restricted samplings of age levels, and idiosyncratic definitions of response measures (e.g., Levin, Silverman, & Ford, 1967). All too often in the past, and even more recently in the 1970s, researchers (e.g., Clay & Imlach, 1971; Mishler & Waxler, 1970) have relied on subjective judgments of location and duration of unfilled pauses. Such subjective procedures represent one of the more serious methodological flaws in most pausological research of speech production. Unless one is studying pause perception, such subjective methodologies are clearly inadequate due to their bias, unreliability, and lack of sensitivity.

To date, computer techniques for measuring unfilled pauses remain far from solving the methodological difficulties of pausological research. A significant problem involves the selection of minimal sampling intervals as long as 300 msec (e.g., Jaffe & Feldstein, 1970), an interval that misses the on-and-off signals of a considerable number of unfilled pauses. However, shortening of the sampling interval increases the restrictions due to computer load. Another serious limitation of computer methodologies involves the failure to provide information on the location of unfilled pauses relative to the speaker's verbal units. Further, current computer techniques have not yet reliably separated speech signal from such intrusive noises as subject-generated coughs, breathing, body movements, etc.

The present program of research has attempted to overcome many of the inadequacies of previous pausological investigations. A uniform, objective methodology has been used in all the studies to locate and measure unfilled pauses and associated measures of rate. The criterion for an unfilled pause, a silent speech hesitation equal to or greater than 270 msec, was similar to the criterion of Goldman-Eisler (1968). In all instances, once the speech samples were obtained, permanent graphic records of the tape recordings were produced in terms of amplitude of acoustic energy over time. In conjunction with the voice recordings, all temporal variables were located and measured from the graphic records.

The developmental picture presented here is based on a series of 12 empirical studies, each conducted by the same investigative team at Saint Louis University over a span of 8 years. Advantages of this continuity have been the design of logically related studies and the use of consistently defined response measures, which make possible meaningful comparisons. The comparison of one study with another allows the present integration of results from 880 subjects representing a wide range of ages (6 to 49 years) and educational levels (kindergarten to college professors). Both males and females were included in the research in fairly equal proportions. The descriptive findings presented here were based on three main types of speech tasks: (1) readings of prose or poetry; (2) retellings of prose readings, and (3) spontaneous narratives based on a sequence of cartoon pictures and in one instance narratives based on a movie sequence and/or audio presentation.

The progression from readings to retellings to spontaneous narratives reflects the movement of our research efforts from tasks highly structured by the experimenter toward the more spontaneous, creative aspects of speech that might be termed "personally structured." The goal of the research is eventually to understand some aspects of the psycholinguistic complexities of everyday dialogic and multilogic conversation. The monologues of the present research are a step in the direction of formulating and refining such a psycholinguistically relevant theory of speech behavior. The data collected thus far reveal that developmental differences due to age, education, and language proficiency are clearly evident and consistently emerge as important factors reflected in a variety of tasks and response measures. A striking characteristic of all the studies is the impressive reliability of the data and the consistent, mutually confirming pattern of results evidenced in the integration of various studies.

RESULTS AND DISCUSSION

The Data Base

A few comments on the organization of the data as presented in the tables and figures will serve as the preface to the detailed discussion of the results. The sample sizes and sources of the data discussed are given in Table 2.1. Since the inferential statistics involving the comparisons made below have been presented in the individual research reports, we have chosen to limit our current presentation to descriptive statistics with an occasional inferential statistic to fill in lacunae.

Tables 2.2, 2.3, and 2.4 each present data for a specific response measure according to chronological age and related educational level. Figure 2.1 presents results for the spontaneous narratives for nine age levels. In Figs. 2.2, 2.3, and 2.4, the data for American subjects have been combined to form four age levels: (1) young children, ages 6 to 8; (2) preadolescents, ages 10 to 13; (3) adolescents, ages 14 to 18; and (4) adults, ages 21 to 49. Two additional educational levels for adults are presented for the reading of poetry: graduate students in English and university professors of English.

Cross-language comparisons are provided in the tables for German and American adolescents and adults based on identical speech tasks of reading and retelling, as well as for Mexican and American adolescents based on narratives about a movie and/or audio presentation. Narrative data for children of different levels of socioeconomic status are likewise presented. In addition, results are reported for a study involving a developmental analogy: Levels of proficiency in the acquisition of German served as the developmental analogy to a child acquiring linguistic ability in his or her native language. Results are also indicated for the readings and retellings of normal versus schizophrenic adults. Except for the aforementioned variables, all the results in the tables are averaged across other stimulus conditions or independent variables. In order that the figures be based on groups of subjects with similar characteristics, data representing different psychological states (readings and retellings of schizophrenics and matched controls), different levels of socioeconomic status (narratives), different native languages (German readings and retellings, and Spanish narratives), and different stimulus presentations (English narratives based on audio and/or visual presentations) are not included.

Three response measures have been selected for detailed presentation, since they clearly reflect the developmental trends and, in addition, are relevant to a conceptual integration of the research. Each response measure to be discussed bears an intimate relation to the temporal aspects of speech. The first measure, speech rate (Table 2.2 and Fig. 2.2), was computed in syllables per second rather than in words (per unit of time), in order to avoid the inherent

TABLE 2.1
Number of Subjects and Data Source[a]

Age (years): Education (grade):	6 K	8 2	10 4	12 5	13 7	14 8	16 10	17 11	18 12	21 Coll.	32 Grad.	36 13	46 Prof.	49 Coll.
Readings														
Prose E[b]		32(f)	32(f)			40(h)				40(h)		20(d)		
Prose E[b]												20(d)*		
Prose G[b]				40(h)						40(i)	20(f)			
Poetry E[b]		24(f)			24(f)				24(f)	24(f)	24(f)		24(f)	
Poetry G[b]		20(f)	20(f)	20(f)										
Retellings														
Prose E[b]		32(f)	32(f)			40(h)				40(h)		20(d)		
Prose E[b]												20(d)*		
Prose G[b]				40(h)						40(i)	20(f)			
Prose E[b]		20(f)	20(f)	20(f)						20(f)				
Narratives														
Audio/visual films S[b]							45(e)							
Audio/visual films E[b]	40(c)	54(c)						45(e)						
Pictures E[b]	24(g)	24(g)	24(g)	24(g)		24(g)	24(g)		24(g)	20(i)				20(j)

[a] Corresponding experimental studies are indicated in parentheses and footnoted below; prose readings are based on the "Child Story;" subjects in retellings are not independent of those in readings.
[b] E(English), G(German), S(Spanish).
[c] Bassett, O'Connell, & Monahan (1977); [d] Clemmer (1976); [e] Johnson (1976); [f] Kowal, O'Connell, O'Brien, & Bryant (1975); [g] Kowal, O'Connell, & Sabin (1975); [h] O'Connell & Kowal (1972); [i] O'Connell et al. (1969); [j] Sabin (1976).
*Schizophrenics

difficulty of using a unit (the word) that varies considerably in mean length depending on the language, speech tasks, and developmental level. The other response measures, the length (total unfilled pause time) and frequency of unfilled pauses, are based directly on the unfilled pause and are highly correlated with speech rate. The length (Table 2.3 and Fig. 2.3) and frequency (Table 2.4 and Fig. 2.4) of unfilled pauses are adjusted to a standardized speech sample of 100 syllables. The adjustment allows valid comparisons among corpora of varying lengths. Furthermore, a 100-syllable sample of speech is long enough to provide a stable index of pause and rate (Goldman-Eisler, 1954).

Spontaneous Narratives

The narratives, based on a task designed to elicit speech of a spontaneous nature, provide a convenient starting point. They represent the largest of our developmental studies (208 of the 880 subjects) and include a systematic sampling of nine age groups ranging from young children to middle-age adults: kindergarten (K), grades 2, 4, 6, and 8, high school sophomores (So), high school seniors (Se), college seniors (CS), and middle-age college alumni (CA) of 25 years. Figure 2.1 presents the developmental trends for speech rate and the length and frequency of unfilled pauses.

As reported previously (Kowal, O'Connell, & Sabin, 1975), significant successive increases in speech rate were found between kindergarten and second grade, between second and fourth grade, and between sixth and eighth grade. When additional data for adults (CS and CA) were included in the analysis, a new successive decrease in speech rate was indicated between high school seniors and college seniors (Newman-Keuls, $p < .01$).

Speech rate dramatically reflects the developmentally related utilization of linguistic skills and cognitive abilities. The general developmental pattern of increasing speech rate from early childhood to a peak rate in adolescence (So level in Fig. 2.1) documents the greater fluency evident in the speech of preadolescents and adolescents. The decline in speech rate following adolescence can be interpreted as the gradual development of reflective and rhetorical dimensions of adult speech.

Trends for the length and frequency of unfilled pauses are also presented in Fig. 2.1. In a comparison of successive age–educational levels, significant decreases in the length of unfilled pauses occur between kindergarten and second grade, during the early years of the child's formal education. From second grade throughout adolescence and adulthood, length of unfilled pause remains very stable. Likewise, the frequency of unfilled pauses provides a corresponding indication of the rapid development of linguistic skills and cognitive abilities of young children. A significant decrease in the frequency of unfilled pauses occurs between kindergarten and second grade, and

TABLE 2.2

Speech Rate (Syl/Sec) by Age-Educational Level and Speech Task

Age (years)		6	8	10	12	13	14	16	17	18	21	32	36	46	49
Education (grade)		K	2	4	5	7	8	10	11	12	Coll.	Grad.	13	Prof.	Coll.
Readings															
Prose	E[a]		2.16	2.97			5.00				4.48		4.16		
													3.58*		
	G[a]				4.28						4.63				
			(2.12)[b]	(3.29)[c]	(3.62)[d]							(4.00)[e]			
Poetry	E[a]		2.13			3.57				4.33	3.97	3.63		3.43	
Retellings															
Prose	E[a]		1.59	2.37			3.49				2.87		2.80		
													2.67*		
	G[a]				3.28						3.25				
	E[a]		(1.72)[e]	(2.79)[c]	(3.03)[d]						(3.12)[b]				
Narratives															
Audio/visual films	S[a]	1.77													
	E[a]		2.53					4.24	3.66						
Pictures	E[a]	2.15	2.87	3.25	3.26		3.83	4.00		3.84	3.07				3.25

[a]E(English), G(German), S(Spanish); [b]no academic or familial training in German; [c]college students with 4 to 6 semesters of German; [d]graduate students in German studies; [e]native speakers of German, resident in the United States 5 years or less.

*Schizophrenics

TABLE 2.3
Length of Unfilled Pauses (Total Sec/100 Syl) by Age-Educational Level and Speech Task

Age (years)	6	8	10	12	13	14	16	17	18	21	32	36	46	49
Education (grade)	K	2	4	6	7	8	10	11	12	Coll.	Grad.	13	Prof.	Coll.
Readings														
Prose E[a]		16.5	7.7			3.9				4.4		4.8		
												8.1*		
Prose G[a]		(17.0)[b]	(8.9)[c]	3.9						3.7				
				(5.5)[d]										
Poetry E[a]		15.6			6.0				3.4	3.5	(4.4)[e]		7.1	
											6.4			
Retellings														
Prose E[a]		43.5	30.3			12.4				17.0		19.2		
												17.9*		
Prose G[a]				15.6						15.0				
Prose E[a]		(37.7)[e]	(18.7)[c]	(15.1)[d]						(20.3)[b]				
Narratives														
Audio/visual films S[a]							7.4	7.5						
Audio/visual films E[a]		42.6	20.9	10.1										
Pictures E[a]		29.3	12.0	11.4		7.7			8.9	13.4				11.5

[a] E(English), G(German), S(Spanish); [b] no academic or familial training in German; [c] college students with 4 to 6 semesters of German; [d] graduate students in German studies; [e] native speakers of German, resident in the United States 5 years or less.
*Schizophrenics

TABLE 2.4

Frequency of Unfilled Pauses (Number/100 Syl) by Age–Educational Levels and Speech Task

Age (years)		6	8	10	12	13	14	16	17	18	21	32	36	46	49
Education (grade)		K	2	4	6	7	8	10	11	12	Coll.	Grad.	13	Prof.	Coll.
Readings															
Prose	E[a]		21.6	13.6			6.5				5.9		6.7		
	G[a]				7.3						5.4		9.9*		
			(22.9)[b]	(13.5)[c]	(8.1)[d]										
Poetry	E[a]		22.5			11.4				7.1	8.4	10.5		10.7	
												(5.6)[e]			
Retellings															
Prose	E[a]		18.8	16.5			14.5				13.9		13.9		
	G[a]				19.1						14.1		13.0*		
			(23.7)[e]	(17.1)[c]	(17.0)[d]						(12.6)[b]				
Narratives															
Audio/visual films	S[a]	23.4													
	E[a]	21.1						9.9	11.7						
Pictures	E[a]	20.1	14.7	14.8	15.1		11.4	10.9		11.0	12.6				10.5

[a] E(English), G(German), S(Spanish); [b] no academic or familial training in German; [c] college students with 4 to 6 semesters of German; [d] graduate students in German studies; [e] native speakers of German, resident in the United States 5 years or less.
*Schizophrenics

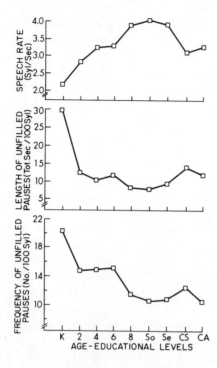

FIG. 2.1. Speech rate (syllables/ second), length of unfilled pauses (total seconds/100 syllables), and frequency of unfilled pauses (number/100 syllables) based on the spontaneous narratives for nine age-educational levels: kindergarten (K), grades 2, 4, 6, 8, high school sophomores (So), high school seniors (Se), college seniors (CS), and college alumni (CA) of 25 years.

between sixth and eighth grade, mirroring the significant increases in speech rate also occurring at that time. With increasing age, less time (shorter total length of unfilled pause) is involved in the production of more fluent speech, while unfilled pauses also occur less frequently.

The spontaneity representative of speech elicited by less structured stimulus settings is characterized in the narratives by the occurrence of vocal hesitations (cf. Kowal, O'Connell, & Sabin, 1975). Consequently, the frequency of four types of vocal hesitations are presented as supplementary response measures for the narratives and compared across four age levels, including (1) young children, (2) preadolescents, (3) adolescents, and (4) adults (as further specified above for Figs. 2.2, 2.3, and 2.4). The frequency (per 100 syllables) of three types of vocal hesitations decreases dramatically with increasing age. These decreases occur for false starts, e.g., "Realizing he's...he suddenly realizes" (2.61, 2.32, 1.14, .67); filled pauses, e.g., "uh, umm" (1.92, 1.75, 1.30, 1.39); and repeats, e.g., "The the girl came" (1.96, 1.19, .67, .68). However, parenthetical remarks, e.g., "well, you know" increased with age through adolescence and then decreased in adulthood (.60, 1.32, 2.39, 1.84), which parallels the trend for speech rate.

Filled pauses, false starts, and repeats disrupt the fluency of spoken language, due to the speaker's inappropriate semantic and/or syntactic productions, and indicate insufficient planning and organization of the utterance. However, the use of parenthetical remarks allows the speaker to rely on overlearned verbal habits that maintain fluency. The content conveyed by the parenthetical remarks is nonessential to the listener but nonetheless does not interfere with the linguistic coherence of the utterance. Adults make more judicious and controlled use of a wider variety of parenthetical remarks than do adolescents.

Speech Task Comparisons

In addition to providing a reliable index of language development, measures of pause and rate are also sensitive indicators of the speaker's task. Although the developmental trends discussed for the spontaneous narratives are further supported by comparisons with results for readings and retellings, a consistent differentiation of tasks is immediately evident. The influence of tasks (narration, reading, and retelling) on speech rate (Fig. 2.2) and the length (Fig. 2.3) and frequency (Fig. 2.4) of the unfilled pauses is discussed for young children, preadolescents, adolescents, and adults (as already defined).

For all tasks, in relation to age, an inverted U-shaped function is found for speech rate (Fig. 2.2) indicating that speech rate is slowest for young children, accelerates during preadolescence to a maximum level in adolescence, and then decreases in adulthood. Specifically, with regard to tasks, retelling a passage just read consistently yields the slowest speech rate for all tasks across age levels. Likewise narrative speech is consistently produced at a more rapid rate than the retellings for all age levels.

The acquisition of skills necessary for reading yields the most dramatic increases in speech rate: The readings emerge with the fastest rate in adolescence and adulthood. With regard to prose and poetry, little

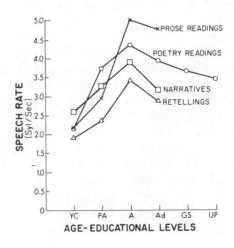

FIG. 2.2. Speech rate (syllables/second) for age–educational levels (young children, YC; preadolescents, PA; adolescents, A; and adults, Ad) according to speech tasks (prose readings and retellings, and narratives). For the task of poetry readings, graduate students (GS) and university professors (UP) are included as well.

differentiation is found between the readings until adolescence, when poetry is read more slowly than prose. However, adolescents' speech rate is faster than adults' for all tasks, which may be one indication of the high activity level of adolescents. It seems that adolescents may concentrate on overt skills of fluency to the sacrifice of covert reflection. For instance, O'Connell and Kowal (1972) found that adolescents are less alert to semantically unusual content than adults; fewer adolescents correctly reproduced the unusual semantic content of a reading in their retellings.

As can be seen in the reading of poetry, speech rate decreases with increased literary sophistication. The adult decline in speech rate reflects increased levels of expressive interpretation. Apparently, this expressive interpretation of the density of meaningfulness inherent in a poetic passage accounts for the greater reduction of speech rate when poetry is read aloud.

As Lenneberg (1967) has noted, speech rate is limited by the "cognitive aspects of language" rather than simply the physical ability to articulate speech. Specifically, we have found (in agreement with Goldman-Eisler, 1968) that speech rate is more closely related to variations in the length and frequency of unfilled pauses than to articulation rate. As an example, speech rate correlated (Pearson product moment correlation coeffecients) -.86 with length and -.86 with the frequency of unfilled pauses based on the narratives of 40 adult subjects (groups CS and CA); whereas speech rate correlated + .59 with articulation rate (syllables per vocal second). Although these correlation coefficients are all significant ($p < .001$), squares of the coefficients indicate that the length (74%) and frequency (74%) of unfilled pauses individually accounted for twice as much variation in speech rate as did articulation rate (35%).

Figure 2.3 presents the U-shaped developmental trends for the total length of unfilled pause time, which decreases dramatically for all tasks from early childhood to adolescence and then, mirroring speech rate, increases in adulthood. The amount of pause time required to produce readings, retellings, or narratives indicates the level of cognitive and linguistic demands made of the speaker. The least amount of pause time is required for the readings where lexical and syntactic decisions have already been made for the speaker, depending of course on his or her ability to read. The production of narratives requires more unfilled pause time. Although the narratives do not depend on skill with written language, the speaker is responsible for specific lexical and syntactic choices in addition to establishing an overall meaningful context and sequence of events for the oral description of a set of pictures.

Though narratives require more time for planning and formulating an utterance than do readings, they do not include the more severe restriction involved in the recall of specific verbal contents characteristic of retellings. Increased memory load is clearly evident in the retellings, which consistently involve the greatest amount of unfilled pause time and in addition exhibit the

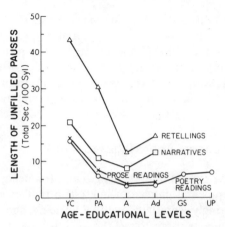

FIG. 2.3. Length of unfilled pauses (total seconds/100 syllables) for age–educational levels (young children, YC; preadolescents, PA; adolescents, A; and adults, Ad) according to speech tasks (prose readings and retellings, and narratives). For the task of poetry readings, graduate students (GS) and university professors (UP) are included as well.

largest decrease in actual pause time from childhood to adolescence. Retellings are the most time-consuming, since the speaker is required to reexpress both the general organization and specific contents from readings composed by someone other than the speaker.

The frequency of unfilled pauses (Fig. 2.4) is closely related to linguistic development and dramatically reflects the acquisition of reading skills. Readings exhibit the greatest reduction in the occurrence of unfilled pauses between early childhood and adolescence. Following adolescence, more frequent use of unfilled pauses in the readings of poetry is related to increased literary sophistication. However, whereas literary scholars use a greater number of unfilled pauses, they locate more of them between, rather than within, syntactic units or words (Kowal, O'Connell, O'Brien, & Bryant, 1975, Experiment 3). The distribution of pauses becomes increasingly associated with the syntactic structure of the text and represents a means of expressive interpretation.

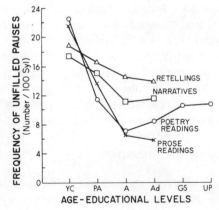

FIG. 2.4. Frequency of unfilled pauses (number/100 syllables) for age–educational levels (young children, YC; preadolescents, PA; adolescents, A; and adults, Ad) according to speech tasks (prose readings and retellings, and narratives). For the task of poetry readings, graduate students (GS) and university professors (UP) are included as well.

The rank ordering of speech tasks in Figs. 2.3 and 2.4 indicates a close relationship between the length and frequency of unfilled pauses. In all but one instance (the frequency of unfilled pauses in the readings of young children), retellings involve the longest and most frequent use of unfilled pauses, with narratives representing an intermediate use, whereas readings resulted in the lowest rate of occurrence and shortest length of unfilled pause across age levels.

Correlational Approaches to the Data

The association between length and frequency of unfilled pauses exhibits a developmental pattern of interest in that these response measures become increasingly correlated with advancing age. Based on results from the spontaneous narratives, the length and frequency of unfilled pauses correlated + .39 for kindergartners, + .65 for second graders, + .77 for preadolescents (grades 4, 6, and 8), and + .91 for adolescents and adults (Pearson product moment correlation coefficients). For the kindergarten group, the correlation between length and frequency of unfilled pauses was nonsignificant. However, by second grade and subsequently, the relationship is statistically significant ($p < .001$), and increases consistently. This increasing level of correlation between the length and frequency of unfilled pauses reflects the increasing association of linguistic and cognitive skills. These same developmental relationships are exhibited for the reading of poetry (Kowal, O'Connell, O'Brien, & Bryant, 1975).

The nature of association between measures of unfilled pause and vocal hesitations is also of interest. In a factor analysis of 40 adult narratives (groups CS and CA), two factors were extracted that together accounted for 95% of the common factor variance (Sabin, 1976). The highest loadings on the first factor were produced by the length (.96) and frequency of unfilled pauses (.87), whereas the highest loadings for the second factor were due to the frequency (.96) and length (in syllables) of vocal hesitations (.94). This factor structure suggests the relative independence of unfilled pause measures from vocal hesitation variables. Furthermore, this factor structure has also been reported by Johnson (1976) for Mexican and American groups of adolescents; she indicates similar structure in Spanish and English. Tables 2.2, 2.3, and 2.4 include data for English–Spanish cross-language comparisons; these results indicate similar levels of performance by adolescents speaking their respective native languages.

Developmental Analogies

Schizophrenic thought has been described as regressed, in the developmentally analogous sense of being childish or of employing defective logic (e.g., Vigotsky, 1934). However, the differences between adult schizophrenic and normal children's speech are too great to ascribe the same dynamics to both (Laffal, 1965). Moreover, Brown (1973) observed none of the properties of child speech in schizophrenics.

In our research, there were no significant differences between adult schizophrenics and matched adult normals for speech rate in the readings or retellings, or for the length or frequency of unfilled pauses in the retellings. In the readings, however, schizophrenics spent almost 70% more pause time (Table 2.3) and produced about 48% more unfilled pauses (Table 2.4) than did matched normals. Schizophrenics actually appear not to allow themselves to be structured by the reality of the materials they read, or they may reorganize and reinterpret the reality of what they read. In addition, they may use pause and rate to obstruct or exclude the listener's involvement in conversation. A more complete treatment of the pausological patterns differentiating schizophrenic from normal speech is provided by Clemmer (1976).

Of special interest are the results from the research involving the developmental analogy of proficiency levels, which corroborate the actual age level findings. Four levels of proficiency in German were investigated: (1) no academic or familial training in German; (2) college students with 4 to 6 semesters of German; (3) graduate students in German studies; and (4) native speakers of German resident in the United States 5 years or less. As proficiency in reading the foreign language increased, speech rate increased (2.12, 3.29, 3.62, 4.00), and accordingly, decreases occurred in the total length (17.0, 8.9, 5.5, 4.4) and frequency (22.85, 13.48, 8.07, 5.62) of unfilled pauses.

Not only does the rank order of the proficiency levels resemble the actual age level findings, but the specific patterns of values for the pause and rate measures are remarkably consistent. For instance, college students with no training in German resemble 8-year-old children learning to read their native language (speech rate: 2.12 vs. 2.16; length of unfilled pause: 17.0 vs. 16.5; frequency of unfilled pause: 22.85 vs. 21.62). Moreover, college students with 4 to 6 semesters of German resemble 10-year-old children reading their native language (speech rate: 3.29 vs. 2.97; length of unfilled pause: 8.9 vs. 7.7; frequency of unfilled pause: 13.48 vs. 13.59).

Whereas all of the passages were read in German with groups representing progressive increases in proficiency, the readings were all retold in English, obviously involving a different order of language proficiency. The most proficient speakers of German also represented the only group where fluency in English was problematic. Likewise, the group with no training in German language retold a passage they did not understand. With these aspects of the retellings in mind, several comparisons are valuable.

Native Germans retelling the German reading in English resemble 8-year-old children retelling in their native language (speech rate: 1.72 vs. 1.59; length of unfilled pause: 37.7 vs. 43.5; frequency of unfilled pause: 23.66 vs. 18.83). The non-native German student groups retelling the German readings in English progressively resembled native Germans retelling the story in

German (speech rate: 2.79 and 3.03 vs. 3.25; length of unfilled pause: 18.7 and 15.1 vs. 15.0; frequency of unfilled pause: 17.10 and 17.01 vs. 14.10).

German–American native language comparisons further indicate the cross-language stability of the results (Tables 2.2, 2.3, and 2.4). Speech rate was faster for adult Germans and Americans reading their native languages (4.63 and 4.48) than for retelling the passage just read in their native languages (3.25 and 2.87). Accordingly, length of unfilled pause time increased for both Germans and Americans from the readings (3.7 and 4.4) to the retellings (15.0 and 17.0), as did the frequency of unfilled pauses when the readings (5.38 and 5.85) are compared to the retellings (14.10 and 13.86).

CONCLUSIONS

The Relevance of Pausology

Although pause and rate phenomena reflect a wide variety of processes that influence speech production—including cognitive, emotional, organismic, social, and situational processes—measures of pause and rate are nonetheless sensitive and reliable indicators of both task and developmental variables. In light of these findings, the relegation of pausological variables by psychologists and linguists to the wastebasket category of *para*linguistics (e.g., Houston, 1972) or "breathing" (Fodor, Bever, & Garrett, 1974) is not only ill-advised; it is untenable.

The terminology that classifies pausological as para- or extralinguistic is logically arbitrary; it represents the historical trend of increasing abstractionism in "orthodox" linguistics and the resulting inability of linguistic theory to integrate pausological data into a realistic theory of speech behavior.

In view of the evidence in the present pausological research for the continuation of speech development through adolescence into adulthood, theories advanced in the 1960s with emphasis on the virtual completion of language development in early childhood (McNeill, 1966) are unwarranted. Accordingly, we maintain that a methodologically rigorous analysis of temporal speech patterns and hesitation phenomena provides a viable and essential psycholinguistic approach to understanding language development. This contention is supported by the mutually confirmatory patterns of developmental differences ascribable to chronological age, level of education, and analogous processes of learning a second language. The reliability of these patterns across languages further substantiates the contention.

The stability of the pausological variables is further illustrated by the factor analytic studies in which the common factor variance accounted for by the two pausological factors increased from a remarkable 81% and 86% for American and Mexican adolescents, respectively, to an extraordinary 95% for American adults.

A meaningful psycholinguistic theory of speech production must be simultaneously linguistic and cognitive. Isolation of linguistic and cognitive variables can be quite artificial, since cognitive and linguistic ability develop simultaneously and operate in consort. Whereas cognition is closely related to semantics, linguistic skill is more closely associated with syntax. In the most general sense, the length of the unfilled pause is related to cognition, and frequency of unfilled pause to linguistic skill. However, since the category of frequency subsumes location, the specific locations of unfilled pauses and vocal hesitations should receive additional attention in future research.

Describing the syntactic location of unfilled pauses in readings is relatively straightforward. We have found that with increasing age, pauses are more often in accord with the syntactic structure of prose and poetry readings. But the locations of pauses are not always in accord with syntactic boundaries. Furthermore, it becomes increasingly difficult to define syntactic units with a high degree of interjudge reliability for more spontaneous speech. Consequently we do not agree with Fillenbaum's (1971) recommendation that pausological research should become dependent on linguistic analysis. This is not to say, however, that spontaneous speech is ungrammatical; we concur with Labov (1970) that the alleged ungrammaticality of spontaneous speech is more myth than reality.

The increasing grammaticality of spontaneous speech through successive developmental stages is reflected in our data by the reduction of disruptive utterances (false starts, filled pauses, and repeats) and the increase of parenthetical remarks over age. However, there is a low overall rate of occurrence for vocal hesitations: An analysis of 40 adult narratives revealed that less than 8% of the total length (in syllables) was due to these vocal hesitations. It should be pointed out that vocal hesitations and other "slips of the tongue" are lawful phenomena that can provide valuable insights into the structure and organization of spoken language (cf. Fromkin, 1971).

The location of unfilled pauses and vocal hesitations can be determined relative to the speaker's units (cf. Clemmer, 1976). However, researchers should be cautioned against engaging in a futile search for *the unit* of speech behavior or the unique proximal *or* distal determinants of pause and rate (cf. O'Connell, 1977; Rochester, 1973).

Speech Task Differences

The tasks of reading aloud, retelling, and narration yield distinct levels of verbal performance, reflecting variations in the complexity or demand characteristics involved in planning, organizing, and formulating utterances; retrieving material from memory; making lexical decisions; monitoring one's utterances, etc. In reading aloud, the overt speech is already mandated for the reader, who nevertheless must organize his or her own interpretation and understanding of the passage. The retellings tend to place more emphasis on memory processes and the recall of specific verbal elements. Both the readings and retellings of the readings originate in a speech task requiring knowledge of the written speech mode.

The developmental decrease in the total length of unfilled pause time is most dramatic for the retellings, whereas the readings yield the most significant decline in the frequency of unfilled pauses from childhood to adolescence. Frequency of unfilled pauses is thus a sensitive measure of reading proficiency, or linguistic skill with written language. The length of unfilled pause is more closely associated with the cognitive dimensions involved in retelling the passage. It should also be noted that the reading of poetry by literary experts results in a more dramatic increase in the frequency of unfilled pauses relative to the more modest increase in length; again the frequency of unfilled pauses reflects the proficient knowledge of written language.

The narratives, on the other hand, were not derived from written stimuli, but from visual and/or aural stimuli. The narratives represented an intermediate level of pause length and frequency relative to the readings and retellings.

Since various response measures are differentially sensitive to the speaker's task and to underlying psychological processes, no single pausological variable provides an exhaustive explanation of the entire speech act. However, multiple response measures can provide an adequate under-standing of speech behavior. Additional response measures become important, depending on the nature of the task and the subject population. For example, in more spontaneous speech such as the narratives, a measure of vocal productivity (narrative length, in syllables) is relevant and yields almost a threefold increase across the nine age–educational levels from kindergarten to middle-age college alumni (Kowal, O'Connell, & Sabin, 1975; Sabin, 1976).

Interpretation of Developmental Differences

Similar overt speech behavior, as reflected in measures of pause and rate, may result from very *different* underlying linguistic and cognitive processes. For example, the young reader pauses more frequently, apparently concentrating on the particulars of the language (syntactic usage, lexical items, organization of the expression). In verbal utterances, the child is wrestling with the basic tools of speech. Adults, once having achieved a level of linguistic skill sufficient for verbal expression, can increasingly focus their attention on the semantic dimensions and develop the reflective and expressive characteristics of adult speech.

Another example of different underlying processes that may result in similar behavior is provided by the identical moderate speech rates in the narratives of fourth graders (3.25 syl/sec) and middle-age college alumni (3.25), relative to the rapid speech rate found for high school sophomores (4.00). Although the fourth graders and adults evidenced the same speech rate, they did so for different reasons. For the child, the rate reflects undeveloped linguistic and cognitive skills; the identical speech rate for the adults represents an increased capacity to utilize language reflectively and expressively.

Characteristic of the adult is the ability to speak and think simultaneously. Unlike the child, the adult, relying on overlearned linguistic skills, produces overt speech and plans future utterances in parallel linguistic and cognitive processes, rather than in serial fashion. Linguistic structuring and vocalization become relatively automatic for the adult in such a way that he or she can direct attention and efforts to cognition.

During the process of language learning, vocal expression must be deliberately controlled and limited because of the requirements of the language system of a specific social community. This initial limitation eventually frees the individual speaker from clumsy restrictions in the use of language and allows him or her to gracefully order syntactic and semantic structure for efficient and creative expression of the thought.

Summary

To summarize our findings and orientation: First, we are in agreement with Goldman–Eisler (1968) that pauses are not per se paralanguage phenomena, but are both essential and functional to the speech act for the speaker and listener. Second, a meaningful psycholinguistic theory of speech development must be simultaneously linguistic and cognitive, in recognition of the multiple determinants of the speech act, and must integrate data based on multiple response measures. Third, our findings indicate that there are critical behavioral differences useful in the comparison of speech tasks. Finally, we vigorously maintain that analyses of temporal patterns and hesitation phenomena provide a viable and necessary approach to understanding the developmental processes involved in the relationship of language and thought at the actual time of speech production.

The Future

Developmental studies show great promise for both the integration of findings and the generation of researchable hypotheses. Currently, attention is being focused on several facets of the developmental perspective, including both very young children and geriatric populations, who have received little systematic study.

Pausological research into literary and dramatic skills and second-language learning, including cross-linguistic comparisons, is expected to yield valuable results, as are studies concerned with pathological language such as schizophrenia, aphasia, and stuttering. Whereas monologic research has emphasized processes essential to the speaker in generating language, a concurrent emphasis on more spontaneous speech, including dialogues and multilogues in naturally occurring situations, will add an emphasis on the perception of pausological variables and their function for the listener. Efforts must also be begun on applications of pausological findings to language education and rehabilitation.

REFERENCES

Bassett, M. R., O'Connell, D. C., & Monahan, W. J. Pausological aspects of children's narratives. *Bulletin of the Psychonomic Society*, 1977, *9*, 166–168.

Brown, R. Schizophrenia, language, and reality. *American Psychologist*, 1973, *5*, 395–403.

Clay, M. M., & Imlach, R. H. Juncture, pitch, and stress as reading behavior variables. *Journal of Verbal Learning and Verbal Behavior*, 1971, *10*, 133–139.

Clemmer, E. J. Linguistic and cognitive aspects of speech hesitations in schizophrenics and normals (Doctoral dissertation, Saint Louis University, 1975). *Dissertation Abstracts International*, 1976, *36*, 3135B–3685B. (University Microfilms No. 76-857, 160)

Fillenbaum, S. Psycholinguistics. *Annual Review of Psychology*, 1971, *22*, 251–308.

Fodor, J. A., Bever, T. G., & Garrett, M. F. *The psychology of language: An introduction to psycholinguistics and generative grammar*. New York: McGraw-Hill, 1974.

Fromkin, V. A. The non-anomalous nature of anomalous utterances. *Language*, 1971, *47*, 27–52.

Goldman-Eisler, F. On the variability of the speed of talking and on its relation to the length of utterance in conversation. *British Journal of Psychology*, 1954, *45*, 94–107.

Goldman-Eisler, F. *Psycholinguistics: Experiments in spontaneous speech*. New York: Academic Press, 1968.

Houston, S. H. *A survey of psycholinguistics*. The Hague: Mouton, 1972.

Jaffe, J., & Feldstein, S. *Rhythms of dialogue*. New York: Academic Press, 1970.

Johnson, T. *Temporal analysis of English and Spanish narratives*. Unpublished doctoral dissertation, Saint Louis University, 1976.

Kowal, S., O'Connell, D. C., O'Brien, E. A., & Bryant, E. T. Temporal aspects of reading aloud and speaking: Three experiments. *American Journal of Psychology*, 1975, *88*, 549–569.

Kowal, S., O'Connell, D. C., & Sabin, E. J. Development of temporal patterning and vocal hesitations in spontaneous narratives. *Journal of Psycholinguistic Research*, 1975, *4*, 195–207.

Labov, W. The study of language in its social context. *Studium Generale*, 1970, *23*, 30–87.

Laffal, J. *Pathological and normal language*. New York: Atherton Press, 1965.

Lenneberg, E. H. *Biological foundations of language*. New York: Wiley, 1967.

Levin, H., Silverman, I., & Ford, B. L. Hesitations in children's speech during explanations and description. *Journal of Verbal Learning and Verbal Behavior*, 1967, *6*, 560–564.

Maclay, H., & Osgood, C. E. Hesitation phenomena in spontaneous English speech. *Word*, 1959, *15*, 19–44.

McNeill, D. The creation of language. *Discovery*, 1966, *27*, 34–38.

Mishler, E. G., & Waxler, N. E. Functions of hesitations in the speech of normal families and families of schizophrenic patients. *Language and Speech*, 1970, *13*, 102–117.

O'Connell, D. C. One of many units: The sentence. In S. Rosenberg (Ed.), *Sentence production: Developments in research and theory*. Hillsdale N.J.: Lawrence Erlbaum Associates, 1977.

O'Connell, D. C., & Kowal, S. Cross-linguistic pause and rate phenomena in adults and adolescents. *Journal of Psycholinguistic Research*, 1972, *1*, 155–164.

O'Connell, D. C., Kowal, S., & Hörmann, H. Semantic determinants of pauses. *Psychologische Forschung*, 1969, *33*, 50–67.

Rochester, S. The significance of pauses in spontaneous speech. *Journal of Psycholinguistic Research*, 1973, *2*, 51–81.

Sabin, E. J. *Pause and rate phenomena in adult narratives*. Unpublished master's thesis, Saint Louis University, 1976.

Vigotsky, L. Thought in schizophrenia. *Archives of Neurology and Psychiatry*, 1934, *1*, 1063–1077.

3 Ultradian Biorhythms in Social Interaction

Donald P. Hayes
Loren Cobb
Cornell University
and
The University of New Hampshire

INTRODUCTION

The natural tendency of human beings to engage in conversation at the slightest provocation—if only a discussion of the weather—is apparent in all cultures and in people of all ages. There is variation across individuals in this tendency, of course, on a range from taciturnity to loquacity, as there is variation depending on the social setting of the interaction and on the content of the conversation, once started. We suspect, however, that there is a further, more subtle source of variation: a periodic trend in the tendency to engage in conversation that moves through a complete cycle perhaps 5 to 10 times daily. Such a latent periodicity would remain largely unnoticed for several reasons: because externally generated schedules and chance events would mask and perturb the latent periodicity so that the manifest (observable) pattern would but dimly reveal its outlines; and because the aspects of conversation that one normally remembers are its content and tone rather than its time of onset and its duration. This hypothetical periodicity is similar to the sleep biorhythm: an irregular and perturbable progression of stages whose complete cycle time is in the 90–100 minute range, first identified by Dement and Kleitman (1957). The sleep biorhythm appears to be a manifestation of a latent periodic physiological process—a biorhythm that probably continues throughout the day as well as night and may manifest itself in a variety of ways. Some of the possible manifestations that have been explored are oral activity (Friedman & Fisher, 1967; Oswald, Merrington, & Lewis, 1970), daydreaming (Othmer, Hayden, & Segelbaum, 1969), work performance (Globus, Drury, Phoebus, & Boyd, 1971), heart rate (Orr & Hoffman, 1974), and gastric activity (Hiatt

& Kripke, 1975). We find it plausible to believe that there is one latent biorhythm underlying all of these manifestations and that it induces a similar periodicity in the tendency to engage in social interaction. The term *ultradian* describes biorhythms that move through a complete cycle in *less* than the roughly 24 hours of the "circadian" biorhythms.

SOCIABILITY AND BIORHYTHMS

Eliot Chapple (1939, 1940, 1970, 1971; Chapple & Lindeman, 1941) was among the first social scientists to propose that individuals have distinct and stable social interaction patterns whose foundations are biological in nature. His thinking was influenced by his association with several pioneers in the study of biorhythms: Pincus, who worked on menstrual cycles; Brazier, who used electroencephalography; and Halberg, one of the founders of the field now called *chronobiology*.

Chapple reasoned that conversational behavior may be linked to a biological oscillator whose cycle time is on the order of a minute in duration. He based his observations on "actions" and "silences," which he defined in operational terms as tension or relaxation of sets of facial muscles. (Chapple's "action" correlates highly with vocalization.) His analyses ignored both the content of the communication and the cognitions of the participants, while focusing on the observable physiological changes during the interaction. Although trained observers detect and record these changes in state, good electromyography could, in principle, provide adequate measurements for his variable. Chapple hypothesized that in human interaction, each person's manifest oscillatory pattern represents an accommodation, in varying degrees, to the people with whom he/she interacts. Rarely is an individual able to interact with others without the necessity of adapting his/her pattern to the other. How then can the hypothesized individual oscillatory pattern be discerned?

Chapple's approach to this complex problem was to devise his so-called Experimental Standard Interview, in which a trained interviewer enacted three different temporal styles of conversation. Recordings of the interviewee's temporal pattern of response yielded measures of his/her adaptability and latent periodicity. Chapple's research led him to assert (1940) that these characteristics are stable features of an individual's personality. Statistical approaches to this same problem have made use of Markov Chain Analysis (Jaffe & Feldstein, 1970) and Time Series Analysis (Cobb, 1973).

Chronobiologists, studying diverse periodic phenomena in animals and plants, confront the same problem; uncontrolled exogenous events in the natural environment can and do perturb these rhythmic processes and obscure their underlying pattern. To estimate the natural periodicities and determine the probable source of their timing (the "oscillator"), biologists have designed "free-running" environments in which as many as possible of those naturally occurring exogenous events suspected to influence the process are eliminated. These "unnatural" environments typically permit experimental control over the main known influences on the process. Should the process continue to oscillate under free-running conditions, the hypothesis of an endogenous biological basis for the oscillation is strengthened (but, of course, not proven). Typically, where the process continues under these conditions, the oscillation is more evident and predictable than when studied under natual conditions. However, when the underlying oscillation is itself not very powerful, as is the case with the 90-minute sleep rhythm, even the free-running data must be analyzed statistically before the periodicity becomes evident.

A FREE-RUNNING SOCIAL ENVIRONMENT

Our interests are in determining whether the oscillation between episodes of sociability and independent activity are sufficiently regular to be classified as "periodic," in the sense understood by chronobiologists. We felt that a free-running environment would provide the best opportunity to observe and estimate the spontaneous cycle of sociability. Since we are describing humans, not fiddler crabs or rats, the environment we created is a compromise between the need to produce as ecologically valid a natural environment as possible to encourage natural interaction and the necessity to eliminate those conditions that might perturb the spontaneous expression of sociability. Our environment was a spacious (75-meter^2) three-room apartment built inside the Social Psychology Laboratory at Cornell University. It consisted of a 47-m^2 carpeted living/dining room, a separate bedroom, and a full bathroom. It was furnished as a conventional apartment, with couches, chairs, a coffee table, desk, double bed, and a full kitchen including stove and refrigerator. The walls were decorated variously with paintings or posters. Subjects brought with them numerous personal belongings, including musical instruments, sewing machines, records, hobbies, games, and books. Subjects purchased their own food prior to the experiment and prepared it whenever it suited them while the experiments were in progress.

In most respects, the apartment was physically more spacious and better equipped than many of the subjects' own quarters in Ithaca. It was however, a laboratory designed for a special purpose. Sound was controlled by concrete walls 23 cm thick and double lead-filled doors. The air was fresh and recirculated continuously at a temperature selected by the subjects, as was the lighting in the rooms. Where the apartment differed from others was in the absence of normal light and time cues: There were no windows and no clocks; no television, radio, or telephone, although there was a stereo set that subjects might use whenever they wished. To provide an opportunity to exercise, there was a stationary bicycle. While the experiment was in progress, subjects had no contacts with anyone other than their spouse or partner, although mail and newspapers were delivered during their sleeping hours.

TELEMETRY AND RECORDING SYSTEM

The spontaneous interactions of subjects were recorded by several means— film, audiotape, chart paper, and ultimately, computer disk. A Bolex 16-mm movie camera took one still-frame picture each minute of the living room only, showing what the subjects were doing, where, and when. Each picture also showed the time of day, subjects' pulse rate, and the presence/absence of vocalization from each subject at the moment of the picture. A television camera covered the living room, providing the staff with a view of the experiment.

The record of vocalization and heartbeats for each subject was obtained by telemetry. Each subject wore a comfortable golf hat, on top of which were two miniature FM radio transmitters and batteries. This arrangement permitted complete freedom of movement for the subjects. It took several years of experimentation to develop an automatic speech-detection system that would permit us to determine which of two or more persons is speaking in a potentially high ambient-noise environment with negligible errors of either omission or commission. Details of this system follow.

One transmitter of each hat broadcasts the sounds picked up by a high-quality condenser microphone mounted on a little boom 3 cm from the side of the mouth. The second transmitter broadcasts the signal from a throat microphone embedded in a cloth neckband. The receivers in the adjacent control room directed these signals to special circuits that determine whether both signals were present. If so, the person was recorded as vocalizing; if not, as silent. The purpose of the dual-micorphone system is to separate background noises such as music, dish washing, and the sounds of the partner's voice from being mistaken for the subject's speech. This configuration of apparatus accomplished this by using the throat microphone to edit the signal coming from the condenser microphone. The throat unit is sensitive to viberations of objects to which it is attached, but it is not sensitive to airborne sounds. Therefore, it will not so easily be activated by background sounds as the condenser unit. Should the latter detect phonograph sounds, the circuit will not report this as speech, because the throat unit will not have detected it. The circuit that performs the comparison of the two signals uses only the low- and mid-frequency waveforms of the FM transmissions, and only if both have such waveforms present will it pass the signal as "speech."

The decision—silence or speech—for each subject is made continuously, generally in a much more fine-grained manner than can be provided by human observers. The decisions of the circuitry are in binary form suitable for computer recording or for activating event recorders. These binary decisions also activated a circuit that recorded the information in the form of frequency-encoded tones on audiotape, synchronously with an audio track containing the content of what the subjects were saying. The tone generation system is adapted from the telephone Touch-Tone system.

Other information recorded included heartbeats, which were transmitted by another miniature FM radio transmitter worn on the belt. This information served as our principle measure of physical activity during the time the subjects were in the living room. Two other binary coded pieces of information were indications of silence/sound and stillness/movement in the bedroom. Such events must be recorded so as to have a complete record of sociability and physical activity. We worked out an agreement with subjects to provide complete privacy of spoken content while permitting us to know when speech occurred through the use of an acoustic threshold device that was triggered by sound pressure. When the sound pressure is above a preset level, the device signals the presence of speech; otherwise, silence. There is also a similar device for detecting movement, which is based on an ultrasonic Doppler-shift detector. From these recordings, we knew the full patterns of sociability and movement around the clock under free-running conditions, with high precision and at low labor costs.

The reliance upon a fully instrumented detection and recording system evolved for several reasons. The initial studies began with time sampling by observers, followed later by continuous human observation when time sampling proved inadequate. The observers reported considerable difficulty producing accurate recordings during periods of active sociability, and they found the long silent periods between sociability episodes boring. As serious as these problems were, the effects of the observers' presence on the subjects was even more serious. The debriefing interviews frequently turned up evidence of disturbing effects attributed to the one-way glass and the knowledge that someone was listening to and watching the subjects' every sound and movement. The observers shared this distaste, feeling that they were unconscious participants in these conversations. Further incentive to develop an automated recording system came from the large expenses of human observations around the clock and the sheer administrative difficulties in arranging shifts, parking permits, and emergency coverage when someone could not make their observations. Since the conversion to a fully instrumented system, the couple report much less of a feeling of constraint, and the films and tapes appear to confirm this. Our recent studies have been so free of human observations that we can assure the couples that only a few minutes a day will be required to check on the operation of the recording system, thus providing them with virtually 24 hours of privacy.

SUBJECTS

From their inception, these studies of free-running sociability have been limited to couples, most often husband/wife or unmarried couples who have lived together for some time. Occasionally, we have had friends of the same sex as subjects. The youngest subject was 18; the oldest, less than 40. They represent a reasonably wide range of occupations: school teachers, poets, musicians, programmers, graduate students, farmers, unemployed commercial artists, and members of religious communes. In the early studies, couples were recruited by advertisement, but all the recent couples have volunteered as a result of personal contact with former participants in the study. No one with very small children has participated, since it is impossible to accommodate infants in the laboratory, and all subjects have to pass a medical examination in advance.   Once subjects are selected to participate, they are fully informed about the experiment; there are no deceptions whatsoever. They are shown the equipment, what it does and how, and are assured that their private communications will be respected and known only to members of the staff. A legal document explaining the nature of the study and the rights and obligations of both subjects and staff is signed before the study gets under way. Subjects are paid $100 each and are given $25 per week as a food allowance. Most experiments last for 7 days; the first is always a day of adaptation that is separated from the experiment proper by a short 4-hour break. Eight couples have completed two uninterrupted week-long confinements.

During the experiments, the subjects have no schedule of activities imposed from the outside. They are free to work, play, eat, sleep, and socialize whenever it suits them. In these respects, their experience is quite different from that of subjects in sensory-deprivation studies and also from that of workers isolated in weather and space stations where life is heavily regulated by exogenous events and schedules.

DAILY PATTERNS OF CONVENTIONAL ACTIVITY

Our central hypothesis concerned the existence of a possible periodicity in conversational activity with a full cycle time (hereafter called *period*) in the vicinity of 100 minutes per cycle. To permit efficient encoding of the data while retaining sufficient precision to test the hypothesis, we elected to use 10-minute intervals as the fundamental temporal unit within which conversational activity would be measured. Thus (in theory) we could with this level of data aggregation detect periodicities with periods as short as 20 minutes per cycle. The typical waking "day" in our experiments would contain an average of 95 points in time, corresponding to 16 hours of activity. As the length of our subjects' waking days ranged between 10 and 20 hours, the length of our daily data records ranged between 60 and 120 points.

At the 10-minute level of aggregation, the vocal activity measures for the two individuals in each couple presented virtually identical patterns, a not unexpected result of the relatively long interval of time during which the measurements were accumulated. Attempts to separate individual characteristics proved impossible at this level of aggregation, although they showed up clearly at the micro level. Thus these measurements reflected the activity of the dyad more than of the individuals in the dyad, and for this reason only the total amount of dyadic conversational activity was encoded for analysis.

As stated earlier, the recordings of the original data were in three forms: audio sound track, audio binary, and event recorder. For these studies at the 10-minute level, the charts from the event recorder were used as the basic reference, and *every* measurement was checked against the audio sound track for validity. We have, therefore, considerable confidence in the accuracy of these data. Physical activity measures were not used in the analyses reported here.

Figures 3.1a, 3.2a, and 3.3a depict successive daily conversational activity patterns for one of our couples. These data are fairly typical in that although there are certain gross similarities in the patterns from one day to the next, there is little real stability visible. On the other hand, the ebb and flow of conversation during these three days is clearly visible, although without some statistical analysis it is difficult to tell whether there are any periodic components in the data.

SPECTRAL ANALYSIS

The appropriate statistical tool for the study of periodicities in time series data is spectral analysis. In the present context, this technique is particularly simple and straightforward to use. The power spectra for the time series shown in Figs. 3.1a, 3.2a, and 3.3a are shown, respectively, in Figs. 3.1b, 3.2b, and 3.3b. On the assumption that few readers have encountered spectral analysis before, a nontechnical explanation follows. Technical details and computer programs can be found in two excellent books: *Fourier analysis of time series: An introductory* by Bloomfield (1976), and *Spectral analysis and its applications* by Jenkins and Watts (1968). Although the fundamental ideas of spectral analysis are very old (dating back to the discovery that a glass prism could separate the individual color components in light), the application of its principles to numerical data is quite recent, having been made practical by the development of computers and the discovery (Cooley, Lewis, & Welch, 1967) of a remarkably efficient algorithm for the calculation of a spectrum.

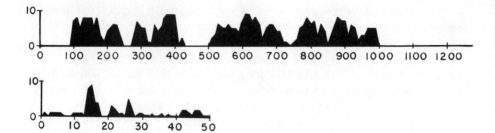

FIG. 3.1a   Conversational activity time series, Day 1. Horizontal axis; time in minutes (0 = time of awakening); vertical axis: amount of talking per 10-minute interval (9 = continuous talking).

FIG. 3.1b   Power spectrum of conversational activity, Day 1. Horizontal axis: frequency of periodic component (in cycles per 1,280 minutes; see Table 3.1); vertical axis: power of each periodic component (in arbitrary units).

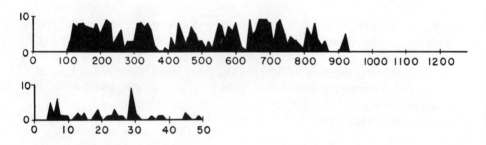

FIG. 3.2a   Conversational activity time series, Day 2. Same units as Fig. 3.1a.

FIG. 3.2b   Power spectrum of conversational activity, Day 2. Same units as Fig. 3.1b.

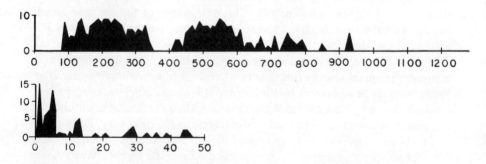

FIG. 3.3a   Conversational activity time series, Day 3. Same units as Fig. 3.1a.

FIG. 3.3b   Power spectrum of conversational activity, Day 3. Same units as Fig. 3.1b.

Whereas the horizontal axis in the graphs of the conversational activity time series indicates *time*, measured in minutes, the horizontal axis of a power spectrum indicates *frequency*, measured in cycles per 1,280 minutes. Thus, for example, a frequency of 10 refers to a periodicity that undergoes 10 full cycles every 1,280 minutes—i.e. a periodicity with a *period* of 128 minutes per cycle. Similarly, a frequency of 20 refers to a periodicity with a period of 64 minutes. The base figure of 1,280 from which the frequencies are computed was chosen for computational convenience: It is a trifle longer than the longest time series, and it represents a series length that—being a power of 2 ($128 = 2^7$)—is computationally efficient. Table 3.1 provides a conversion chart, so that the reader may more easily translate frequency into period, and vice versa.

Whereas the vertical axis in the graphs of the time series indicate *amount* of conversational activity per 10-minute interval of time, the vertical axis of the power spectra indicate the strength (or "power") of the periodicities at each frequency. The power of each frequency component of a spectrum is, in fact, its contribution to the total variance of the time series about its mean; so that the height of each peak can, if desired, be interpreted in "explained variance" terms. The highest point in the power spectrum shown in Fig. 3.1b is at a frequency of 15, which corresponds to a period of 85 minutes. Thus, in that day, the strongest periodicity contained in the data had a period of 85 minutes per cycle. The two secondary peaks in the power spectrum are at frequencies of 21 and 26, corresponding to weaker periodicities with periods of 61 and 49 minutes, respectively.

Thus, it can be seen that by noting the frequency (or period) and relative height of the peaks in a power spectrum, a time series can be decomposed into its constituent periodic components (if it has any). A time series that has a perfectly flat power spectrum is called "white noise," a signal that when realized acoustically sounds like the hissing of radio static. A time series that has a power spectrum with a single sharp peak located at a given frequency

TABLE 3.1
A Conversion Table for Frequency (Cycles/1,280 Min) and Period
(Min/Cycle)

Frequency	Period	Frequency	Period	Frequency	Period
1	1280	11	116	21	61
2	640	12	107	22	58
3	427	13	98	23	56
4	320	14	91	24	53
5	256	15	85	25	51
6	213	16	80	26	49
7	183	17	75	27	47
8	160	18	71	28	46
9	142	19	67	29	44
10	128	20	64	30	43

closely resembles a sine wave, whose acoustic realization would sound like a pure tone. Typical applications of spectral analysis occur when it is suspected that a periodic process has been masked in noise to the extent that it is not visible in the time series. In these situations, examination of the power spectrum provides information about the power of hypothetical periodicities at each frequency.

A comparison of the three time series and their associated power spectra shown in Figs. 3.1, 3.2, and 3.3 demonstrates many of the most useful functions of spectral analysis. Figure 3.2 for example, shows an activity pattern that is noticeably more "choppy" than the relatively smooth patterns seen in Figs. 3.1 and 3.3. This is reflected in the power spectrum of Fig. 3.2: There is a sharp peak at a high frequency, 29, which corresponds to a comparatively rapid 44-minute period. Similarly, the activity pattern in Fig. 3.3 shows two long episodes of generally high levels of conversational activity. These are reflected in the power spectrum by the very high peak at the low-frequency end of the spectrum, covering a band of frequencies from 3 to 5. These frequencies correspond to a range of period from 256 to 427 minutes, matching what is plain to the eye in the original conversational activity series. Of interest in this power spectrum, however, is the secondary peak at a frequency of 13. This is an indication that in addition to the visible phenomena, there is a hidden rhythm with a period of 98 minutes. It is precisely in the detection of such otherwise hidden periodicities that spectral analysis finds its greatest utility.

The analysis reported here is based on a recent set of 45 experimental days, representing 17 different individuals. The length of the experiments varied from 4 to 8 days, and all initial and final days were disregarded. The power spectra for these daily activity records show a degree of variation from day to day similar to that seen in Figs. 3.1, 3.2, and 3.3. The central question is, therefore, whether there are any features in the spectra that recur from day to day. The answer to this question is found in the average power spectrum for the entire set of 45 days. This power spectrum is shown in Fig. 3.4.

The average power spectrum of Fig. 3.4 exhibits four major features, of which two were completely unexpected. The first feature, marked with an encircled numeral 1, is a broad peak extending from a frequency of 1 to a frequency of 5. As exemplified in Fig. 3.3, this kind of feature in a power spectrum results from the occurrence during the day of one or two major episodes of conversational activity that extend across many hours each. A card game, for example, would generate such a feature in a power spectrum. This kind of feature was expected and has little substantive significance.

The feature marked with an encircled numeral 3 is a moderate peak covering a band of frequencies from 12 to 15, corresponding to a range of period between 85 and 107 minutes per cycle. This is the evidence that we were looking for: a clear indication that there is a periodicity in daytime

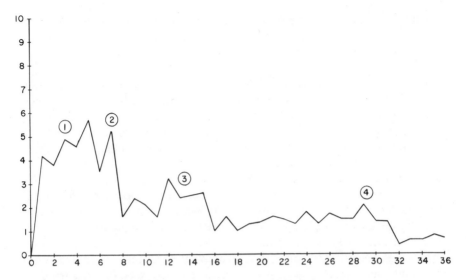

FIG. 3.4 Average power spectrum of conversational activity, 45 days. Same units as Fig. 3.1b.

conversational activity that has a period in the same range as the observed nighttime sleep/dream cycle, i.e., 90–100 minutes per cycle.

Two features appeared that were not at all expected, marked 2 and 4, respectively. Feature 2 is at a frequency of 7, and feature 4 is at a frequency of 29, corresponding to periodicities with periods of 183 and 46 minutes per cycle. It is interesting to note that these periods are almost exactly double and half of the hypothesized period (about 90 minutes). An interpretation of these features and a discussion of their implications follows.

DISCUSSION

There are several alternative explanations for the existence of the three peaks seen in the average power spectrum (Fig. 3.4). It may be suggested, for one, that the peaks with periods of 91 and 46 are *harmonics* of the fundamental periodicity at 183 minutes per cycle. We feel that this explanation can be rejected for several reasons:

1. The harmonic hypothesis implies that peaks should be found at frequencies that are multiples of the fundamental, i.e. at periods of 91, *61*, 46, *37*,... minutes per cycle; but the two italicized periodicities did not appear in the power spectrum.

2. Harmonics occur primarily in acoustical applications for spectral analysis, in which context they imply a nonsinusoidal shape in the

fundamental periodic waveform; but our data do not show any periodicity that is strong and stable enough to be called "fundamental" in any sense similar to that of acoustics.

For these reasons, we feel that the peaks at periods of 91 and 46 are not harmonics of a fundamental periodicity whose period is 183 minutes per cycle.

A more plausible explanation for these three periodicities suggests that sociability is influenced by a biorhythm whose period is roughly 91 minutes per cycle. Kleitman (1963, p. 367) holds that there is just such a basic rest–and–activity cycle, which modulates the circadian sleep–wakefulness cycle at all times. During sleep, this modulation produces the cyclic progression in sleep stages, and during wakefulness it produces cyclic variation in all activity, and in social interaction in particular. Given that this hypothetical biorhythm is easily perturbed and entrained by exogenous events, e.g., the other person initiating (or avoiding) an interactional episode, it is quite conceivable that episodes would frequently be omitted from or inserted into what would otherwise have been a more regular periodicity. This would yield apparent periods of double or half that expected; in other words, it would produce the peaks at 183 and 46 minutes per cycle. Similar phenomena have been found in Rhesus monkeys (Maxim, Bowden, & Sackett, 1976). It is interesting to note that 46, 91, and 183 minutes per cycle are, respectively, exactly 1/32, 1/16, and 1/8 of the 24.75-hour (average), free-running circadian period of our subjects. They may well be, therefore, a fundamental link between the circadian and the ultradian biorhythms.

The stability of the daily periodic structure of conversational activity was substantially less than our earlier pilot studies and the literature had led us to believe. The absence of a single large stable peak in the daily power spectra may simply mean that the tendency to engage in conversational activity is not affected by an endogenous biological oscillator. Our findings of three relatively unstable periodic components would (if this is accepted) still remain unexplained, since they relate to no known or suspected environmentally produced source of entrainment. It remains, therefore, to identify the possible sources of destabilization. We have considered two major sources: attention span, and the circadian cycle itself.

The possible effects of attention span and boredom on interactional rhythms emerged out of the postexperimental interviews with out subjects. Although they brought a great many of their personal belongings with them into the experiments and were free to do as they pleased around the clock, all subjects reported periods of boredom. After devoting some time to an activity such as reading, cooking, or playing cards, subjects would spontaneously (and often suddenly) shift their attention to a new activity. This phenomena is particularly apparent when viewing the motion pictures of the experiments at normal speeds (recall that the pictures were taken at the rate of one frame per minute). Whatever the underlying processes that control attention, there are clear transitions in attention over time. When these shifts involve the other person, then episodes of conversation develop. Further, if an activity is inherently interesting (e.g., an exciting card game), then the next transition may be delayed for some time, and conversely. Thus, there may well be interference between attention span and the hypothetical ultradian biorhythm.

The destabilizing influence of the free-running circadian rhythm operates indirectly. Without clocks or other temporal cues, our couples retired to bed roughly 45 minutes later each night *on the average*; but there were some variations from day to day in the length of the circadian period, ranging between the extremes of 19 and 30 hours. Thus the circadian biorhythm itself was subject to (endogenous) perturbations of some magnitude in our experiments, resulting in considerable fluctuations in our subjects' restedness or fatigue. We suspect that compensatory behavior (such as napping, etc.) may have interfered with the interactional rhythms that we have hypothesized.

In sum, we feel that the appearance of three peaks in the average power spectrum of conversational activity for 45 days of free-running social behavior argues for the influence of daytime ultradian biorhythms on social interaction. Such biorhythms, if they do indeed exist during the waking hours, must be easily perturbable—as, in fact, the 90-minute sleep biorhythm is. The free-running social conditions that our experimental design was intended to produce constitute a novel approach to the scientific study of human social interaction—an approach that could be used for many purposes other than the narrow range of hypotheses that motivated our study. We have demonstrated the feasibility of moving a much larger slice of "life" into the laboratory than heretofore attempted. Only on this scale are effects as subtle as that of the ultradian biorhythm visible at all, and only on this scale can the complete daily cycle of interpersonal dynamics be studied.

ACKNOWLEDGMENTS

This research was supported by grants from the National Science Foundation and the National Institute of Mental Health.

REFERENCES

Bloomfield, P. *Fourier analysis of time series: An introduction.* New York: Wiley, 1976.

Chapple, E. D. Quantitative analysis of the interaction of individuals. *Proceedings of the National Academy of Sciences, U.S.*, 1939, *25*, 58–67.

Chapple, E. D. Personality differences as described in invariant properties of individuals in interaction. *Proceedings of the National Academy of Sciences, U.S.*, 1940, *26*, 10–16.

Chapple, E. D. *Culture and biological man.* New York: Holt, Rinehart & Winston, 1970.

Chapple, E. D. Toward a mathematical model of interaction: Some preliminary considerations. In P. Kay (Ed.), *Explorations in mathematical anthropology.* Cambridge, Mass.: MIT Press, 1971.

Chapple, E. D. & Lindeman, E. Clinical implications of measurements of interaction rates in psychiatric patients. *Applied Anthropology,* 1941, *1,* 1–10.

Cobb, L. *Time series analysis of the periodicities of casual conversations.* Unpublished Ph. D. dissertation, Cornell University, Ithaca, N.Y., 1973.

Cooley, J. W., Lewis, P. A. W., & Welch, P. D. Historical notes on the fast Fourier transformation, *Institute of Electrical and Electronics Engineers, Transactions on Audio and Electroacoustics,* 1967, *AU-15,* 75–79.

Dement, W. C., & Kleitman, N. Cyclic variations in EEG during sleep and their relation to eye movements, body motility, and dreaming. *Electroencephalography and Clinical Neurophysiology,* 1957, *9,* 673–690.

Friedman, S. & Fisher, C. On the presence of a rhythmic, diurnal oral instinctual drive cycle in man. *Journal of the American Psychoanalytic Association,* 1967, *15,* 317–343.

Globus, G. G., Drury, R., Phoebus, E., & Boyd, R. Ultradian rhythms in performance. *Psychophysiology,* 1971, *9,* 132. (Abstract).

Hiatt, J. R., & Kripke, D. F. Ultradian rhythms in waking gastric activity. *Psychosomatic Medicine,* 1975, *37,* 320–325.

Jaffe, J. & Feldstein, S. *Rhythms of dialogue.* New York: Academic Press, 1970.

Jenkins, G. M., & Watts, D. G. *Spectral analysis and its applications.* San Francisco: Holden–Day, 1968.

Kleitman, N. *Sleep and wakefulness.* Chicago: University of Chicago Press, 1963.

Maxim, P. E., Bowden, D. M., & Sackett, G. P. Ultradian rhythms of solitary and social behavior in Rhesus monkeys. *Physiology and Behavior,* 1976, *17,* 337–344.

Orr, W. C., & Hoffman, H. J. A 90-minute cardian biorhythm: Methodology and data analysis using modified periodograms and complex demodulation. *IEEE Transactions on Audio and Electroacoustics,* 1974, *BME-21,* 130–143.

Oswald, I., Merrington, J., & Lewis, H. Cyclical "on-demand" oral intake by adults. *Nature,* 1970, *225,* 959–960.

Othmer, E., Hayden, M. P., & Segelbaum, R. Encephalic cycles during sleep and wakefulness in humans: A 24-hour pattern. *Science,* 1969, *164,* 447–449.

II PERSONALITY AND SOCIAL INFLUENCES

4

Self-Attributed Personality Characteristics and the Pacing of Conversational Interaction

Stanley Feldstein
University of Maryland Baltimore County

Luciano Alberti
University of Bern

Mohammed BenDebba
The Johns Hopkins University

How much of what we think of ourselves is reflected in the ways in which we pace our conversations? How are the ways in which we pace our conversations influenced by how our conversational partners see themselves? Given, for instance, that an individual's contribution to a dialogue involves relatively long bursts of speech with relatively long silences among them, can we say anything about how he views himself? Does he believe that he is cautious, thoughtful, and/or complaisant? Or does he believe himself to be hesitant, indecisive, and/or stubborn? Does such an individual keep the floor for long periods of time, and, if so, does it reflect a self-perception of maturity, solemnity, and perseverance? Or is his doing so related somehow to his partner's self-perception?

These questions are not meant to necessarily imply that an individual paces his conversational interactions in a particular way *because* he views himself as he does; no intimation of deliberateness is intended. (On the other hand, it might be noted that actors often alter the pacing of their speech quite deliberately to more adequately depict the people they are portraying.) The questions are meant rather to raise the possibility that the timing of an individual's participation in a dialogue may be related to those characteristics that individual attributes to him- or herself, characteristics that are usually considered to be aspects of personality. If such timing is capable of distinguishing among individuals, and if personality attributions about oneself and others are conceded to have psychological reality (Scherer, in press), then whether the relationship is causal or correlational is not of immediate concern, since either type contains potentially predictive information (Blass, 1977). Implied here is the general notion that people tend, in interpersonal situations, to behave in ways that are consonant with their self-attributions. Thus, it may be the case that (a) information about such attributions can be helpful in predicting behavior, and (b) conversational time patterns can provide some of the information. The study we report here was that part of a larger investigation (Marcus, Welkowitz, Feldstein, & Jaffe, 1970) designed to explore the relations between self-attributed personality characteristics and the temporal parameters that define the pacing of conversational interaction.

Studies of the relationship of personality characteristics to the time patterns, or rhythm, of speech are beginning to appear in the literature with greater frequency. Siegman (1977) reviews at some length investigations relating introversion–extraversion to speech pausing and speech rate. Most of the studies indicated that the speech of extraverts was faster than that of introverts and that this difference in tempo seemed to be primarily a function of the shorter silences used by extraverts. The results of a recent experiment by Sloan and Feldstein (1977) also showed that their extraverts did use a faster tempo and shorter pauses in their speech (monologues) than their introverts. In addition, however, the experiment attempted to explore the characteristics associated with the vocal stereotype of introversion–extraversion by having each of the introverted and extraverted participants role play introverted and extraverted speech. The role-played speech seemed to be an exaggeration of the actual speech of the introverts and extraverts. Specifically, when they role played extraverts, all the participants not only used shorter pauses and faster tempos than when they role played introverts, but the probability of their continuing to talk was greater. Of perhaps more interest is the fact that even in their role playing of the extraverted and introverted speech, the extraverts used shorter pauses and faster tempos than the introverts.

An even more recent study (Feldstein & Crown, 1978) examined the conversational speech of introverts and extraverts. The results clearly indicated that the ways in which introverts and extraverts paced their conversational interactions depended upon their race and, to a somewhat lesser extent, their gender. For example, although the probability of continuing to pause was greater for black introverts than for black extraverts, it was not different for white introverts and extraverts. Again, the speech rate of black extraverts was faster than that of black introverts, but the rates of white introverts and extraverts did not differ. It is not easy to explain why these results are at variance with those of most previous studies although it should be noted that none of the previous studies appears to have involved ordinary conversations. Nor have previous studies reported the racial composition of their participants.

As Siegman (1978) points out, however, there is still relatively little information available about the relation of speech rhythm to personality characteristics other than introversion–extraversion. Gallois and Markel

(1975) examined the use of the *speaking turn* as an index of "social personality." What is meant by "social personality" is never clearly elaborated. The study that most closely approaches the present one was conducted by Markel, Phillis, Vargas, and Howard (1972). In that study, however, the authors compared their subjects' scale scores on the *Sixteen Personality Factor Questionnaire* (16PF) and the *Minnesota Multiphasic Personality Inventory* (MMPI) with ratings of their subjects' "voice quality," i.e., ratings of whether their speech was "loud–fast," "loud–slow," "soft–fast," or "soft–slow." One of the analyses yields a significant interaction of the four voice quality groups with the 16 factor scores of the 16PF, indicating that different factors were associated with each of the groups. The authors describe the four groups in terms of the popular adjectives provided by the original *Handbook* (Cattell & Eber, 1957) for the 16PF.

Temporal Parameters

At perhaps its crudest level, a conversation can be viewed as a sequence of sounds and silences having at least two sources. The knowledge of which segment of the sequence emanates from which source allows us to derive from the sequence five parameters: *speaking turns, vocalizations, pauses, switching pauses,* and *simultaneous speech.*

Speaking Turns. The *speaking turn* is the superordinate member of the temporal classification in that it not only distinguishes the source, so to speak, but its frequency indexes the pivotal feature of a conversation, which is the alternation of the sources, or speakers. Moreover, it includes up to three of the other parameters and allows for the categorization of simultaneous speech.

In spite of the seemingly clear description implicit in the words *to take turns speaking,* the definition of a *turn* varies from one investigator to another. Reasons for this divergence are presented in some detail elsewhere (Feldstein & Welkowitz, 1978). Suffice it to say that definitions of a turn vary according to the criteria used to determine its boundaries. The criteria may be semantic, kinesic, temporal, or combinations thereof. The definition used here is purely temporal; a speaker's turn begins the instant he or she starts to talk alone and ends immediately prior to the instant another speaker starts to talk alone (Jaffe & Feldstein, 1970). Having a turn is synonymous with having the floor. Having a turn is not at all dependent upon what a speaker says, nor upon the time taken to say it. In the present study, the durations of the turns used by the subjects ranged from about 1½ to 15 seconds and averaged about 5 seconds. Theoretically, however, they can range from a fraction of a second to many minutes.

Relatively few studies of speaking turns have appeared in the literature. Schegloff's (1968) examination of how turns are sequenced at the beginnings of conversations is often cited as a pioneering effort. Yngve (1970) proposed that the turn be explored as a behavior that could provide information about the structure of what he calls "state of mind." Duncan (1972, 1973, 1974) has been engaged in a series of studies that seek to define the turn in terms of the paralinguistic and kinesic behaviors that accompany it. Markel (1973), who defines the turn in exactly the same way in which it is defined here, suggested that it might usefully be considered a unit of conversational analysis analogous to the "phone" in phonological analysis. He proposed the interesting notion that it may be possible to distinguish contrasting classes of turns based upon differing functions and coverbal behaviors. As was mentioned earlier, Gallois and Markel (1975) also investigated the turn as an index of social personality. Finally, an intriguing experimental study by Martindale (1971) demonstrated that participants in task-oriented discussions retained the floor longer when the discussions were held on their own territories than when they took place on the territories of the persons with whom they were talking. This territorial effect, however, appears to be at least partially dependent upon whether the task is competitive or cooperative (Conroy & Sundstrom, 1977).

The minimal turn consists of a single vocalization. However, a turn can also consist of vocalizations and pauses; of a vocalization and switching pause; or of vocalizations, pauses, and a switching pause. The consistency of the average durations of speaking turns within the conversations of the present study yields an estimate of .63; their stability from conversation to conversation, an estimate of .64 (Feldstein & Welkowitz, 1978). These estimates are high enough to permit the inference that turn behavior is not only reliable within and across conversations, but also that it displays sufficient interindividual variability to warrant further attention.

Vocalizations, Pauses, and Switching Pauses. A *vocalization* is a segment of sound uninterrupted by any silence that can be detected by the unaided human ear. The sound can be speech or a laugh or a cry; it can consist of part of a word, a full word, or several words; it is uttered by, and credited to, the speaker who has the floor. A *pause* is an interval of joint silence bounded by the vocalizations of the speaker who has the floor and credited to that speaker. A *switching pause* is an interval of joint silence that is initiated by the speaker who has the floor but terminated by a vocalization of the speaker who did not have the floor but who thereby obtains it. Inasmuch as it occurs within the turn of the speaker by whom it is initiated, it is credited to him or her.

Previous research as well as the present study have established the reliabilities of the parameters within and across conversations (Jaffe & Feldstein, 1970). In the present study, the within-conversation reliability estimates for pauses, switching pauses, and vocalizations are .71, .72, and .76, respectively; the across-conversation estimates are .65, .66, and .68, respectively. It has also been shown that vocalizations are statistically unrelated to either pauses or switching pauses, that pauses are related to switching pauses in unrestrained conversations but not in interviews, and that the average durations of the three parameters do not fully account for the variability of the average durations of turns (Feldstein & Welkowitz, 1978).

Pauses have been used as a dependent variable under several names (e.g., *hesitations, pauses, unfilled pauses, silences*) in a wide variety of research studies, many of which have been adequately reviewed elsewhere (e.g., Rochester, 1973; Siegman, 1978). A major issue of concern continues to be the relation of pauses to cognitive processes, particularly those involved in the making of syntactic and lexical choices. Most investigations of pauses have used monologues as their speech samples and have not been interested in the pause as a conversational event. Those that have (Feldstein & Welkowitz, 1978) have noted that participants in conversations tend to match each other's durations of pauses and switching pauses. The degree of matching or, as it is also called, *congruence*, appears to be related to a number of characteristics such as mutual attraction, psychological differentiation (Marcus et al. 1970), socialization level (Welkowitz, Cariffe, & Feldstein, 1976), and perceived interpersonal similarity (Welkowitz & Feldstein, 1969). However, an unpublished study of conversations (Dabbs, Uwanno, Evans, Meiners, Stokes, Kennedy, & Bakeman, 1977) examined the durations of pauses and switching pauses in relation to length of acquaintanceship. Beattie (Chapter 6) has conducted a provocative series of studies, the results of which indicate that rate of pausing can be systematically altered by the use of reinforcement and punishment. Not many other studies have explored the function or correlates of the switching pause as it is defined here. Nor have vocalizations as defined here been used as the dependent variable in much research. One study (BenDebba, 1974) did indicate that the frequency of vocalizations can be altered as a function of conditioning.

Simultaneous Speech. A vocalization initiated by the speaker who does not have the floor while the other speaker is talking is considered *simultaneous speech*. By dint of its outcome, simultaneous speech can be divided into *interruptive* and *noninterruptive simultaneous speech* (Feldstein, BenDebba, & Alberti, 1974). Inasmuch as the relationship of the two categories to the self-attributes examined in the present study was reported elsewhere (Feldstein, Alberti, BenDebba, & Welkowitz, 1974), simultaneous speech is not discussed here in any detail.

Personality Attributes

The instrument used to measure self-attributed characteristics was the *Sixteen Personality Factor Questionnaire* (16PF) of Cattell. The 16PF was first published in 1949 and since that time has undergone extensive investigation with regard to the reliabilities and validities of its scales and their applicability in diverse types of contexts. The questionnaire consists of 16 factor-analyzed scales considered by Cattell and his associates to index "personality source traits" that have been found to be dimensions of personality that operate across all age ranges and, to a great extent, cross-culturally.

The 16PF seemed particularly suitable for the present study because it is a self-report instrument, one that requires the respondent to describe what he or she does, prefers, thinks, and feels. It is true that the technical and popular labels used to describe the factors derived from the given answers are themselves inferences. A seemingly more straightforward approach would ask the respondent to describe himself by choosing adjectives from a given set. A major problem with such a strategy, however, is that it is never clear that the adjectives mean the same things to different people. The advantage of the adjectives used to describe the factors of the 16PF is that their behavioral referents are provided by the items on which they are based.

The *Handbook* for the 16PF (Cattell, Eber, & Tatsuoka, 1970) suggests that the technical names of the factors be used in intraprofessional communications. It seems to us, however, that unless one is quite conversant with the 16PF, the technical names mean little or indeed are more misleading than the "best *popular* terms" given for each factor by the *Handbook*. In this report, therefore, only the popular terms are used.

METHOD

The participants of the study were 24 female college students whose ages ranged from 17 to 23. They were divided into 6 subgroups of equal size, or "quartets." The study required that each member of a quartet converse with every other member of the quartet for half an hour on each of 8 occasions about one or more of a range of topics provided for the purpose. Thus, each subject engaged in 3 conversations on each occasion. On the day preceding the first occasion, the subjects were asked to complete Form A of the 16PF as well as a variety of other questionnaires designed to examine other questions.

The conversations took place in a sound-attenuated room furnished as a comfortable office. The two participants engaged in conversation sat facing each other in upholstered chairs, and each subject's microphone was suspended from the ceiling immediately in front of her but above her line of vision. The conversations were recorded on a professional model Ampex stereo tape recorder located outside the experimental room.

The completed forms of the 16PF (Form A) were scored by computer. The sound–silence sequences of the conversations were analyzed by a special analogue-to-digital converter system (Jaffe & Feldstein, 1970) that divided the sequences into speaking turns, vocalizations, pauses, switching pauses, and simultaneous speech and output their frequencies and durations for each subject in each conversation.

Recall that each of the 24 women were engaged in 3 dialogues on each occasion. Thus, for each parameter of interest, there were 72 average durations per occasion. They were then averaged across occasions to provide the values used in the statistical analyses.

Statistical Analysis

The intent of the study was to assess the possibility that the personality characteristics of the participants influenced the average amounts of time they kept the floor each time they obtained it and their average durations of pauses, switching pauses, and vocalizations. It seemed not unreasonable, however, to take into account in the analysis of the data the possibility that the average parameter durations of each participant in a conversation were influenced not only by her personality characteristics but also by those of her conversational partner. Thus, the data were analyzed by hierarchical multiple regression analyses. Sixteen regression equations were used for the analysis of each of the temporal parameters. Each of the equations was concerned with one of the 16 personality factors. Specifically, each equation used the average durations obtained by the subjects on one of the temporal parameters as its dependent variable. In addition, three independent variables were entered into each equation. The first to enter was a variable called *Subjects* that consisted of scores of the participants on one of the factors. The scores of their conversational partners on the same factor formed the second independent variable (called *Partners*). The third and last variable to enter was called *Subjects by Partners* and consisted of the algebraic products of the subjects' and partners' factor scores. As a function of its order in the equation, this last variable assessed the proportion of variance contributed to the average parameter durations by the interaction of the factor scores of the participants and their partners.

RESULTS

A by-product of the regression analyses is an intercorrelation matrix of the 16 factors. The matrix is presented in Table 4.1. Note that there are significant relationships among several of the factors that are partially involved in the relations between the factors and the temporal parameters.

The results of the multiple regression analyses are shown in Table 4.2 and can be discussed in terms of individual factors. On the other hand, it may provide a more coherent picture to present them in terms of the individual parameters. It should be noted, however, that only three of the factors were

TABLE 4.1

Product Moment Correlation Coefficients Yielded by Comparisons Among the 16 Factors of the 16 Personality Factor Questionnaire

	B	C	E	F	G	H	I	L	M	N	O	Q_1	Q_2	Q_3	Q_4
								Factors							
A	-.06	.56	.14	.52	.05	.68	.05	-.04	-.23	.13	-.29	-.11	-.63	-.09	.23
B		-.12	.51	.11	-.28	.08	.05	.11	.39	.13	-.01	.18	.23	-.12	.07
C			-.13	-.07	.19	.32	-.05	-.63	-.19	-.24	-.73	.09	-.28	.42	.70
E				.45	-.40	.58	-.12	.45	.50	.26	.11	.07	-.34	.45	.33
F					-.08	.66	-.19	.19	-.23	.36	.18	-.41	-.57	-.46	.30
G						-.12	-.24	-.10	-.38	.10	-.13	.04	.13	.46	-.29
H							.27	-.03	-.05	.27	-.25	-.14	-.67	-.37	-.06
I								-.09	.25	-.37	.22	-.19	.20	.02	.15
L									.22	.11	.51	-.22	-.07	-.45	.70
M										.25	-.10	.18	.19	-.24	.15
N											.15	.17	-.19	-.03	.16
O												-.32	-.01	-.43	.78
Q_1													.22	.41	.42
Q_2														.32	-.05
Q_3															.66

Note: With 22 df, an r of .40 is significant at or beyond the 5% level.

found to be unrelated to any of the parameters. The three factors are B, M, and Q_1: B has to do with intelligence, M with the difference between practical and impractical approaches to everyday concerns, and Q_1 with the comparison of radical and conservative attitudinal orientations. It might also be noted that Factor A is the only factor related, in some way, to all the parameters. Among the adjectives used by the *Handbook* to describe persons who score high on Factor A are *warmhearted, easygoing, cooperative,* and *attentive to people;* among those used to describe the persons who score low are *reserved, detached, critical, distrustful,* and *skeptical.*

Speaking Turns

Perhaps the most interesting aspect of the analysis of speaking turns is that their average durations were influenced not by the personality characteristics of the individuals who produced them but by those of their conversational partners. The characteristics involved are indexed by Factors A, F, H, and N. Those partners who scored low on these factors elicited longer average turn durations than partners who scored high. In other words, the subjects used longer turns when their partners were reserved, detached, taciturn, sober, shy, and restrained than when their partners were warmhearted, outgoing, talkative, cheerful, adventurous, and socially bold. They also took longer turns when their partners were forthright and unpretentious rather than astute and worldly.

Switching Pauses

The personality characteristics of the partners also affected the average durations of the participants' switching pauses to a greater extent than did the participants' own characteristics. Thus, participants who produced longer switching pauses tended to score low on Factors A and G. Such persons are described by the *Handbook* as reserved, detached, rigid, and prone to sulk and, at the same time, self-indulgent, indolent, and undependable. On the other hand, four factors were involved in the effect of the partners on the participants' switching pauses. That is, the participants produced longer switching pauses when their partners scored low on Factors A and C and high on Factors O and Q_4. Such partners can be described as reserved, detached, easily upset, changeable, apprehensive, self-reproaching, tense, and frustrated.

Pauses

The average durations of the participants' pauses were mostly a function of their own personality characteristics. Participants who scored low rather than high on Factors A, C, and H and high rather than low on Factors L, O, Q_2,

TABLE 4.2

Hierarchical Multiple Regression Analyses of the Relations Between the Average Durations of Vocalizations, Pauses, Switching Pauses, and Speaking Turns of the Participants in Conversations and Their Scores on the Factors of the Sixteen Personality Factor Questionnaire

16 PF Factors		Vocalizations			Pauses			Switching Pauses			Speaking Turns		
		Subjects	Partners	S × P	Subjects	Partners	S × P	Subjects	Partners	S × P	Subjects	Partners	S × P
A	R_i^2	.168**	.020	.002	.270**	.083**	.000	.110**	.099**	.003	.004	.103**	.001
	r_p	.410	-.154	-.054	-.519	-.338	.038	-.331	-.334	.056	.061	-.321	-.037
B	R_i^2	.027	.008	.014	.032	.001	.000	.000	.002	.008	.001	.000	.007
	r_p	.165	.093	-.120	.179	.029	.019	.002	.045	-.087	.036	.007	-.084
C	R_i^2	.001	.018	.008	.058*	.027	.001	.017	.065*	.002	.001	.009	.005
	r_p	-.024	-.134	-.092	-.241	-.168	-.026	-.131	-.257	-.044	-.029	-.095	-.074
E	R_i^2	.099**	.005	.002	.003	.001	.012	.000	.007	.009	.009	.017	.000
	r_p	.314	-.073	-.052	.058	.025	.109	.003	-.084	.094	.093	-.129	.008
F	R_i^2	.170**	.047	.015	.040	.013	.000	.004	.000	.000	.000	.083*	.001
	r_p	.412	-.237	-.138	-.201	.117	.013	-.059	-.017	-.016	-.013	-.288	.025
G	R_i^2	.001	.022	.051	.035	.054	.089**	.060*	.030	.022	.025	.022	.012
	r_p	-.036	.148	-.230	-.188	-.236	.313	-.244	-.178	.154	.158	-.149	.112
H	R_i^2	.146**	.030	.000	.106	.005	.042	.037	.041	.044	.011	.068*	.000
	r_p	.382	-.186	-.015	-.325	-.074	.216	-.193	-.205	.219	.107	-.263	-.022
I	R_i^2	.066*	.025	.000	.007	.069*	.000	.023	.033	.000	.054	.012	.018
	r_p	-.257	-.163	-.005	.081	-.264	.013	-.152	-.184	.006	-.232	-.112	.137
L	R_i^2	.001	.010	.000	.099**	.014	.000	.027	.056	.000	.020	.001	.000
	r_p	.031	.099	.018	.314	.123	.012	.164	.240	.003	.141	-.025	.011

M R_i^2	.001	.001	.011	.034	.000	.009	.005	.010	.000	.010	.009	.017
r_p	.033	−.024	−.102	.184	.002	.095	.072	−.100	−.008	.102	.096	−.130
N R_i^2	.011	.022	.005	.002	.002	.030	.014	.000	.001	.017	.078*	.002
r_p	.103	−.150	−.073	.046	−.006	.172	−.117	.003	−.035	.129	−.282	.043
O R_i^2	.009	.000	.000	.058*	.012	.013	.010	.064*	.008	.003	.001	.006
r_p	.093	.010	−.004	.241	.113	−.120	.099	.255	−.090	.053	−.029	−.078
Q_1 R_i^2	.024	.004	.016	.007	.007	.000	.004	.004	.006	.002	.003	.007
r_p	−.155	.066	.129	.083	−.086	−.021	−.061	−.060	.075	.045	.051	.083
Q_2 R_i^2	.106**	.045	.006	.086*	.002	.012	.010	.007	.016	.036	.013	.009
r_p	−.326	.224	.086	.293	.046	.114	.100	.086	.128	−.190	.116	.098
Q_3 R_i^2	.042	.008	.004	.000	.077*	.013	.042	.022	.008	.000	.001	.000
r_p	−.204	.092	.062	−.013	−.277	−.118	−.205	−.150	−.093	.000	−.023	.021
Q_4 R_i^2	.023	.003	.002	.085*	.031	.031	.037	.058*	.021	.000	.000	.001
r_p	.151	.059	.048	.291	.182	−.185	.192	.245	−.153	.016	−.020	−.032

Note: The dependent variables in the regression analyses were the average durations of vocalizations, pauses, switching pauses, and speaking turns. The independent variables entered into each equation were the participants' factor scores ("Subjects"), the factor scores of their conversational partners ("Partners"), and the products of the two sets of scores ("S × P"). The solution of each equation is presented in terms of proportion of variance by which the dependent variable is incremented at each step (R_i^2) and the partial correlation coefficient (r_p) that indexes the magnitude and direction of the relation of the independent variable to the dependent variable with the effects of prior independent variables removed. The table presents the solutions of 48 equations (4 dependent variables and 16 factors). Although each participant is multiply represented at each step of each equation by virtue of having had three partners, the significance of the F ratio associated with each R was evaluated on the basis of 1 df for the numerator and 23 −k df for the denominator, where k = 1 for the first step and is incremented by 1 for each successive step.

*p < .05
**p < .01

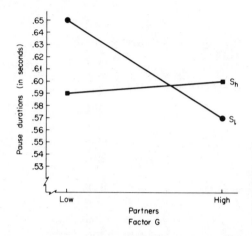

FIG. 4.1. Estimated durations of pauses for subjects who scored high (S_h) and subjects who scored low (S_l) on Factor G of the 16PF as a function of whether their partners scored high or low on the factor.

and Q_4 tended to produce longer pauses. The characteristics associated with Factor A and, to some extent, with C and H have already been given. Persons who score low on C and H tend to be easily upset, worrying, shy, restrained, and somewhat restricted in their interests. Persons who score high on Factors L, O, Q_2, and Q_4 are described as suspicious, jealous, insecure, troubled, fussy, tense, driven, and, at the same time, self-sufficient and resourceful.

The lengths of the participants' pauses were to some degree also affected by their partners' characteristics. The participants tended to use longer pauses when their partners were persons who scored low on Factors A, I, and Q_3, i.e., persons who are reserved, self-reliant, and unsentimental but also uncontrolled and careless about social rules.

Finally, the analysis of Factor G yielded an interaction effect (Fig. 4.1) such that those participants who scored low on the factor—who might be described as expedient, fickle, frivolous—used longer pauses with partners who scored low than with partners who scored high. However, those persons who scored high on Factor G—presumably responsible, conscientious, and moralistic—tended to use pauses of relatively similar durations whether their partners scored high or low.

Vocalizations

The average durations of the participants' vocalizations appear to have been determined solely by their own personality characteristics. Those participants who scored high on Factors A, E, F, and H and low on Factors I and Q_2 were the ones who produced the longer vocalizations. They were persons who, according to the *Handbook*, could be described as warmhearted, outgoing, assertive, enthusiastic, socially bold, and unsentimental, but also group dependent.

DISCUSSION

The results are interesting in a number of ways. Perhaps the most important is that although they obviously need to be replicated, they do seem to indicate that personality characteristics play some role in determining how conversational participants pace their interactions. Moreover, given the behaviorally oriented descriptions provided by Cattell and his colleagues (1970), the relationships revealed by the study appear, for the most part, to be intuitively reasonable. It does not seem unduly strange that speakers take longer turns when talking with persons who are reserved, detached, and taciturn than with persons who are talkative, cheerful, and cooperative. Nor is it difficult to believe that persons who are reserved, cold, suspicious, insecure, and tense tend to produce longer pauses.

On the other hand, it is intriguing to have discovered that personality characteristics of the speakers exerted relatively little influence on the amount of time they tended to hold the floor. Similarly intriguing was the finding of a shift in responsibility for each of the parameters from the characteristics of the person speaking to those of the person to whom the speaking was addressed. To reiterate briefly, the results suggest that:

1. The average durations of the participants' vocalizations appeared to have been solely a function of their own personality characteristics.
2. The average lengths of time the participants paused while speaking were primarily a function of their own characteristics, although those of their partners clearly exerted influence.
3. The average durations of the participants' switching pauses were determined to a greater extent by their partners' characteristics than by their own.
4. The average amounts of time they held the floor each time they spoke appears to have been wholly determined by the characteristics of their partners.

This shift is supportive of expectations derived from the topology of the temporal events. Specifically, speaking turns and switching pauses are dyadic events; they do not exist in a monologue. Moreover, switching pauses and consequently turns are terminated not by the speaker who initiates them but by his or her partner. It seems reasonable, therefore, that the influence of the partners' characteristics was greater for both parameters than that of the participants' characteristics. Pauses and vocalizations, however, are—topologically, at least—dependent only upon the individual speaker in the sense that they are the two temporal events that occur in a monologue. It would be expected that they are less susceptible to interpersonal influence than switching pauses and speaking turns. Note, then, that pauses are less influenced by the personality characteristics of the partner than by those of the speaker, and vocalizations much less so. These differences among the parameters are also partially supported by previous research concerned with another type of interpersonal influence. A series of studies (Feldstein & Welkowitz, 1978) has shown that the participants in a dialogue tend to match the average durations of each other's pauses and switching pauses, but not of each other's vocalizations. The same studies also suggest that switching pauses are more susceptible to such matching than are pauses, and that the matching of switching pauses occurs earlier developmentally than does that of pauses (Welkowitz, Cariffe, & Feldstein, 1976). The interpersonal matching of speaking turns has not yet been explored systematically.

It may be important to mention again, as a caution, that the participants in the present study were women. In the investigation of which this study was a part, Marcus et al. (1970) found that the conversational time patterns of those women who tended to be field dependent were more influenced by the time patterns of their conversational partners that were those of the women who tended to be field independent. However, Witkin, Dyk, Faterson, Goodenough, and Karp (1974) have reported finding that women in general seem to be more field dependent than men. Regardless of the possible reasons for this difference, it suggests that the temporal parameters of male speakers may be less influenced by the personality characteristics of their conversational partners than are those of women.

ACKNOWLEDGMENTS

The authors are indebted to the Statistics Center of the University of Maryland Baltimore County and to the Computer Center of the University of Maryland College Park for the generous amounts of computer time they provided.

REFERENCES

BenDebba, M. *Vocalization rate as a function of contingent "mm-hmms."* Paper read at the annual meeting of the Eastern Psychological Association, Philadelphia, April 1974.

Blass, T. (Ed.). *Personality variables in social behavior.* Hillsdale, N.J.: Lawrence Erlbaum Associates, 1977.

Cattell, R. B., & Eber, H. W. *Handbook for the sixteen personality factor questionnaire.* Champaign, Ill.: Institute for Personality and Ability Testing, 1957.

Cattell, R. B., Eber, H. W., & Tatsuoka, M. M. *Handbook for the sixteen personality factor questionnaire.* Champaign, Ill.: Institute for Personality and Ability Testing, 1970.

Conroy, J., III, & Sundstrom, E. Territorial dominance in a dyadic conversation as a function of similarity of opinion. *Journal of Personality and Social Psychology,* 1977, *35,* 570–576.

Dabbs, J. M., Uwanno, T., Evans, M. S., Meiners, M. L., Stokes, N. A., Kennedy, J., & Bakeman, R. *Acquaintanceship patterns of speech and gaze.* Unpublished manuscript, Georgia State University, 1977.

Duncan, S., Jr. Some signals and rules for taking speaking turns in conversations. *Journal of Personality and Social Psychology,* 1972, *23,* 283–292.

Duncan, S., Jr. Toward a grammar for dyadic conversations. *Semiotica,* 1973, *9,* 29–46.

Duncan, S., Jr. On the structure of speaker–auditor interaction during speaking turns. *Language in Society,* 1974, *3,* 161–180.

Feldstein, S., Alberti, L., BenDebba, M., & Welkowitz, J. *Personality and simultaneous speech.* Paper read at the annual meeting of the American Psychological Association, New Orleans, August 1974.

Feldstein, S., BenDebba, M., & Alberti, L. *Distributional characteristics of simultaneous speech in conversation.* Paper read at the Acoustical Society of America, New York, April 1974.

Feldstein, S., & Crown, C. L. *Conversational time patterns as a function of introversion and extraversion.* Paper read at the Eastern Psychological Association, Washington, D.C., March 1978.

Feldstein S., & Welkowitz, J. A chronography of conversation: In defense of an objective approach. In A. W. Siegman & S. Feldstein (Eds.), *Nonverbal behavior and communication.* Hillsdale, N.J.: Lawrence Erlbaum Associates, 1978.

Gallois, C., & Markel, N. N. Turn taking: Social personality and conversational style. *Journal of Personality and Social Psychology,* 1975, *31,* 1134–1140.

Jaffe, J., & Feldstein, S. *Rhythms of dialogue.* New York: Academic, 1970.

Marcus, E. S., Welkowitz, J., Feldstein, S., & Jaffe, J. *Psychological differentiation and the congruence of temporal speech patterns.* Paper presented at the meeting of the Eastern Psychological Association, Atlantic City, April 1970.

Markel, N. N. Coverbal behavior associated with conversation turns. In A. Kenson, R. Harris, & M. R. Key (Eds.), *The organization of behavior in face-to-face interaction.* The Hague: Mouton, 1973.

Markel, N. N., Phillis, J. A., Vargas, R., & Howard, K. Personality traits associated with voice types. *Journal of Psycholinguistic Research,* 1972, *1,* 249–255.

Martindale, D. A. Territorial dominance behavior in dyadic verbal interaction. *Proceedings of the 79th Annual Convention of the American Psychological Association,* 1971, *6,* 305–306.

Rochester, S. R. The significance of pauses in spontaneous speech. *Journal of Psycholinguistic Research,* 1973, *2,* 51–81.

Schegloff, E. A. Sequencing in conversational openings. *American Anthropologist,* 1968, *70,* 1075–1095.

Scherer, K. R. Personality markers in speech. In H. Giles & R. St. Clair (Eds.), *Language and social psychology.* Oxford: Blackwell, in press.

Siegman, A. W. The telltale voice: Nonverbal messages of verbal communication. In A. W. Siegman & S. Feldstein (Eds.), *Nonverbal behavior and communication.* Hillsdale, N.J.: Lawrence Erlbaum Associates, 1978.

Sloan, B., & Feldstein, S. *Speech tempo in introversion and extraversion.* Unpublished manuscript, University of Maryland Baltimore County, 1977.

Welkowitz, J., Cariffe, G., & Feldstein, S. Conversational congruence as a criterion of socialization in children. *Child Development,* 1976, *47,* 269–272.

Welkowitz, J., & Feldstein, S. Dyadic interaction and induced differences in perceived similarity. *Proceedings of the 77th Annual Convention of the American Psychological Association,* 1969, *4,* 343–344.

Witkin, H. A., Dyk, R. B., Faterson, H. F., Goodenough, D. R., & Karp, S. A. *Psychological differentiation.* Hillsdale N.J.: Lawrence Erlbaum Associates, 1974.

Yngve, V. H. On getting a word in edgewise. In M. A. Campbell et al. (Eds.), *Papers from the Sixth Regional Meeting, Chicago Linguistic Society.* Chicago: University of Chicago Department of Linguistics, 1970. Pp. 567–578.

5 The Voice of Attraction: Vocal Correlates of Interpersonal Attraction in the Interview

Aron Wolfe Siegman
University of Maryland Baltimore County

Interpersonal attraction is one of the major foci of interest in contemporary social psychology. Almost every contemporary textbook and reader in social psychology devotes at least a whole chapter, if not a complete section, to this topic, and the journals are replete with studies trying to identify the critical variables that affect interpersonal attraction. Much less is known, however, about the impact of interpersonal attraction on behavior, i.e., about the effects of interpersonal attraction as an independent variable. Exline and his associates (Exline & Fehr, 1978) have studied the effects of attraction on eye contact, and Hess and his associates have investigated the relationship between attraction and changes in pupil size (Hess & Petrovich, 1978). However, few, if any, experimental investigations have addressed themselves to the question of how interpersonal attraction affects voice quality and other vocal parameters of speech. Yet in everyday life, people continually make inferences regarding other people's feelings toward them not only on the basis of *what* is being said to them, but also (if not mostly) on the basis of *how* it is said, i.e., on the basis of noncontent voice and speech characteristics.

Studies on the effects of attraction on noncontent aspects of speech are of interest not only in their own right but also because of their potential contribution to the solution of a serious methodological problem that plagues most laboratory studies on interpersonal attraction. In most of these studies, attraction is measured by asking subjects to indicate on a Likert-type scale how much they liked the person with whom they were interacting—this person usually being a confederate of the experimenter. A major problem with such studies is that paper–and–pencil measures of interpersonal attraction are undoubtedly influenced by a variety of response biases, including the ubiquitous social desirability bias. If, however, interpersonal attraction can be shown to have a significant impact on one or more speech parameters, they may in turn serve as behavioral indices of attraction. Clearly, such indices are less subject to intentional and unintentional manipulation by the subject than the paper-and-pencil questionnaires now in use. Besides being relatively unobtrusive and less amenable to conscious manipulation by subjects than the usual paper-and-pencil, self-rating procedures, speech-derived variables have other advantages as well.

In the typical social-psychological laboratory experiment, the investigator assesses the effects of some manipulation on subjects' feelings or attitudes toward another person or object. This assessment is usually made at one point in time by means of rating scales. The relevance of such data to behavior in the "real world," which is continuous and ongoing and very seldom frozen in time, is at best limited. A major advantage of using conversation-derived speech variables for the testing of social-psychological theories is that they readily allow for the evaluation of time effects, for the monitoring of moment-to-moment changes over time.

Conversations, be they dyadic or group conversations, have a greater verisimilitude to everyday social interactions than the typical social-psychological laboratory experiment. Furthermore, by their very nature dyadic conversations are interactive and sequential, which is, of course, another feature of social behavior in the real world. In the real world, our behavior elicits feedback from others, which in turn modifies our subsequent behavior—a feature that is built into dyadic and group conversations. Such conversations, then, would seem to provide an ideal testing ground for social-psychological hypotheses and theories.

The studies reported in this chapter all involve analogues of the initial interview. A major objective of our interview research program has been to identify the factors that facilitate interviewee productivity, self-disclosure, and verbal fluency. In our search for variables that are likely to facilitate or to inhibit the flow of communication between the interviewee and the interviewer, we have turned for guidance to both communication theory and social psychology (Pope & Siegman, 1972; Siegman & Pope, 1972). The results of some of these studies have occasionally led us to reverse the procedure and to use the interview as the testing ground for general social-psychological principles. The research reported in this chapter illustrates this two-way relationship: the application of a social-psychological perspective to a clinical issue and the use of the interview for testing a widely cited social-psychological principle.

The first part of this chapter focuses on the relationship between interpersonal attraction and silent pausing in speech, within the context of initial interviews. Previous correlational data suggest that interviewee-interviewer attraction is associated with fewer and/or shorter silent pauses in interviewees' speech. These findings provided the impetus for two experimental studies, the results of which are consistent with the previous findings. The second part of this chapter discusses the implications of two interview studies for Aronson's gain–loss principle of interpersonal attraction. The third part of the chapter focuses on the meaning of silent pauses in speech and advances the hypothesis that such pauses are most parsimoniously explained in terms of information processing that is taking place at the time of the pausing. The inverse relationship between interpersonal attraction and silent pausing is explained in terms of this information-processing approach to silent pauses in speech.

THE EFFECTS OF INTERVIEWEE–INTERVIEWER ATTRACTION ON THE TEMPORAL PATTERNING OF INTERVIEWEES' SPEECH

Previous Findings

As part of one of our first studies on the initial interview (Pope & Siegman, 1965; Siegman & Pope, 1965, 1966, 1972), we were interested in the effects of interviewees' attraction to their interviewer on interviewees' productivity and on several temporal aspects of interviewees' responses. The basic assumption of that study was that interviewees would be more willing to talk to an interviewer whom they liked than to one whom they disliked, and that they would be less reluctant to disclose personal material to the former than to the latter. Specifically, we hypothesized a positive correlation between interviewees' attraction-to-interviewer scores and their productivity scores, and a negative correlation between their attraction scores and their response latencies and within-response silent pauses. Interviewees' attraction to their interviewer was assessed by a modified version of the Libo Picture Impressions Test (Libo, 1956), a projective TAT-like instrument. All interviewees were administered one Libo card (depicting a woman sitting close to a door on which is displayed a sign reading, "Doctor is in. Please be seated.") immediately preceding the interview and another card (showing a standing woman with her hand on a door knob and behind her the sketchy outline of a man behind a desk, displaying a card with the name, "Dr. James") immediately after the interview. Subjects' stories to each of these cards yielded an attraction score. Thus, both a base level of attraction to the interviewer and a postinterview increase or decrease of attraction over the base level was obtained for each subject, with the pre- to postinterview change in attraction score assumed to be a consequence of the interview experience. The greater the positive change, the higher the subject's attraction score; the greater the negative change, the lower the attraction score.

The correlation (r) between interviewees' attraction and productivity scores was .054, clearly not significant. On the other hand, the correlation between interviewees' attraction scores and a pausing index that combined their response latencies and within-response silent pauses of more than 2 sec. was in the expected direction and clearly significant ($r = -.38, p < .01$). A significant negative correlation between patient attraction to the therapist and a measure of silent pauses in the patient's speech was also reported by Goldstein (1971).

To summarize the findings thus far: The expectation that interviewees would talk more to an interviewer whom they like than to one whom they dislike was not confirmed. On the other hand, the hypothesis that interviewees would evidence less pausing when responding to an interviewer whom they like than when talking to one whom they dislike was supported in two separate studies. Yet, the correlational nature of these studies impels us to view both the negative and the positive findings with caution.

It became increasingly clear that we needed to manipulate interviewee–interviewer attraction experimentally and to monitor its effects on interviewees' verbal behavior, although at first it was not at all obvious how such a manipulation could be achieved. The answer to this dilemma was provided by correlational data that indicated that interviewees are more attracted to an interviewer whom they perceive as warm and accepting rather than to one seen as cold and rejecting ($r(71) = .46$ and better). These findings suggest that it should be possible to manipulate interviewees' attraction to their interviewer by manipulating the interviewer's level of friendliness or warmth.

The Effects of Interviewer Warmth on Interviewees' Speech Tempo: First Experiment

In this study (Pope & Siegman, 1968, 1972), 32 female students in a university-affiliated school of nursing were interviewed twice—once by a warm and friendly interviewer and once by a neutral and reserved interviewer. The interviewer-warmth manipulation was achieved by arousing in the interviewees contrasting expectations regarding the two interviewers and by programming the interviewer's behavior to accord with the aroused expectation or set. During the warm and friendly interview, the interviewer smiled, nodded her head, and spoke warmly. During the neutral and reserved interview, she refrained from smiling, did not nod her head, and kept her voice drab and cold. Two female interviewers alternated between the two interview conditions, and the interviewees alternated between the sequence of the two conditions (warm first versus reserved first). The interview itself consisted of two topical areas, family relations and school experiences, which were always presented in that order. Within each topical area, one-half of the questions were moderately ambiguous, the others highly specific (see Table

TABLE 5.1
Interviewer Questions in the First
"Interviewer Warmth" Study

Interview A1
1. Tell me something, anything you wish about your father.
2. Now tell me something, anything about your brother X.
3. Tell me with which parent you got along better.
4. (Use one as appropriate)
   ____Has your father been very strict with you?
   ____Did your father do many things with you?

I'd like now to talk with you about your school history, O.K.? (Pause)
5. Tell me something, anything about your schools before college.
6. Now, something about your first 2 years in college.
7. Which school, elementary, junior high, high, did you prefer?
8. Which of these schools had the best library facilities?

Interview B1
1. Tell me something, anything you wish, about your mother.
2. Now tell me something, anything about your sister X.
3. Please tell me with which parent you were closest.
4. (Use one as appropriate)
   ____Has your mother been very strict with you?
   ____Did your mother do many things with you?

I'd like now to talk with you about your school history, O.K.? (Pause)
5. Tell me something about the elementary school you attended.
6. Now tell me something about the School of Nursing.
7. Did you have many extracurricular interests before college?
8. Did your precollege schools have good gym facilities?

5.1). One-half of the subjects were started on the ambiguous questions, the others on the specific ones.

The dependent measures directly concerned with the temporal dimension of interviewees' speech were: response latency or reaction time (RT), silence quotient (SQ), and production rate (PR). RT was defined as the interval between the end of the interviewer's question and the beginning of the interviewee's response. SQ was defined as the summed duration of interviewee's within-response silent pauses of 2 sec and over, divided by the duration of interviewee's response minus the silent pauses. PR was defined as the number of words per response divided by the reponse latency plus the response duration. Thus, PR is a function of the duration of the utterance plus two types of silent pauses: the pre-response silent pause or RT and the within-response silent pauses. Of the temporal measures that were used in this study, the PR index is the most comparable to the pausing index that was used in our earlier correlational study (Pope & Siegman, 1966). Unlike that index, however, the PR index taps not only relatively long within-response silent pauses (2 sec and more), but brief ones as well.

In this study, all the temporal measurements were made by hand with a stopwatch. With adequate training, the reliability and validity of such measurements are quite satisfactory, provided the measured time units are at least of 2 sec duration (Siegman, 1978b). Since quite a few interviewee responses to the highly specific interviewer probes consisted of only two or three words and thus were of extremely short duration, we only analyzed the SQ and PR scores associated with interviewees' responses to the relatively ambiguous interviewer remarks. The mean number of words for these interviewee responses was 292 (SD = 155.06), with none below 25 words.

A post-interview questionnaire, completed by the interviewees after each interview, included an interviewee–interviewer attraction index. This index consisted of interviewees' responses—on a 6-point scale—to the following questions: "Did you like the interviewer?" "How happy would you be with today's interviewer as a counselor or a psychotherapist?" This index is very similar to one used by Byrne (1971) in his interpersonal attraction studies.

Results.   As expected, the interviewees were significantly more attracted to the warm interviewers than to the reserved ones ($p < .001$) with no overlap between conditions.

Interviewer warmth had a borderline effect on interviewees' RT scores ($F(1,30)$ = 3.585, $.10 < p > .05$), and a clearly significant effect on their PR scores ($F(1,30)$ = 5.673, $p < .05$).[1] Interviewees responded with shorter RTs and higher PRs in the warm interview conditions than in the reserved ones. However, the experimental manipulation had no significant effect on interviewees' SQ's ($F(1,30)$ = < 1).

The discrepancy between the SQ and PR findings suggests that perhaps interviewer warmth reduces relatively short silent pauses, but not the relatively longer ones (2 sec and more), which are indexed by the SQ measure. Alternatively, the discrepancy may result from the fact that the SQ measure is a less reliable index than the PR measure. In the present study, there were quite a few interviewee responses that had no silent pauses of 2-sec duration— i.e., zero SQ scores. At any rate, the variability of interviewees' SQ scores was considerably greater than the variability of their PR scores. Whatever the explanation, these findings suggested the need for yet another study, one that would allow for a fine-grained analysis of interviewees' pausing behavior as a function of their attraction to their interviewer. This, then, was the objective of the next experiment—to determine more precisely which aspects of the interviewees' pausing behavior are affected by their level of attraction to the interviewer.

---

[1]This finding does not appear in the original report of this experiment (Pope & Siegman, 1968, 1972), because the production-rate data were not analyzed at that time.

Second Experiment

In the previous study, there was not only a manipulation of the interviewer's behavior—i.e., warm and friendly versus reserved and distant—but additionally, interviewees were given a set that prepared them for the interviewer's behavior. The purpose of these instructions was to assure that the interviewees would indeed perceive the interviewer's behavior as it was intended to be perceived: warm and friendly in the warm condition and reserved and distant in the reserved condition. As a result, however, the two variables—i.e., interviewee expectation and interviewer behavior—were thoroughly confounded. In the present study, an attempt was made to unconfound these two variables and to assess the contribution of each of these factors on the interviewees' verbal fluency as measured by a variety of temporal indices. In order to make such an assessment, one-half of the subjects were given a set that was consistent with the interviewer's actual behavior, whereas the others were given a set that was inconsistent with the interviewer's actual behavior. Altogether, then, there were the following four experimental conditions.

1. *Warm–Warm (W–W) Condition.* The interviewees are led to believe that their interviewer is a warm and friendly person, and the interviewer behaves in a manner that is consistent with the interviewees' expectations.
2. *Reserved–Warm (R–W) Condition.* The interviewees are led to believe that their interviewer is a reserved person, and the interviewer behaves in a manner that is opposite to interviewees' expectations; i.e., the interviewer is warm and friendly.
3. *Reserved–Reserved (R–R) Condition.* The interviewees are given a reserved set, and the interviewer behaves in a reserved manner.
4. *Warm–Reserved (W–R) Condition.* The interviewees are led to expect a warm and friendly interviewer, but in fact the interviewer behaves in a neutral and reserved manner.

This design makes it possible to assess the effects of (a) the interviewees' expectations, (b) the interviewer's behavior, and (c) the interaction between these two factors on a variety of temporal speech indices.

Interviewer and Interviewees. One female interviewer interviewed 56 female interviewees, with 14 subjects in each of the 4 experimental conditions. The present study used a between-subjects comparison design, unlike the previous study, which was based on within-subjects comparisons. It should be pointed out that the interviewer in the present study, who was especially trained for conducting experimental interviews, was considerably older than the interviewees, who were recruited from introductory psychology classes.

Dependent Variables and Manipulation Checks. In addition to RT and SQ, the present study included the following measures: pause duration ratio (PDR), average pause duration (APD), pause frequency ratio (PFR), speech rate (SR), and articulation rate (AR). With the exception of SQ, which was obtained in the same manner as in the previous study, the temporal components of all the other indices were measured automatically by means of the Automatic Vocal Transaction Analyzer or AVTA (Jaffe & Feldstein, 1970). This instrument made it possible to include in the pausing indices silent pauses as brief as 300 msec. The PDR represents the summed duration of interviewee's within-response pauses—300 msec and over—divided by interviewee's vocalization time. As is the case with SQ, the rationale for expressing this index as a ratio of pauses to vocalizations is that pauses tend to increase as a function of response duration. The more, or the longer, a person speaks, the greater the person's pausing time. However, this particular method of adjusting for response productivity or duration—the two being used interchangeably—has been criticized on a variety of methodological grounds (Marsden, Kalter, & Ericson, 1974), which prompted the addition of the APD index. The latter is simply the mean duration of interviewee's within-response pauses—300 msec and over—and is immune to the criticisms that have been made against measures that include an adjustment for response productivity. The PFR is obtained by dividing the total number of within-response pauses 300 msec and over by vocalization time. This measure was included, the above-mentioned methodological strictures notwithstanding, because we wanted some indication of the effect of the experimental manipulation on pause frequency. SR consists of the total number of words in an interviewee's response divided by response time—which includes the silent pauses. AR, on the other hand, is obtained by dividing the total number of words in an interviewee's response by vocalization time, i.e., response time minus all pauses 300 msec and over.

No assumption is made regarding the independence of the various within-response pause duration indices, i.e., SQ, PDR, and APD. As can be seen in Tables 5.2 and 5.3, they are in fact highly intercorrelated. The consistently high correlations between SQ and PDR and between SQ and APD are important, because they put to rest our previous qualms about the validity of the manually obtained SQ index. On the other hand, RT—the measure of subjects' initial delays—correlates only moderately with the within-response pausing indices (Tables 5.2 and 5.3). The fairly high correlations between SR and the various within-response pausing indices are not unexpected, since speech rate is—among others—a function of such pausing.

As in the previous study, the interviewees completed a post-interview questionnaire that included two items ("Did you like the interviewer?" and "How happy would you be with today's interviewer as a counselor or a psychotherapist?") designed to measure interviewees' attraction to their interviewer. They also responded to four bipolar adjective scales designed to

TABLE 5.2
Intercorrelations (r) of Verbal Indices in the W-W and R-W
Conditions in Second Interviewer Warmth Study[a]

	RT	SQ	PDR	APD	PFR	SR	AR
RT		.150	.333	.338	.355	-.489*	-.166
SQ	.569*		.718**	.866**	.531*	-.719*	.055
PDR	.484*	.925**		.893**	.929**	-.755**	.397
APD	.499*	.785**	.865**		.700**	-.802**	.177
PFR	.282	.730**	.782**	.389		-.723**	.336
SR	-.351	-.691**	-.629*	-.486*	-.544*		.288
AR	.072	.079	.160	.173	.109	.630**	

*$p < .05$
**$p < .01$
[a]The correlations for the W-W condition are above the diagonal, those for the R-W
condition below the diagonal.

TABLE 5.3
Intercorrelations (r) of Verbal Indices in the R-R and W-R
Conditions in Second Interviewer Warmth Study[a]

	RT	SQ	PDR	APD	PFR	SR	AR
RT		.459*	.430	.315	.595*	-.544*	-.071
SQ	.197		.797*	.694*	.824**	-.765**	.032
PDR	.439	.770**		.925**	.776**	-.762*	.281
APD	.507*	.757**	.990**		.607*	-.738**	.284
PFR	.065	.724**	.747*	.680**		-.738**	.030
SR	-.168	-.660**	-.732**	-.682*	-.715**		.300
AR	.108	-.084	-.131	-.073	-.165	.723**	

*$p < .05$
**$p < .01$
[a]The correlations for the R-R condition are above the diagonal, those for the W-R
condition below the diagonal.

assess the interviewees' perception of interviewer warmth. Another assessment of interviewees' perception of interviewer warmth was based on their
post-interview recall of the frequency with which the interviewer emitted
certain discrete social reinforcers—specifically, the frequency of smiling,
nodding approval, leaning forward, and showing interest in the interviewees'
responses.

Results. Interviewer warmth was a highly significant source of variance
in the two indices designed to assess the interviewees' perception of the
interviewer's behavior on this dimension (Table 5.4). The interviewees who
were in the warm conditions (W-W and R-W) perceived their interviewer as
warmer than did the interviewees who were in the reserved conditions (R-R

TABLE 5.4
Analysis of Varaince Results of Manipulation Check Variables and of Interviewees' Attraction Scores in Second Interviewer Warmth Study

| | | Mean Squares | | |
Source of Variance	df	Warmth (ratings)	Warmth[a] (recall)	Attraction
Interviewer Warmth (A)	1	74.67**	1161.0**	67.58**
Interviewee Expectation (B)	1	27.52**	223.3**	18.07**
A × B	1	.60	41.0	.08
Ss within groups	52	1.92	27.4	.90

**$p < .01$

[a]For this variable, data were available only on 10 subjects in each of the conditions. The proper df associated with the error term for this variable are therefore, 36.

TABLE 5.5
Mean and SD (Standard Deviation) of Subjects' Scores in the Second Interviewer Warmth Condition

| | W–W Condition | | R–W Condition | | W–R Condition | | R–R Condition | |
Variable	Mean	SD	Mean	SD	Mean	SD	Mean	SD
Warmth (ratings)	5.47	.676	4.78	.853	4.26	.680	3.33	.960
Warmth[a] (recall)	17.15	4.74	10.40	8.43	4.35	3.66	1.65	1.49
Attraction	5.14	.97	4.28	.775	3.53	.665	2.78	.850
Reaction Time[b]	.990	.476	.987	.290	1.147	.535	1.09	.708
Silence Quotient	.074	.071	.080	.073	.143	.140	.148	.096
Pause Duration Ratio	.411	.227	.530	.252	.711	.718	.823	.685
Average Pause Duration	.834	.218	.989	.292	1.188	.781	1.321	.586
Pause Frequency Ratio	.154	.047	.169	.042	.178	.048	.197	.059
Speech Rate	2.560	.375	2.420	.417	2.142	.577	2.151	.613
Articulation Rate	1.039	.084	1.082	.188	.971	.163	1.052	.143

[a]For this variable, data were available only on 10 subjects in each of the conditions.
[b]Logarithmic transformations of mean number of words per response.

and W–R) (Table 5.5). Interviewee expectation was also a significant source of variance in relation to these two variables, with a reserved set attenuating the interviewees' perception of interviewer warmth in the warm condition, and a warm set attenuating the interviewees' perception of interviewer reserve in the reserved condition (Tables 5.4 and 5.5). In other words, the sets influenced the interviewees' perception of interviewer warmth or reserve in the direction of the sets. Even the interviewees' recall of discrete interviewer behaviors—such as the frequency of her smiling— was influenced by the sets or expectations, even though objectively the interviewer's behavior in the R–W condition was the same as her behavior in the W–W condition; and likewise there was no difference in the interviewer's behavior between the R–R and the W–R conditions. That there were no such objective differences, we know from ratings of the interviewer's behavior made by two judges (from behind a one-way mirror) who did not know that some of the interviewees had been given discrepant sets. Nor, of course, was the interviewer aware of this experimental manipulation.

Interviewees' attraction scores corresponded to their perception of interviewer warmth. Interviewees were more attracted to the interviewer when she behaved in a warm and friendly manner rather than in a neutral and reserved manner, and a positive expectation increased their attraction scores whereas a negative expectation had the opposite effect (Table 5.5). The interaction between interviewer warmth and interviewee expectations had no significant influence on the above measures (Table 5.4).

In relation to the temporal indices, we were interested, not only in whether they were affected by the interviewer's behavior (warm versus reserved), by the interviewees' expectations, and by the interaction of these two variables; but also in whether these effects, if any, fluctuated over time. In order to make this determination, the interview was divided into two parts, with sequence as a within-subjects variable.

Interviewer warmth was a significant source of variance in relation to interviewees' SQ, PDR, APD, and SR[2] scores and a near-significant source of variance in relation to their PFR scores (Table 5.6). Interviewees exhibited less within-response pausing and a faster speech rate in the warm conditions (W–W and R–W) than in the reserved ones (R–R and W–R) (Table 5.5). Neither interviewee expectation nor the interaction between interviewee

---

[2]In a recent paper, Feldstein (1976) proposed an index based on automatically measured sound–silence sequences as an adequate estimate of speech rate. Specifically, this index consists of the proportionality constant of a speaker's vocalizations divided by the proportionality constant of his pauses (PC_v/PC_p). In the present study, the correlation (r) between this index and subjects' speech rates, based on actual word counts, in the W–W, R–W, R–R and W–R conditions were .793, .694, .840, and .752, respectively. Furthermore, the PC_v/PC_p index discriminated between the warm and reserved conditions somewhat better than the conventional but more laborious SR measure ($F(1,52) = 8.321$, $p < .01$, vs $F = 6.836$, $p < .05$).

TABLE 5.6

Analysis of Variance Results of Interviewees' Verbal Behavior Scores in Second Interviewer Warmth Study

Source of Variance	df	Mean-Square						
		RT	SQ	PDR	APD	PFR	SR	AR
Interviewer Warmth (A)	1	4.58	.1713*	22.13*	265.73*	.172†	31.51*	2.65
Interviewee Expectation (B)	1	.12	.0003	3.34	47.07	.001	.01	7.08
A × B	1	.33	.0011	.01	.25	.075	4.99	3.44
Ss within groups	52	4.95	.0362	4.96	44.08	.044	4.61	3.99
Sequence (C)	1	.113	.0478*	3.36*	38.72*	.057*	6.95**	.63
A × C	1	6.38*	.0009	.05	.89	.001	.01	12.43*
B × C	1	.13	.0035	.49	4.33	.000	.49	11.03*
A × B × C	1	.01	.0098	.01	.42	.004	.70	.07
Ss within A × B × C	52	1.056	.0080	.27	5.53	.008	.87	2.37

*$p < .05$
**$p < .01$
†$.10 < p > .05$

expectation and interviewer warmth were significant sources of variance in relation to any of the above indices (Table 5.6), even though the latter source of variance clearly affected the interviewees' perception of interviewer warmth and their attraction to the interviewer as measured by both the questionnaire and the recall data (Table 5.4). It should be pointed out that the strong effect of interviewer warmth on the various pausing indices is not merely a result of the combining of the two warm conditions (W–W plus R–W) and the two reserved conditions (R–R plus W–R), which gives this analysis greater power than was the case in the previous experiment. The differences between the interviewees' scores in the W–W condition and in the R–R condition in relation to PDR, APD, and SR were all clearly significant ($t(26)$ = 2.133, 2.906, and 2.209 respectively), although there were only 14 subjects in each of these conditions. The difference in relation to SQ, however, was only of borderline significance ($t(26)$ = 1.943, p = .063).[3] Taking the inteviewees' mean PDR score in the W–W and the R–R conditions as a cutoff point, only two subjects in the former group were found to score above this point, and only three subjects in the latter group scored below it. Corresponding figures for interviewees' APD and SR scores were 2 and 6 and 5 and 4.

Although interviewer warmth did not account for a significant proportion of the variance in interviewees' RT scores, the interaction between interviewer warmth and sequence did (Table 5.6), reflecting the fact that during the first part of the interview, the subjects responded with significantly shorter RTs in the warm than in the reserved conditions ($F(1,52)$ = 4.07, $p < .05$). This difference, however, was not sustained during the second half of the interview (F = <1).

Warmth was also not a significant source of variance in interviewees' articulation rates, but the interaction between sequence and interviewer warmth as well as the interaction between sequence and interviewee expectation were both significant sources of variance (Table 5.6). Separate analyses were made for the two parts of the interview, with interviewer warmth, interviewee expectation, and their interactions as the sources of variance. In the first part of the interview, only interviewee expectation had a significant effect on interviewees' articulation rates ($F(1, 52)$ = 5.85, $p < .05$), with interviewees who expected a neutral and reserved interviewer exhibiting faster articulation rates than interviewees expecting a warm interviewer. This effect dissipated during the second half of the interview, with none of the independent variables having a clear-cut significant effect on the interviewees' AR scores in the second part of the interview. These findings in regard to articulation rate are of interest for two reasons. First, they challenge

---

[3]The W–W and R–R conditions were selected for this comparison, because they correspond to the warm and the reserved conditions in the previous study.

Goldman–Eisler's (1968) claim that articulation rate is a highly stable personality characteristic that is not readily influenced by task manipulations. Second, the experimental manipulations of this study had different effects on interviewees' speech rates (number of words per response, including silent pauses) than on their articulation rates (number of words per response, not including silent pauses). Whereas one index, i.e., speech rate, was influenced by the interviewer's actual behavior, the other was influenced by interviewees' expectations. Furthermore, whereas interviewer warmth has an accelerating effect on interviewees' speech rates (by reducing their silent pauses), expecting a warm and friendly interviewer has the opposite effect on their articulation rates. These findings, plus the fact that interviewees' SR scores and AR scores did not correlate significantly in two of the four interview conditions ($r(13) = .288$ in the W–W condition and .300 in the R–R condition), suggest that these two variables measure different psychological processes. Some speculations about the meaning of these findings are offered later in this chapter.

Discussion. The results of this study are clearly consistent with the hypothesis that interviewees respond with shorter within-response pauses, and hence with a faster speech rate, to warm and friendly interviewers than they do to reserved and neutral interviewers. Furthermore, interviewer warmth reduces not only very brief within response silent pauses, but also the relatively longer ones (2 sec and more) as measured by the SQ index. The findings also suggest that attraction has a more clear-cut effect on within-response pauses than on response latencies, and on the duration of the within-response pauses than on their frequencies. Considering the strong link between interviewer warmth and interviewees' attraction to their interviewer, the results of this study suggest that pausing indices can provide us with unobtrusive measures of interpersonal attraction. More direct evidence, albeit of a correlational nature, for an inverse relationship between interpersonal attraction and pausing is provided by other previously cited studies (Goldstein, 1971; Pope & Siegman, 1966).

It should be noted that the pausing indices were influenced only by the interviewer's actual behavior, but not by the experimenter's preinterview sets. The experimenter's suggestion to the interviewees that their interviewer was generally reserved and distant did not increase the interviewees' pausing behavior if in fact the interviewer behaved in a warm and friendly manner; nor did the warm set influence the interviewees' pausing behavior if the interviewer was in fact reserved and distant. This is in contrast to interviewees' ratings of interviewer warmth and attraction to the interviewer, which were influenced by the experimenter's preinterview sets. One possible explanation of this discrepancy is that the ratings are more susceptible to response bias than the pausing indices.

The advantage of pausing indices as measures of interpersonal attraction is not only their unobtrusive nature, but also that they allow us to monitor changes in subjects' behavior over time. Thus, the effects of interviewer warmth on interviewees' response latencies and articulation rates were temporary and dissipated as the interview progressed.

THE GAIN-LOSS PRINCIPLE OF
INTERPERSONAL ATTRACTION:
SOME CONTRADICTORY FINDINGS

As noted earlier, the study just discussed was undertaken primarily in order to ascertain the effects of interviewer warmth and of interviewees' expectations regarding interviewer warmth on interviewees' attraction to the interviewer and on their pausing behavior. Yet, the design of this study was such that its results have implications for Aronson's gain-loss principle of interpersonal attraction (Aronson, 1969). According to the gain part of this principle, people are more attracted to someone whose evaluation of them has changed from negative to positive than to someone who liked them from the very beginning. According to the loss part of this principle, people are less attracted to someone whose evaluation of them has changed from positive to negative than to someone who never did think much of them in the first place.

Aronson (1969) has offered several explanations for the gain phenomenon. One explanation involves anxiety reduction. When someone dislikes us, we tend to experience some negative affect—anxiety, hurt, self-doubt, etc. When that same person then changes his or her feelings from disliking us to liking us, the positive affect is not only rewarding in its own right, but also tends to reduce the previously aroused anxiety. The total reward value of that positive behavior is therefore greater than if the individual never disliked us. Another explanation of the gain phenomenon is in terms of effectance or competence. The success in changing someone's opinion about us from negative to positive is taken as a personal triumph, as a sign of our worth and effectiveness. This positive feeling may generalize to its cause. We may therefore like someone whom we converted into an admirer much more than someone who always liked us. The two processes—anxiety reduction and gain in effectance—are of course not mutually exclusive, and both may play a role in a particular gain phenomenon. Yet a third explanation for the gain phenomenon may be in terms of a simple contrast effect. A positive evaluation stands out more if it follows previous negative evaluations. According to Aronson, the same reasonings in reverse account for a loss effect.

The aforementioned explanations seem equally relevant to the case of discrepant expectations regarding interviewer warmth or reserve. Interviewees who expect a reserved interviewer are likely to feel more apprehensive about their forthcoming interview than interviewees who expect a warm interviewer. If the interviewer then turns out to be warm and accepting, the interviewee should experience anxiety reduction. Also, an interviewee who is treated warmly by someone who is generally reserved toward interviewees should feel a sense of effectance, a sense that there is something about him- or herself that turned this reserved interviewer into a warm and friendly one. Finally, according to the contrast effect, a generally reserved individual who shows warmth and friendliness should appear warmer than someone who is consistently warm and friendly. According to all three explanations, then, interviewees who expect a reserved interviewer and instead find a warm and friendly one should demonstrate a gain in interpersonal attraction. All three explanations, of course, could also account for a loss effect—i.e., for interviewees being less attracted to a reserved interviewer who was expected to be warm and friendly than to a reserved interviewer who was expected to behave in a reserved manner.

In a previous study (Siegman, 1974), interviewees indicated that they were more attracted to a warm interviewer whom they had expected to be cold and rejecting than to one whom they expected to be warm and friendly. This is of course consistent with Aronson's gain principle of interpersonal attraction. However, in the study described earlier, there is no indication for either a gain or a loss in attraction, whether we rely on interviewees' ratings or whether we rely on their pausing behavior as an index of attraction.

It should be pointed out, however, that there is an obvious difference between the procedures used by Aronson and his associates in order to obtain gain and loss effects and those procedures used in our studies. In the studies by Aronson and his associates, subjects' own prior experiences with a confederate served as the basis for their expectations. In our studies, however, the interviewees' expectations regarding the interviewer's warmth or reserve were based on information given to them by the experimenter prior to the interview about the interviewer's typical affective relationship with inter-viewees. Perhaps under these circumstances, interviewees are less likely to attribute a change in the interviewer's style to something they have done or not done, especially since the interviewer behaved in this unexpected manner from the very moment of introduction. This difference in procedures may be of significance if the gain and loss effects in interpersonal attraction are mediated by gain and loss in effectance. It is not at all clear, however, that the difference in procedure should be of significance if anxiety reduction/arousal or the contrast effect are the mediating variables. Nevertheless, a more appropriate design for testing the gain and loss principles within the context of the interview would be one in which the interviewer's behavior toward the interviewee changes during the course of the interview from distant and reserved to warm and friendly and vice versa. Then the interviewees' responses to such interviewers could be compared with their responses to interviewers who behave in a consistently warm or in a consistently reserved manner. A study that was conducted in our laboratory (Siegman, 1976) seems to fit the above criteria.

We, therefore, analyzed some of the findings of this study, which have not been reported before, from the point of view of the gain and loss principle of interpersonal attraction.

Another Study, Similar Findings

One of the interview studies conducted in our laboratory used a paradigm that is analogous to the one used by Aronson and his colleagues. The basic objective of that study, which is described in some detail elsewhere (Siegman, 1976), was to investigate the effects of noncontingent interviewer verbal "reinforcement," in the form of "mm-hmm" and similar expressions, on interviewees' productivity levels. The subjects in that study participated in two brief, consecutive interviews. Following each of the two interview sessions, the subjects filled out a questionnaire focusing on their feelings during the interview and on their perceptions of the interviewer's behavior. In one of the four experimental conditions in that study, the interviewers responded with "mm-hmm's" during both interview sessions (R–R); in another condition, they made such responses only during the second of the two interviews (NR–R); in yet another condition, they refrained from making such responses throughout both interviews (NR–NR); and in yet another condition, they made such responses only during the first of the two interviews (R–NR). Previously reported findings (Siegman, 1976) indicate that in the interviews during which the interviewers responded with "mm-hmm's" and other such verbal "reinforcers," they were perceived as warm and accepting and that in the interviews during which the interviewers refrained from making such responses, they were perceived as relatively cold and unfriendly. In the present paper, we focus on the levels of interviewees' attraction to their interviewers during the second of the two interviews, and we do so from the perspective of the gain and loss principles.

First, we are hypothesizing greater interviewee attraction to the responsive than to the nonresponsive interviewers, irrespective of the interviewer's behavior in the first interview. Second, in accord with the gain principle, it is hypothesized that the inteviewees will be more attracted to the responsive interviewers if this responsiveness represents a change from a previous lack of responsiveness (NR–R condition) than if it does not represent such a change (R–R condition). Conversely, in accord with the loss principle, it is hypothesized that interviewees will be less attracted to the nonresponsive interviewers who changed their behavior from a prior responsive style to a nonresponsive one (R–NR condition) than to the interviewers who are consistent in their lack of responsiveness (NR–NR condition).

As in the previous study, interviewee–interviewer attraction was measured by their responses to the following two questions: "How much did you like your interviewer?" and "How happy would you be with today's interviewer as a counselor or psychotherapist?" On the basis of the results obtained in the previous study, we feel that within-response pausing is a valid index of interviewee–interviewer attraction. Consequently, we also analyzed the interviewees' within-response pauses, as measured by the APD index.

In this study, there were 6 interviewers who alternated between the 4 interview conditions and 12 interviewees in each condition. For further details on methods and procedures, the reader should consult Siegman (1976).

Results. The interviewees were more attracted to the responsive than to the nonresponsive interviewers, with the questionnaire index yielding clearly significant results and the pausing index just missing the conventional .05 significance level (p = .062) (Tables 5.7 and 5.8). From the overall perspective of this chapter, the most significant aspect of these findings is that silent pausing again emerged as an index of interpersonal attraction.

As to gain and loss effects, there is some indication for a gain effect in interviewees' questionnaire scores, but it was not significant ($t(23)$ = 1.622, $p < .10$). There is no indication for a loss effect in either the questionnaire or the pausing data. In fact, both the questionnaire and the pausing data are in the *opposite* direction of such an effect.

A review of the experiments carried out by Aronson and his associates on the gain–loss model of interpersonal attraction indicates that there never really was any solid experimental evidence to support the loss part of the model. Thus, in the Aronson and Linder (1965) study—the first to investigate the gain–loss principle—the subjects indicated in a postexperimental

TABLE 5.7
Mean and *SD* (Standard Deviation) of
Subjects' Scores in the Second Interview of
the Verbal "Reinforcement" Study

	Variables			
	Attraction		*Average Pause Duration*[a]	
Condition	*Mean*	*SD*	*Mean*	*SD*
R–R	8.16	1.33	.921	.274
NR–R	9.33	2.10	1.009	.434
NR–NR	6.83	2.73	1.444	.888
R–NR	7.33	.88	1.066	.343

[a]In seconds

TABLE 5.8
Analysis of Variance Results:
Verbal "Reinforcement" Study

| Source of Variance | df | Mean Squares | |
		Attraction	APD^a
Interviewer Responsiveness (A)	1	33.34**	8.519+
Interviewee Expectation (B)	1	1.33	2.070
A × B	1	8.33	.203
Error	43	3.69	2.274

**$p < .01$; $+ .10 < p > .05$
^{a}Based on logarithmic transformations of interviewees' APD scores.

interview that they had liked a confederate who had changed his evaluation of them from negative to positive (negative–positive condition) significantly more than a confederate who had always liked them (positive–positive condition). Although subjects indicated less liking for the confederate in the positive–negative condition (in which the evaluation of the subjects changed from positive to negative) than in the negative–negative condition, this difference failed to reach significance. In a later study by Sigall and Aronson (1967), the major dependent variable was the subjects' opinion change in the direction of a confederate whose evaluation of them was manipulated in a manner similar to that in the Aronson and Linder study. A major assumption of the study was that subjects' attitude changes would reflect their liking of the confederate. Again, the data support a gain phenomenon, but not a loss phenomenon. There never was, then, any real confirmation of the "loss" part of the gain–loss principle. Although an assumption of symmetry between the effects of positive and negative affective experiences underlies many theories of human behavior, including Aronson's gain–loss model of interpersonal attraction, the empirical data frequently belie this assumption.

Whereas the data reported by Aronson and his associates suggest a gain effect but no loss effect, our own findings are inconsistent even as far as the gain effect is concerned. As noted earlier, the results of an early interview study (Siegman, 1974) were consistent with a gain effect in interpersonal attraction, but these findings have not been confirmed by the results of two subsequent studies. Clearly, much more research needs to be done on the gain and loss principles of interpersonal attraction before they can be considered confirmed phenomena of interpersonal attraction. At the very least, the negative findings reported in this paper suggest certain limits in regard to these phenomena, which should be considered in any theoretical discussion of the possible mediating mechanisms.

ON THE MEANING OF SILENT PAUSES
IN SPEECH

What is the meaning of the inverse relationship between interviewer warmth and interviewee within-response silent pausing? Traditionally, silent pauses within the interview, especially the relatively long silent pauses of 2 sec and over, have been viewed within a motivational framework as evidence of anxiety and resistance and defensiveness. However, for some time now, evidence has been accumulating that silent pauses in speech are an indication of cognitive processes.

One of the first to investigate the relationship between cognition and silent pauses in speech was Goldman-Eisler (1968). On the basis of the results of several studies, she concluded that silent pauses in speech are indicative of information processing that is taking place at the time of the pausing.

In an early study, Goldman-Eisler (1961a) used a guessing technique in order to determine the predictability of words following hesitation pauses in a speaker's communications. She found that "where guessers found themselves at a loss for predicting the next word as spoken originally...the original speaker also seemed to have been at a loss for the next word, for it was at these points that he tended to hesitate" (Goldman-Eisler, 1968, p. 42). On the basis of these findings, Goldman-Eisler concludes that hesitation pauses reflect the speaker's lexical decision-making process, that is, his or her word choices.

Boomer (1970) has raised a number of methodological questions in relation to the aforementioned study and maintains that hesitation pauses involve primarily structural, syntactic decisions. In part, his position is based on the finding that hesitation pauses tend to cluster immediately following the first word in a phonemic clause (Boomer, 1978). In contrast to Boomer, Goldman-Eisler (1968) believes that syntax is a matter of habit or skill rather than of cognitive planning. Both agree, however, that hesitation pauses in speech involve some kind of information processing that is taking place at the time of the pausing.

In a subsequent study, Goldman-Eisler (1961a, 1961b, 1968) compared the ratio of silent and filled pauses ("ah's" and similar expressions) in speech associated with tasks of varying levels of difficulty. Specifically, she asked subjects first to describe and then to interpret a series of *New Yorker* cartoons. A comparison of the descriptions versus the interpretations showed that the latter were associated with a significantly higher silent-pause ratio than the former. This was not only true for the group as a whole, but every single subject in the study evidenced a higher silent-pause ratio in the interpretations than in the descriptions. There was no significant difference between the two tasks (interpretations vs. descriptions) in relation to the filled pauses ratio. Although the reaction times, or initial delays, for the descriptions were roughly the same as the initial delays for the interpretations, Goldman-Eisler argues that it took subjects proportionately more time to plan and to organize the interpretations than the descriptions, since the former contained considerably fewer words than the latter. The difference in within-utterance pauses between the two tasks, she attributes primarily to the more complex, lexical decision making associated with the interpretations than with the descriptions.

This study, too, has been criticized on a number of methodological grounds (Rochester, Thurston, & Rupp, 1977; Siegman, Chapter 7, this volume), with the most serious criticism perhaps being that this study confounded the major experimental manipulation with the instructions to the subject to be concise—instructions that occurred only in the interpretation condition. There is evidence that an effort to eliminate redundancy and to formulate concise responses is associated with an increase in silent pausing (Siegman & Reynolds, 1978). A recent study (Siegman, Chapter 7, this volume), however, that took these methodological criticisms into account, succeeded in replicating Goldman-Eisler's original findings. The interpretation condition, in contrast to the description condition, was clearly associated with significantly longer response latencies and within-response silent pauses. There is, then, clear-cut evidence for the proposition that cognitive planning and decision making are associated with silent pauses in speech.

In fact, a case can be made for the proposition that a cognitive, information-processing interpretation of silent pauses provides the most parsimonious explanation for the various findings that have been reported in literature in relation to silent pausing. A cognitive approach certainly has no difficulty in accounting for the inverse relationships between intelligence and socioeconomic background on one hand and silent pausing on the other hand (Siegman, 1978a). Even the reported relationship between introversion and silent pauses in speech (Ramsay, 1966, 1968; Siegman, 1978a) could be mediated by cognitive factors. Introverts are reported to be more thoughtful and less impulsive than extraverts, which could account for their pausing behavior. In fact, in a recent reanalysis of previously obtained data, we found a significant negative correlation between interviewees' silence quotients and their scores on the impulsivity items in the Eysenck Extraversion Scale, but no significant correlation between their silence quotients and their scores on the social-introversion items that make up this scale (Siegman, 1978a).

The finding that intimate interviewer probes are associated with more frequent and longer silent pauses than are nonintimate ones (Siegman, 1978a) is also readily explained in terms of an increase in self-monitoring when one is discussing intimate subjects. Intimate and potentially embarrassing interviewer questions present the interviewee with difficult decisions as to what to say: what to include and what to exclude and how to phrase that which is said.

In other words, the defensiveness that is associated with intimate interviewer questions can be conceptualized in terms of cognitive decision making.

As far as anxiety and stress are concerned, Siegman (1978a) has shown that anxiety arousal per se is in fact associated with a decrease in silent pausing, unless the speaking task is a difficult one involving complex decision making. The clinical observation that anxiety-arousing topics are sometimes associated with silent pauses and hesitant speech is probably an accurate one, but this too can readily be explained in cognitive, decision-making terms. Some anxiety-arousing interviewer queries, like intimate questions, may very well present some interviewees with difficult choices as to what to say and what to conceal. To the extent, then, that there is an association between anxiety and silent pausing, it is suggested that this relationship, too, is mediated by cognitive processes rather than by anxiety arousal per se. Silent pauses in speech may be a result of anxiety-arousing or intimate questions, but they may also be related to other factors such as trying to make a good impression or trying to recall some forgotten material. The crux of the argument is that silent pauses in speech, as well as some other indices of hesitant speech (Siegman, Chapter 7, this volume), are fundamentally a manifestation of cognitive decision making that is taking place at the time of the pausing or the hesitations.

As far as the inverse relationship between interviewer warmth and interviewee pausing and by implication between interpersonal attraction and pausing is concerned, it is suggested that they too are cognitively mediated. Interviewees who do not like their interviewer are likely to be more guarded in what they say and to engage in more self-monitoring than those who feel at ease with their interviewer. The same should apply to other types of interpersonal attraction, as well, although elsewhere (Siegman, 1977) it has been suggested that under certain circumstances—for example, in opposite-gender dyads—attraction may lead to greater self-monitoring and that under such circumstances, attraction would be associated with more rather than with less silent pausing.

With the exception of articulation rate, none of the pausing indices was significantly affected by interviewees' expectations regarding interviewer warmth. In relation to AR, the interviewees who were led to expect a reserved and distant interviewer exhibited a significantly faster articulation rate than the interviewees who expected a warm and friendly interviewer, although this difference was significant only during the first part of the interview. One possible explanation is in terms of anxiety arousal. Previous findings (Siegman, 1978a; Siegman & Pope, 1965, 1972) indicate that anxiety arousal per se accelerates articulation rate by decreasing silent pauses, especially brief pauses, although it could have a similar effect even on the relatively longer silent pauses. In light of this finding, it is suggested that the preinterview instructions to the interviewees that their prospective interviewer was generally reserved and distant may have had an anxiety-arousing effect, and hence the increase in interviewees' articulation rates that was associated with these instructions. The reader should keep in mind, however, the post-hoc nature of this explanation, which should be put to a direct test.

SUMMARY AND CONCLUDING REMARKS

A major objective of this chapter was to summarize several studies, the results of which indicate that there is an inverse relationship between interviewee–interviewer attraction and silent pausing within the interview. Furthermore, data were cited that indicate that this relationship can be conceptualized within an information-processing approach to silent pauses in speech.

The original evidence for an inverse relationship between attraction and pausing came from a correlational study (Pope & Siegman, 1966) in which we found an inverse relationship between interviewee's attraction to their interviewer and a composite pausing index, based on interviewees' latencies and within-response silent pauses of 2 sec and more. In a subsequent experimental investigation, in which we manipulated interviewer warmth (a warm and friendly style versus a reserved and distant one), it was found that the interviewees were significantly more attracted to the warm than to the reserved interviewers, with no overlap between the conditions. Furthermore, the interviewees had significantly higher production rates, defined as number of words per response duration (which in this case included the response-latency period), when responding to the warm than to the reserved interviewers. In this study, there was no significant relationship between interviewer warmth and interviewees' RT and SQ scores. In a follow-up experiment in which interviewees' silent pauses were measured automatically rather than by hand with a stopwatch, as was the case in the earlier study, interviewer warmth had a highly significant effect on a wide array of pausing indices, except in relation to articulation rate. The interviewees responded with less silent pausing to the warm than to the reserved interviewers. The differences in relation to most of the pausing indices were highly significant. Of course, no claim is made to any independence between the various pausing measures; they are obviously related to each other. Finally, in yet another study in which the interviewers either responded with verbal "reinforcers" or failed to do so—a manipulation that clearly affected interviewees' attraction to their interviewers, with interviewees more attracted to the responsive interviewers than to the nonresponsive ones—it was found that the interviewees also showed less pausing ($p = .062$) to the responding than to the nonresponding interviewers. Taken together, these findings strongly suggest an inverse relationship between attraction and silent pausing.

It should be noted that the major finding that was reported in this chapter—namely, that there is an inverse relationship between interpersonal attraction and silent pauses in speech—was obtained within the context of the interview. To test the generalizability of this finding, it should be cross-validated within the context of other types of conversation. Moreover, such studies should also monitor the effects of interpersonal attraction on other vocal parameters of speech besides that of pausing behavior.

ACKNOWLEDGMENTS

The author is very much indebted to Drs. Thomas Blass, Stanley Feldstein, and Jonathan Finkelstein for their valuable comments on this paper. The author is especially grateful to Dr. Marilyn Wang for her thorough and helpful critique of an earlier draft of this chapter. The author is also profoundly indebted to Mark Reynolds for his help with the data analyses.

REFERENCES

Aronson, E. Some antecedents of interpersonal attraction. *Nebraska Symposium on Motivation,* 1969, *17,* 143–173.

Aronson, E., & Linder, D. Gain and loss of esteem as determinants of interpersonal attractiveness. *Journal of Experimental Social Psychology,* 1965, *1,* 156–171.

Boomer, D. S. Review of F. Goldman-Eisler, Psycholinguistics: Experiments in spontaneous speech. *Lingua,* 1970, *25,* 152–164.

Boomer, D. S. The phonemic clause, speech unit in human communication. In A. W. Siegman & S. Feldstein (Eds.), *Nonverbal behavior and communication.* Hillsdale, N.J.: Lawrence Erlbaum Associates, 1978.

Byrne, D. *The attraction paradigm.* New York: Academic Press, 1971.

Exline, R. V., & Fehr, B. J. Applications of semiosis to the study of visual interaction. In A. W. Siegman & S. Feldstein (Eds.), *Nonverbal behavior and communication.* Hillsdale, N.J.: Lawrence Erlbaum Associates, 1978.

Feldstein, S. Rate estimates of sound–silence sequences in speech. *Journal of the Acoustical Society of America,* 1976, *60* (Supplement No. 1), 546. (Abstract)

Goldman-Eisler, F. Hesitation and information in speech. In C. Cherry (ed.), *Information theory.* London: Butterworth, 1961. (a)

Goldman-Eisler, F. A comparative study of two hesitation phenomena. *Language and Speech,* 1961, *4,* 18–26. (b)

Goldman-Eisler, F. *Psycholinguistics: Experiments in spontaneous speech.* New York: Academic Press, 1968.

Goldstein, A. P. *Psychotherapeutic attraction.* New York: Pergamon Press, 1971.

Hess, E. H., & Petrovich, S. B. Pupillary behavior in communication. In A. W. Siegman & S. Feldstein (Eds.), *Nonverbal behavior and communication.* Hillsdale, N.J.: Lawrence Erlbaum Associates, 1978.

Jaffe, J., & Feldstein, S. *Rhythms of dialogue.* New York: Academic Press, 1970.

Libo, L. M. *Manual for the Picture Impression Test.* University of Maryland School of Medicine, Baltimore, 1956.

Marsden, G., Kalter, N., & Ericson, W. A. Response productivity: A methodological problem in content analysis studies in psychotherapy. *Journal of Consulting and Clinical Psychology,* 1974, *42,* 224–230.

Pope, B., & Siegman, A. W. Interviewer specificity and topical focus in relation to interviewee productivity. *Journal of Verbal Learning and Verbal Behavior,* 1965, *4,* 188–192.

Pope, B., & Siegman, A. W. Interviewer–interviewee relationship and verbal behavior of interviewee. *Psychotherapy,* 1966, *3,* 149–152.

Pope, B., & Siegman A. W. Interviewer warmth in relation to interviewee verbal behavior. *Journal of Consulting and Clinical Psychology,* 1968, *32,* 588–595.

Pope, B., & Siegman, A. W. Relationship and verbal behavior in the initial interview. In A. W. Siegman & B. Pope (Eds.), *Studies in dyadic communication.* New York: Pergamon Press, 1972.

Ramsay, R. W. Personality and speech. *Journal of Personality and Social Psychology,* 1966, *4,* 116–118.

Ramsay, R. W. Speech patterns and personality. *Language and Speech,* 1968, *11,* 54–63.

Rochester, S. R., Thurston, S., & Rupp, J. Hesitation as clues to failures in coherence: A study of the thought-disordered speaker. In S. Rosenberg (Ed.), *Sentence production: Developments in research and theory.* Hillsdale, N.J.: Lawrence Erlbaum Associates, 1977.

Siegman, A. W. The gain–loss principle and interpersonal attraction in the interview. *Proceedings of the Division of Personality and Social Psychology,* 1974, 85–88.

Siegman, A. W. Do noncontingent interviewer mm-hmm's facilitate interviewee productivity? *Journal of Consulting and Clinical Psychology,* 1976, *44,* 171–182.

Siegman, A. W. *Effects of cross-gender pairing on vocal behavior.* Symposium paper presented at the 85th Annual Convention of the American Psychological Association, San Francisco, 1977.

Siegman, A. W. The meaning of silent pauses in the interview. *The Journal of Nervous and Mental Disease,* 1978, *166,* 642–654. (a)

Siegman, A. W. The telltale voice: Nonverbal messages of verbal communication. In A. W. Siegman & S. Feldstein (Eds.), *Nonverbal behavior and communication.* Hillsdale, N.J.: Lawrence Erlbaum Associates, 1978. (b)

Siegman, A. W., & Pope, B. Effects of question specificity and anxiety-producing messages on verbal fluency in the initial interview. *Journal of Personality and Social Psychology,* 1965, *1,* 188 192.

Siegman, A. W., & Pope, B. The effect of interviewer ambiguity specificity and topical focus on interviewee vocabulary diversity. *Language and Speech,* 1966, *9,* 242–249.

Siegman, A. W., & Pope, B. The effects of ambiguity and anxiety on interviewee verbal behavior. In A. W. Siegman & B. Pope (Eds.), *Studies in dyadic communication.* New York: Pergamon Press, 1972.

Siegman, A. W., & Reynolds, M. *Economy and hesitation in speech.* Symposium paper presented at the Eastern Psychological Association Annual Meetings, April 1978.

Sigall, H., & Aronson, E. Opinion change and the gain–loss model of interpersonal attraction. *Journal of Experimental Social Psychology,* 1967, *3,* 178–188.

6 The Modifiability of the Temporal Structure of Spontaneous Speech

Geoffrey W. Beattie
University of Sheffield, England

> *Men are born with two eyes, but with one tongue, in order*
> *that they should see twice as much as they say.*
> Charles Caleb Colton (1826)

This chapter presents an overview of a series of three experiments that demonstrate how the basic temporal organization of spontaneous speech is affected by visually perceived contingencies both in a highly artificial situation and in a less artificial, interpersonal context. They demonstrate the importance of the human visual system in directing adaptive changes in the basic temporal organization of speech, and they indicate that the underlying temporal structure is much more flexible than many had previously assumed.

The relevance of unfilled pauses (UPs) to cognitive processing in speech has been shown by a number of studies that have demonstrated a positive relationship between the frequency and/or duration of such pauses and the difficulty or abstractness of experimental tasks involving speech production (Goldman-Eisler, 1961a; Lay & Paivio, 1969; Levin, Silverman, & Ford, 1967; Reynolds & Paivio, 1968; Taylor, 1969). Attempts have been made to determine the cognitive functions of these pauses through analyses of their speech locations. These analyses have revealed that UPs tend to precede unpredictable lexical items (Butterworth, 1972; Goldman-Eisler, 1958a, 1958b), that they occur with greater than chance frequency at the beginnings of phonemic clauses (Boomer, 1965), and that they are associated with (intuitively determined) "idea" boundaries in the speech text (Butterworth, 1975). Thus it has been concluded that UPs are used for lexical selection,

115

holistic planning of phonemic clauses, and suprasentential ideational planning.

However, on the basis of these studies, a strong cognitive hypothesis that all UPs are used for cognitive planning is not immediately tenable, since in each study some proportion of the pause variance has not been associated with the particular cognitive process under investigation. In the Goldman-Eisler (1958a) study, which employed a highly selected speech sample, 17.7% of UPs did not precede a word of low transitional probability and thus could not be used for lexical selection. In the Boomer (1965) study, only 49.1% of UPs could be used for holistic planning of the clause, since 50.9% of UPs occurred later than the second word in the clause. No attempt was made to determine the function, if any, of these residual pauses. In the studies of cognitive cycles in speech (Goldman-Eisler, 1967; Henderson, Goldman-Eisler, & Skarbek, 1966) the fluent phases of cycles, reflecting the execution of semantic plans formulated in hesitant phases, are not hesitation free; rather, the mean pause–phonation ratio appears to be in the region of 1:10 (Beattie, 1978b). Some of these pauses in fluent phases are at grammatical junctures and thus may have a listener-directed function (Barik, 1968); others may be used for lexical selection, where this selection is guided by a preformulated semantic plan (Butterworth & Beattie, 1978). Approximately 73% of UPs occurring within the fluent phases of cycles fall into one or the other of these categories (Butterworth, 1976). This leaves 27% of UPs in fluent phases whose function has not been elucidated. Moreover, the amount of pause time in hesitant phases necessary for the planning of these ideational units remains to be determined. And it has yet to be demonstrated that the mean hesitancy of such phases cannot be diminished without a deleterious effect on ideational content.

In the light of these caveats, a strong cognitive hypothesis—that all UPs have a cognitive planning function—must currently be untenable. Nevertheless, this hypothesis appears to be widely subscribed to, as evidenced first by such statements as "hesitation pauses are an index of cognitive activities" (Goldman-Eisler, 1967, p. 122), which suggests that UPs are universally cognitive in function; and second by the interpretations of social and affective-state studies of pauses (see Rochester, 1973). The interpretation of those studies that have found pause rate to be positively related to anxiety (Lay & Paivio, 1969; Reynolds & Paivio, 1968) has been that anxiety interferes with the cognitive processes underlying speech and that when subjects are anxious, such processes require more time. In this particular area, however, this argument could only be substantiated by establishing that the effects of anxiety on pausing are confined to increases in the duration of those UPs whose cognitive function can be demonstrated through analyses of pause location.

A similar interpretative trend is discernible in those studies that have found UPs to be sensitive to certain social variables. Levin and Silverman (1965), having observed that "high exhibitionist" subjects paused for longer periods of time than "low exhibitionist" subjects, described the "high exhibitionist" child as a "slow, thoughtful speaker [p. 82]." Ramsay (1966, 1968) found that introverts used longer pauses in speech than extraverts and concluded that "the results support the idea that the introvert is the thoughtful type; he thinks before acting and weighs his words more than the extravert" (Ramsay, 1968, p. 61). However, in none of these studies was any attempt made to assess the quality of speech produced to validate this concept of "thoughtfulness." Furthermore, the relative locations of UPs were not reported in these studies. It is conceivable that the reported differences between the groups lay in differences in the numbers of "social" pauses occurring at grammatical junctures. This hypothesis is supported by Ramsay's (1968) observation that introverts and extraverts differed significantly in pausing even in one of the reading tasks, where UPs tend to be confined to grammatical junctures (Goldman-Eisler, 1972). Thus, conclusions on differences in the "thoughtfulness" of the various groups are rather peremptory.

A radically different hypothesis can be offered to account for the observed differences in pause behavior between introverts and extraverts—namely that such groups differ in the level of noncognitive pauses habitually displayed (where such noncognitive pauses need not be confined to grammatical junctures, as traditionally assumed by Lounsbury, 1954, among others). This hypothesis is consonant with the observation that introverts and extraverts typically engage in different types of interaction (Stern & Grosz, 1966a, 1966b) that influence both interactional style and speech pattern. One example of this influence is response matching (Argyle, 1969), where certain aspects of behavior and speech of interactants become similar during the course of an interaction and increasingly so with repeated interactions (Lennard & Bernstein, 1960; Welkowitz & Feldstein, 1969). Response matching has been found for a wide variety of behaviors: length of utterance (Matarazzo, 1965); frequency of interruption (Argyle & Kendon, 1967); speech rate (Webb, 1972); posture (Scheflen, 1965); and also for pausing. Jaffe and Feldstein (1970) observed a significant tendency for interviewers and interviewees to adopt similar temporal structures (average congruence coefficients of 0.39 were recorded for pause durations). The temporal structure of speech has also been found to change in contexts that do not necessarily involve response matching. Goldman-Eisler (1952; 1968, Appendix 1) observed that certain aspects of temporal patterning (notably the ratio of the total number of short silences to the total number of long silences) of the speech of depressive or highly anxious psychiatric patients varied across interviews with different psychiatrists. The temporal structure of the psychiatrists' speech, on the other hand, was found to be much more consistent. The temporal structure of speech directed at children has been found to differ in several respects from that directed at adults. Speech rate is significantly slower to children (132.0 words/min. compared with 169.6

words/min. to adults; Sachs, Brown, & Salerno, 1976), and although there appears to be some drop in articulation rate with certain content words (Garnica, 1977), the drop in speech rate is still probably largely a function of an increase in pause time (Goldman-Eisler, 1956). It has also been discovered that in child-directed speech, the majority of pauses occur at syntactic junctures and especially between sentences (Dale, 1974), whereas this is clearly not the case in most adult-directed speech (Goldman-Eisler, 1968, Chap. 1.). There has been some debate over the actual mechanism involved in the changing of temporal structure, particularly with respect to response matching (Matarazzo, 1965; Webb, 1972), but a reinforcement hypothesis has recently found support (Fielding, 1972; Pope & Siegman, 1972). Ethological studies of adult conversations have revealed that possible contingencies do exist for both reinforcement and punishment of pauses in speech. Signals of attention from the listener often occur during speaker pauses (Dittmann & Llewellyn, 1967, 1968; Duncan, 1974; Kendon, 1967); in other contexts and/or at other times, speaker switches and interruptions predominate at speaker pauses (Beattie, 1977a; Jaffe & Feldstein, 1970). Beattie (1977a) discovered a relationship between certain aspects of the temporal structure of speech and temporal properties of interruption. In conversational interactions in which interruption was likely to occur after relatively short delays, UPs within a speaker turn were shorter in duration and more likely to be followed by filled pauses ("ah," "er," "um," etc.) than UPs occurring in conversations where listener interruption occurred after long delays. It has also been hypothesized that in adult–child conversations, even prelinguistic children may actively modify the temporal structure of adult speech by ignoring inappropriately structured speech and by reinforcing (with eye contact, etc.) other types of speech (Gleason, 1977).

If we assume that pause rate can be modified by these social contingencies, then we can hypothesize that the differences in pausing between introverts and extraverts reported by Ramsay (1966, 1968) are due to variations in the habitual level of socially conditioned UPs, which may not have a cognitive function. Such variations could result from differences in the conditionability of the two groups—from the relative ease with which introverts can be conditioned as compared with extraverts (Eysenck, 1955, 1957), even in verbal conditioning tasks (Eysenck, 1959; Jawanda, 1970).

STUDY 1: THE EFFECTS OF REINFORCEMENT ON THE MODIFIABILITY OF TEMPORAL STRUCTURE

The first study[1] has thus two principle aims: first, to test the hypothesis that the temporal structure of speech is modifiable by attempting to change the incidence of UPs of a preselected duration through automatically delivered

---

[1]This study is reported in more detail in Beattie and Bradbury (in press).

reinforcement and punishment in an operant conditioning situation. The majority of verbal conditioning studies have used the Taffel (1955) procedure—in which the subject has a limited choice of responses (for example, the selection of a word from a small number of alternatives in a sentence completion task)—and have usually attempted to manipulate content classes of speech with minimal cues from the experimenter, on the premise that head-nods and "mm-hmms" indicate attention and are therefore reinforcing. The problems with this methodology are that the task is not sufficiently complex to prevent subjects from speculating about the real nature of the experiment during its course (a more complex free operant paradigm reduces the probability of such speculation); and that the experimenter cues employed have been found not to be universally reinforcing (subjects interpret them differently) (Mandler & Kaplan, 1956). This latter problem can be overcome by using an explicitly defined, automated reinforcer. McNair (1957), for example, successfully reinforced rate of verbalization in a discussion group using a bell tone defined as signifying approval. Oakes, Droge, and August (1960) reinforced the same behavior using a light defined as signifying "psychological insight." A light defined as signifying "lack of psychological insight" acted as an effective punisher. Simkins (1963) used a count meter to reinforce continous speech (i.e., speech in which all pauses were less than 750 msec). The present study therefore attempts to employ a more effective verbal conditioning paradigm in reinforcing/punishing pauses in a free monologue condition, using automatically delivered signals.

The second aim of the present study is to test the hypothesis that there is a class of noncognitive UPs in spontaneous monologue by employing a punishment procedure to determine what proportion, if any, of UPs can be eliminated without significantly affecting speech content. A strong cognitive hypothesis would maintain that all UPs displayed (except perhaps brief UPs, i.e., UPs ≤ 500 msec, at grammatical junctures; Lounsbury, 1954; Barik, 1968) are necessary for speech planning and would predict that none (except those noted) could be eliminated without causing a decrement in the quality of the utterance. Alternatively, the hypothesis that posits a class of socially conditioned UPs might predict that some indeterminate proportion of UPs could be eliminated without affecting semantic content.

Method

Apparatus. A voice-operated switch (VOS) was used to detect UPs. A light was activated by the VOS whenever a subject paused for longer than 600 msec.[2] The light remained on until a further speech sound was emitted. A

---

[2]Six hundred msec is approximately equal to the mean value of the shortest pauses whose cognitive function has been elucidated (pauses used for lexical selection in the fluent phase of a temporal cycle, Butterworth, 1976).

multi-X digital recorder attached to the VOS was used to count the number of UPs $\geq$ 600 msec. In some cases, this was checked using an Ediswan pen-oscillograph. Ferrograph and AKAI recorders were used to record the subjects' speech.

Subjects.   Twenty undergraduates from the Universities of Birmingham and Cambridge acted as subjects. Eleven were female, nine were male. All were native English speakers free of any obvious speech defect.

Procedure

A warm-up period in which subjects could become accustomed to the experimental situation preceded testing. All Ss were tested by the same E (the author). There were five Ss in each experimental group. The task for Ss was to compose a short story (from a beginning that was provided) on nine trials each of 2 minutes duration.

Reinforcement Condition

The instructions read to experimental group E_1 and control group C_2 were as follows:

> We are investigating the effects of feedback on story-telling. I would like you to choose one of these cards and silently read what is printed on it. Your task is to compose a story using these lines as the beginning. Do not repeat what is written on the card, simply continue from where it left off. You continue with this story for 2 minutes, you do not have to complete the story in the 2 minutes allocated, but try not to complete the story in less than 2 minutes. In the first phase of the experiment, which covers the first two trials, your performance will be assessed but you will receive no feedback on how well you are telling the story. In the next phase, which covers the next five trials, your performance will again be assessed but you will receive feedback on how well you are telling the story. A green light will come on when you are doing particularly well. The green light means "good." The more frequently this light comes on the better is your telling of the story. In the last phase, which covers the final two trials, your performance will again be assessed but you will receive no feedback. In all you will tell nine stories. It is important to note that every aspect of your story-telling will be assessed. The actual content and how you tell the story are both taken into account in your assessment. Do you understand these instructions?

Ss' story telling was recorded, but reinforcement was not contingent upon actual speech content. For group E_1 reinforcement (in the form of a light signifying "good" performance) was contingent upon 600-msec UPs on a full schedule in trials 3 to 7. In the case of C_1 reinforcement was delivered on a variable time (VT) schedule (i.e., approximately the same number of reinforcers were delivered but at random time intervals). No reinforcement was delivered in baseline trials 1 and 2 or in extinction trials 8 and 9.

Punishment Condition

The instructions read to Ss in experimental group E_2 and control group C_2 were identical to those described for E_1 and C_1 except that they were informed: "A green light will come on when your performance is judged to be poor. The green light means 'poor.' The more frequently this light comes on the poorer is your telling of the story."

For group E_2 the punisher (the light signifying "poor" performance) was contingent upon 600-msec UPs, on a full schedule in trials 3 to 7. In the case of the C_2 the punisher delivered on a VT schedule. After the final trials, Ss were interviewed to determine if they had been aware of the reinforcement/punishment contingency. Their views about the experiment were also noted. The tapes for all groups were transcribed and the number of words counted; filled pauses (FPs) and incomplete words were excluded from the word count. The following categories of filled hesitation were also noted:

1. repetitions (R): all repetitions of any length that were judged to be nonsignificant semantically.
2. false starts (FS): all incomplete or self-interrupted utterances.
3. parenthetic remarks (PR): words and phrases that seem irrelevant to semantic communication, e.g., "I mean," "sort of," "you know."
4. filled pauses (FP): any of the following speech sounds / $\alpha, \epsilon, æ, \tau, e, m$ /.

Filled hesitations were quantified in terms of number of words or parts of words. In the case of groups E_2 and C_2 (punishment condition), the speech locations of the UPs were noted. The definition of grammatical location employed by Goldman-Eisler (1968, p. 13) was used. In order to determine if the punishment manipulation significantly affected the content of speech, edited versions of the transcripts (all filled hesitations being excluded) from trials 1 and 2 and 6 and 7 were presented to three independent judges who were asked to rate the story on a 5-point rating scale, taking into account both the semantic content and style. It was decided to use edited versions of the transcripts, since it was felt that judges might otherwise have paid undue regard to the presence or absence of filled hesitations and neglected other important aspects of the performance.

Results

A. Reinforcement Condition

Rate of Pausing. Table 6.1 shows the change in the rate of pausing across trials for groups E_1 and C_1. These changes are illustrated in Fig. 6.1, which shows the percentage change in pause rate across trials.

TABLE 6.1
Number of UPs for Groups E_1 and C_1 (Reinforcement Condition).[a]

		Baseline		Conditioning					Extinction	
Group	Ss	1	2	3	4	5	6	7	8	9
	S_1	22	36	21	19	24	37	35	26	20
	S_2	53	46	57	59	60	59	59	44	44
E_1	S_3	30	34	33	32	37	46	37	39	29
	S_4	37	39	53	49	50	54	57	41	42
	S_5	43	34	35	47	47	37	48	34	41
	Mean	37.0	37.8	39.8	41.2	43.6	46.6	47.2	36.8	35.2
	S.D.	11.9	5.0	14.9	15.7	13.7	9.9	11.1	7.1	10.3
	S_6	46	52	51	53	57	49	52	48	44
	S_7	41	46	44	55	53	45	50	42	50
C_1	S_8	54	51	58	61	63	43	70	54	63
	S_9	40	41	36	33	31	42	36	45	54
	S_{10}	47	48	42	50	49	53	52	46	49
	Mean	45.6	47.6	46.2	50.4	50.6	46.4	52.0	47.0	52.0
	S.D.	5.6	4.4	8.5	10.5	12.1	4.6	12.1	4.5	7.1

[a]From Beattie and Bradbury (in press).

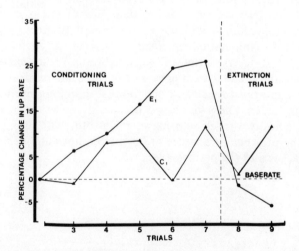

FIG. 6.1. Percentage change in unfilled-pause (UP) rate across trials for groups E_1 and C_1 (full schedule of visual reinforcement of UPs in composition task). From Beattie and Bradbury (in press).

An analysis of variance and trend analysis were used to compare the rate of pausing in baseline trials (1 & 2), final conditioning trials (6 & 7), and extinction trials (8 & 9) for groups E_1 and C_1. The trials effect (MS = 435.04, df = 2, F = 9.84, $p < .01$) and the groups × trials interaction effect (MS = 319.23, df = 2, F = 7.22, $p < .01$) were both significant. The groups effect, however, was nonsignificant (MS = 2083.34, df = 1, F = 3.79, $p > .05$). The quadratic component of the trials effect was significant (MS = 858.82, df = 1, F = 18.10, $p < .01$) and accounted for 98.71% of the trials variance. The quadratic component of the groups × trials effect was also significant (MS = 546.01, df = 1, F = 11.50, $p < .01$) and accounted for 85.52% of the interaction variance.

The significant quadratic component of the groups × trials interaction effect suggests that reinforcement had a significant effect on pause rate, and so too did the termination of reinforcement. Thus, pause rate can be significantly increased through reinforcement; once the reinforcement is withdrawn, extinction is rapid.

Rate of Speech.   There was little change in the speech rate between baseline trials (1 & 2) and conditioning trials (6 & 7). Mean speech rate 156.4 words/min in baseline trials and 163.1 in final conditioning trials for E_1 compared with 144.4 words/min and 151.7 words/min in the corresponding trials for C_1. An ANOVA revealed that the groups effect (MS = 10951.2, df = 1, F = .48, $p > .05$), the trials effect (MS = 3864.2, df = 1, F = .85, $p > .05$), and the groups × trials interaction effect (MS = 7.2, df = 1, F = .0016, $p \gg .05$) were all nonsignificant.

Thus despite the fact that there was a significant increase in the incidence of 600-msec UPs, there was no significant tendency for speech rate (number of words per unit time) to decline. Evidence has suggested that articulation rate (number of words per unit time of phonation) displays a "remarkable invariance" (Goldman-Eisler, 1956, p. 139; see also, Goldman-Eisler, 1961b) and that differences in speech rate are largely a function of differences in the amount of time spent pausing. This suggests that the reinforcement contingency in the present study affected the overall distribution of pauses without significantly changing the absolute amount of time spent pausing. A significant decline in speech rate across trials would have been necessary before we could have assumed that the latter had occurred.

Filled Hesitation.   There was a slight decrease in the amount of filled hesitation in speech across trials, from .073 words per unit word spoken in baseline trials to .058 per unit word in final conditioning trials for E_1, and from .039 per unit word to .034 for C_1. An ANOVA revealed that the groups effect (MS = 4057.55, df = 1, F = 3.85, $p > .05$), the trials effect (MS = 584.6, df = 1, F = 1.64, $p > .05$), and the groups × trials interaction effect (MS = 108.35, df = 1, F = .30, $p > .05$) were all nonsignificant.

B. Punishment Condition

Rate of Pausing.   Table 6.2 shows the change in the rate of pausing across trials for groups E_2 and C_2. These changes are illustrated in Fig. 6.2, which shows the percentage change in pause rate across trials.

Comparing the rate in baseline trials (1 & 2) and punishment trials (6 & 7), an ANOVA revealed a significant trials effect ($MS = 897.8$, $df = 1$, $F = 12.02$, $p < .01$), a significant groups × trials effect ($MS = 1344.8$, $df = 1$, $F = 18.0$, $p < .01$), but a nonsignificant groups effect ($MS = 96.8$, $df = 1$, $F = .08$, $p > .05$).

Thus we can assume that the punishment manipulation was effective in reducing the number of 600-msec UPs displayed. Inspection of Fig. 6.2 also reveals that when the punisher was withdrawn, the return to base rate of pausing was rapid. Recovery of rate of pausing occurred in the first 2-min extinction trial.

Rate of Speech.   Speech rate was found to increase from baseline trials to final conditioning trials from 151.1 words/min to 184.7 words/min in the case of E_2, and from 137.6 words/min to 151.1 words/min in the case of C_2. An

TABLE 6.2
Number of UPs for Groups E_2 and C_2 (Punishment Condition).[a]

| | | *Trials* | | | | | | | | |
| | | *Baseline* | | *Conditioning* | | | | | *Extinction* | |
Group	*Ss*	*1*	*2*	*3*	*4*	*5*	*6*	*7*	*8*	*9*
	S_{11}	62	64	45	41	44	41	29	34	34
	S_{12}	29	20	15	10	11	7	15	26	27
E_2	S_{13}	46	51	43	40	46	50	39	42	46
	S_{14}	58	57	45	45	52	44	44	81	84
	S_{15}	33	34	27	25	21	17	19	27	29
	Mean	45.6	45.2	35.0	32.2	34.8	31.8	29.2	42.0	44.0
	S.D.	14.6	17.9	13.5	14.6	17.8	18.7	12.5	22.7	23.6
	S_{16}	33	38	39	38	38	36	36	40	39
	S_{17}	32	28	21	18	22	32	34	26	28
C_2	S_{18}	29	36	33	27	27	31	38	32	36
	S_{19}	47	48	46	49	41	48	49	50	49
	S_{20}	52	51	48	47	51	54	51	48	52
	Mean	38.6	40.2	37.4	35.8	35.8	40.2	41.6	39.2	40.8
	S.D.	10.2	9.3	10.9	13.2	11.5	10.3	7.8	10.3	9.8

[a]From Beattie and Bradbury (in press).

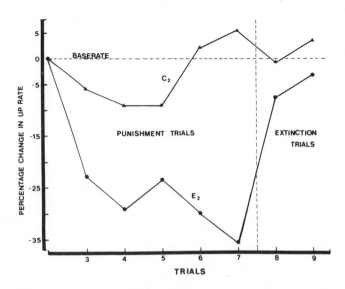

FIG. 6.2. Percentage change in unfilled-pause (UP) rate across trials for groups E_2 and C_2 (full schedule of visual punishment of UPs in composition task). From Beattie and Bradbury (in press).

ANOVA revealed a nonsignificant groups effect (MS = 44,274.0, df = 1, F = 1.76, $p > .05$), but a significant trials effect (MS = 44,274.0, df = 1, F = 12.81, $p > .01$) and a nonsignificant groups × trials effect (MS = 8040.1, df = 1, F = 2.33, $p > .05$).

Thus, again assuming a constancy of articulation rate, we must conclude that the absolute amount of time spent in pausing significantly declined across trials, since there was a significant increase in speech rate across trials. This seemed to occur more for the experimental group than for the control group (although this trend failed to reach significance). There was a 22.2% increase in speech rate from baseline trials (1 & 2) to punishment trials (6 & 7) in the case of experimental group E_2, compared with a 9.8% increase in the case of control group C_2.

Pause Location. The percentage of UPs occurring at grammatical junctures in baseline trials (1 & 2) and punishment trials (6 & 7) was noted. The definition of grammatical location employed by Goldman-Eisler (1968, p. 13) was used. No significant trend emerged across trials. For some Ss, the percentage of UPs at grammatical junctures increased (experimental group E_2–S_{11}, S_{14}, S_{15}; control group C_2–S_{16}, S_{17}, S_{20}, and for some Ss, the percentage of UPs at grammatical junctures decreased (E_2–S_{12}, S_{13}; C_2–S_{19}).

Filled Hesitations. Table 6.3 shows the change in the amount of filled hesitation per unit word between baseline trials (1 & 2) and punishment trials (6 & 7) for groups E_2 and C_2.

TABLE 6.3
Filled Hesitation Rate per Unit Word Spoken for Groups E_2 and C_2 ($\times 10^3$) (Punishment Condition).[a]

Group	Ss	Baseline trials (1 & 2)					Punishment Trials (6 & 7)				
		Repetition	False Starts	Parenthetic Remarks	Filled Pauses	Total	Repetition	False Starts	Parenthetic Remarks	Filled Pauses	Total
E_2	S_{11}	21.49	42.98	5.06	8.85	78.38	53.27	39.95	2.42	3.63	99.27
	S_{12}	32.00	32.00	16.00	18.67	98.67	65.88	57.24	0	3.24	126.35
	S_{13}	16.77	8.39	0	0	25.16	8.39	16.78	2.80	1.40	29.37
	S_{14}	23.15	43.98	0	18.52	85.65	55.56	24.69	0	14.40	94.65
	S_{15}	26.22	31.47	3.50	12.24	73.43	58.11	28.38	1.35	8.11	95.95
	Mean	23.73	31.75	4.91	11.66	72.05	48.34	33.41	1.31	6.16	89.29
	S.D.	5.58	14.33	6.58	7.75	27.99	22.83	15.72	1.31	5.23	35.88
C_2	S_{16}	9.54	5.73	0	3.48	19.08	10.84	7.74	0	1.55	20.13
	S_{17}	31.01	25.19	0	77.52	133.72	18.15	12.70	0	49.00	79.85
	S_{18}	8.03	18.07	8.03	58.23	92.36	37.33	12.44	12.44	20.22	82.43
	S_{19}	30.41	10.14	0	15.20	55.75	26.23	11.48	0	13.11	50.82
	S_{20}	16.08	24.12	3.22	17.69	61.09	17.48	31.47	5.24	17.48	71.68
	Mean	19.01	16.65	2.25	34.42	72.40	22.01	15.17	3.54	20.27	60.98
	S.D.	11.10	8.55	3.52	31.75	43.03	10.16	9.33	5.47	17.57	25.99

[a]From Beattie and Bradbury (in press).

An ANOVA revealed that the groups effect was nonsignificant (MS = 979.58, df = 1, F = .46, $p >$ .05), and so too was the trials effect (MS = 37.02, df = 1, F = .21, $p >$ .05). However, the groups × trials effect was significant (MS = 999.55, df = 1, F = 5.57, $p <$ .05). In the case of the control group, there was a tendency for the amount of filled hesitations per unit word to decline (as with groups E_1 and C_1 in the reinforcement condition), whereas with experimental group E_2, there was a tendency for the amount of filled hesitation to increase. This increase was accounted for largely by an increase in the amount of repetition in speech (there was a mean percentage increase of 104% in the case of repetition). Interestingly, the amount of parenthetic remarks and filled pauses actually declined across trials with this group.

The correlation between the percentage decrease in UP rate and the increase in amount of filled hesitation from baseline trials (1 & 2) to punishment trials (6 & 7) for Ss in group E_2 is r_s = 1.000 (Spearman rank correlation coefficient, $p <$ .01). The correlation between the percentage decrease in UP rate and the increase in amount of repetition from baseline trials (1 & 2) to punishment trials (6 & 7) for Ss in group E_2 is r_s = .700, which is not significant ($p >$ .05).

Judges' Ratings of Content of Stories. The mean ratings for stories in baseline trials (1 & 2) and punishment trials (6 & 7) for the experimental group were 2.1 and 2.8 respectively, and for the control group, 2.2 and 3.0 respectively. There was no significant change in judges' ratings across trials for either group (in both cases, Sign Test, $p >$ .05).

Awareness of Experimental Contingency.

Interviews with subjects after the final trial revealed that none had been aware of the experimental contingency. A number of subjects reported that the reinforcer was delivered on certain occasions when they had not been talking, but they had apparently thought that the reinforcer referred to something said prior to the pause.

Discussion

Study 1 demonstrated that the temporal structure of spontaneous speech can be significantly modified through reinforcement of UPs of a preselected duration. The absolute amount of pausing was not, however, affected by the contingency. It was also discovered that pause rate can be significantly diminished by punishing UPs, without any discernible decrement in the judged content of speech, although this change was accompanied by a significant increase in the amount of filled hesitations, particularly repetition. These results do not support the hypothesis that there is a class of noncognitive pauses in spontaneous monologue, but they do suggest that the form and structure of hesitations in speech are susceptible to change.

STUDY 2: THE EFFECTS OF TASK DIFFERENCES ON THE MODIFIABILITY OF TEMPORAL STRUCTURE

Study 2 attempts to determine if the cognitive demands of the speech task, which do influence the temporal structure, affect its susceptibility to change. Little attention has been paid to this question. Jaffe and Feldstein (1970) noted that there were similar degrees of congruence for the duration of pauses in a verbal task involving the resolution of attitudinal differences and in free discussion (.56 and .43, respectively). They thus concluded that "the topical focus of a conversation exerts relatively little effect on pattern matching [p. 48]." However, since they do not elucidate the topics covered in the free discussion, it is impossible to compare the two tasks in terms of the cognitive demands made on the speakers. In the present study, a more controlled situation is employed to assess the modifiability of the temporal structure of two types of speech—one involving spontaneous composition (as in Study 1) the other the retelling of a story. The effects of reinforcement of UPs of a certain duration in these two speech tasks are compared.

Method

Apparatus.   As in Study 1.

Subjects.   Twenty-three undergraduates from the Universities of Birmingham and Cambridge acted as subjects. Thirteen were female, 10 were male.

Procedure

The usual warm-up procedure preceded testing. All Ss were tested by the same E (the author). There were eight Ss in experimental group E_r (repetition task) and five Ss in each of the other groups. There were nine trials, each of 2 minutes duration.

Composition Task.   Groups E_1 and C_1 of Study 1 were used; therefore, see Procedure, Study 1.

Repetition Task.   The instructions given to experimental group E_r and control group C_r (repetition task) were identical to those used in the Reinforcement Condition, Study 1, except that subjects were told: "Your task is to read a story and retell it into the microphone. You do not have a set time in which to read the story, but please read it as quickly as possible. You must retell the story for two minutes. You do not have to complete the story in the two minutes allocated, but try not to complete it in less than two minutes."

Reinforcement of pauses on a full schedule in trials 3 to 7 in the repetition task was compared with reinforcement of pauses in the composition task. As in Study 1, no reinforcement was delivered in baseline trials (1 & 2) or extinction trials (8 & 9).

Results

A. Repetition Task

Rate of Pausing. Table 6.4 shows the change in the rate of pausing across trials for groups E_r and C_r. These changes are illustrated in Fig. 6.3, which shows the percentage change in pause rate across trials for groups E_r and C_r. An ANOVA was used to compare the rate of pausing in baseline trials (1 & 2) with the rate of pausing in the final conditioning trials (6 & 7). The groups effect was not significant (MS = 831.63, df = 1, F = .81, $p > .05$). However, there was a significant trials effect (MS = 1981.88, df = 1, F = 8.52, $p < .05$) and a significant groups × trials interaction effect (MS = 2592.47, df = 1, F = 11.14, $p < .01$). Thus the 600-msec pause rate significantly increased

TABLE 6.4
Number of UPs for Groups E_R and C_R (Repetition Task)

Group	Ss	Baseline		Conditioning					Extinction	
		1	2	3	4	5	6	7	8	9
E_R	S_{21}	35	41	60	69	56	57	61	30	27
	S_{22}	57	54	58	67	60	57	54	46	44
	S_{23}	38	37	47	40	44	43	53	34	37
	S_{24}	55	46	80	64	86	92	89	40	37
	S_{25}	45	59	56	68	62	74	76	44	38
	S_{26}	34	32	45	49	39	42	47	33	36
	S_{27}	34	32	51	66	58	58	49	38	33
	S_{28}	33	28	38	28	34	32	42	28	31
	Mean	41.4	41.1	54.4	56.4	54.9	56.9	58.9	36.6	35.4
C_R	S_{29}	37	35	33	31	33	43	30	37	35
	S_{30}	56	55	61	54	60	64	57	65	51
	S_{31}	48	45	39	31	37	32	32	38	36
	S_{32}	55	40	42	47	46	52	34	44	44
	S_{33}	44	42	47	46	40	35	39	42	36
	Mean	48.0	43.4	44.4	41.8	43.2	45.2	38.4	45.2	40.4

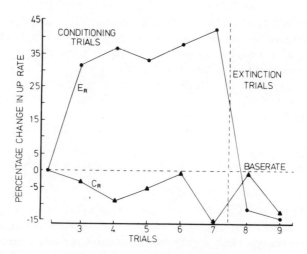

FIG. 6.3. Percentage change in unfilled-pause (UP) rate across trials for groups E_R and C_R (full schedule of visual reinforcement of UPs in repetition task).

across trials, and there was a significant difference in the rate of change of pause rate between the experimental and control group. This means that in a repetition task, pause rate can be significantly increased through reinforcement.

Rate of Speech. There was a slight increase in the speech rate from baseline trials (1 & 2) to conditioning trials (6 & 7), from 140.4 words/min to 154.5 words/min in the case of E_R, and from 140.9 words/min to 141.1 words/min in the case of C_R. An ANOVA revealed that the groups effect ($MS = 2394.31$, $df = 1$, $F = .13$, $p > .05$), the trials effect ($MS = 10280.35$, $df = 1$, $F = 4.58$, $p > .05$), and the groups × trials interaction effect ($MS = 2911.15$, $df = 1$, $F = 1.30$, $p > .05$) were all nonsignificant.

Thus, despite the fact that there was a significant increase in the incidence of 600-msec UPs, there was no significant tendency for speech rate to decline; in fact, there was a slight tendency for it to increase. Again assuming a constancy of articulation rate, it can be concluded that the reinforcement contingency in the present study affected the overall distribution of pauses without significantly changing the absolute amount of time spent pausing.

Comparison of the Effects of Reinforcement of Pauses In Two Different Speech Tasks

Table 6.5 displays the change in the rate of pausing across baseline trials (1 & 2), initial conditioning trials (3 & 4), final conditioning trials (6 & 7), and extinction trials (8 & 9) for groups E_R (pauses reinforced in a task involving repetition) and E_I (pauses reinforced in a task involving composition).

An ANOVA revealed a significant trials effect (MS = 3548.05, df = 3, F = 19.3, $p < .001$), and a significant groups × trials interaction effect (MS = 558.02, df = 3, F = 3.04, $p < .05$). The groups effect, however, was nonsignificant (MS = 2714.12, df = 1, F = 1.68, $p > .05$). These results suggest that reinforcement of pauses had a significantly different effect when subjects were engaged in different speech tasks. A trend analysis (see Table 6.6) revealed that the linear, quadratic, and cubic components of the trials effect were all significant and that the linear and quadratic components of the groups × trials interaction effect were significant.

In the case of the trials effect, the quadratic component was dominant, accounting for 92.62% of the total variance, compared with 1.30% for the linear component and 6.07% for the cubic component. In the case of the groups × trials interaction effect, the quadratic component was again dominant, accounting for 88.96% of the total variance, compared with 8.77% for the linear component. These results suggest that reinforcement of pauses in a speech task involving repetition had a greater and more immediate effect than in a task involving composition. There was a 34.24% increase in 600-msec pause rate from baseline trials (1 & 2) to initial conditioning trials (3 & 4) in the repetition task, compared with an 8.29% increase in pause rate in the corresponding trials in the composition task. There was also a more precipitous drop in pause rate during extinction for the repetition group than for the composition group.

TABLE 6.5

Number of UPs for Groups E_R (Repetition Task) and E_1 (Composition Task).

Group	Ss	Baseline Trials (1 & 2)	Initial Conditioning Trials (3 & 4)	Final Conditioning Trials (6 & 7)	Extinction Trials (8 & 9)
	S_{21}	76	129	118	57
	S_{22}	111	125	111	90
	S_{23}	75	87	96	71
E_R	S_{24}	101	144	181	77
	S_{25}	104	124	150	82
	S_{26}	66	94	89	69
	S_{27}	66	117	107	71
	S_{28}	61	66	74	59
	Mean	82.5	110.8	115.8	72.0
	S_1	58	40	72	46
	S_2	99	116	118	88
E_1	S_3	64	65	83	68
	S_4	76	102	111	83
	S_5	77	82	85	75
	Mean	74.8	81.0	93.8	72.0

TABLE 6.6
Summary of Trend Analysis for Groups E_R (Repetition Task)
and E_1 (Composition Task).

Source	df	MS	F Ratio
Between Ss	12		
Groups	1	2714.12	1.68
Ss within groups	11	1620.12	
Within Ss	39		
Trials	3	3548.05	19.3**
Linear Trend	1	46.28	2.91*
Quadratic Trend	1	3286.26	28.00**
Cubic Trend	1	215.51	4.27*
Groups × Trials	3	558.02	3.04*
Linear Trend	1	48.96	3.08*
Quadratic Trend	1	496.41	4.23*
Cubic Trend	1	12.64	.25
Trials × Ss within Groups	33	183.79	
T × Subj. w Groups (Lin)	11	15.91	
T × Subj. w Groups (Quad)	11	117.38	
T × Subj. w Groups (Cub)	11	50.50	

*$p < .05$
**$p < .001$

Interviews with subjects after the final trial revealed that none had been aware of the experimental contingency, but as in Study 1, a number of subjects reported that the reinforcer appeared on occasions when they were not talking.

STUDY 3: VERBAL CONDITIONING IN AN INTERPERSONAL CONTEXT

Study 3 investigates the effects of reinforcement of pauses in a more natural situation—employing a human reinforcement agent (with the inherent problem of potential delay in reinforcement) and a partial rather than full reinforcement schedule (since it is unlikely that every pause is responded to in conversation). One reason for employing an interpersonal context is to introduce normal social constraints on continuous gaze into this experimental situation, to determine if conditioning still occurs. It was noted in Studies 1 and 2 that a number of subjects gazed continuously at the light signal. In natural conversations, interactants often avert gaze while speaking (Libby, 1970), particularly during hesitations in speech (Kendon, 1967). Recent analyses of the patterning of gaze accompanying speech in natural conversations have revealed, however, that a high proportion of hesitations are accomplished by direct gaze at the listener—52.95% in the case of hesitations at clausal junctures and 49.06% in the case of other hesitations (Beattie, in press). This suggests that even in natural interactions, speakers are potentially receptive to visual signals during hesitations, but obviously not to the extent that subjects who gazed continuously at the light signal were in Studies 1 and 2. By employing a human reinforcing agent in Study 3, it is hoped to "normalize" the overall amount of gaze and to determine if conditioning can still occur. This study also compares the relative efficacy of visual (head-nods) and auditory ("goods") cues in influencing pause behavior.

Method

Apparatus. In this experiment, the VOS triggered a delay timer that drove a relay connected to the tone generator. Pauses $\geq$ 550 msec triggered the relay, delivering a tone to E's earphone, which acted as a signal to deliver reinforcement. An Ediswan pen-oscillograph and pause detector counted the number of UPs $\geq$ 550 msec.

Subjects. Twenty-four undergraduates from the University of Cambridge acted as subjects. Seventeen were male, seven were female.

Procedure

The usual warm-up procedure preceded testing. All Ss were treated by the same E.[3] There were five Ss in each experimental group. The same task as in Study 1 was employed. There were 14 trials, each of 2 minutes duration.

The instructions given to experimental groups E₃ (auditory reinforcement) and E₄ (visual reinforcement) and to control groups C₃ and C₄ were identical to those described for E₁ and C₁ (Study 1), except that concerning feedback, they were told: "In the next phase which covers the next ten trials, your performance will be assessed, and I will give you feedback as to how well you are doing. I will do this by saying 'good' [in the case of E₃ and C₃, auditory reinforcement] or by nodding [in the case of E₄ and C₄, visual reinforcement]. The more often I say 'good,' or nod, the better is your telling of the story." For the experimental groups, reinforcement was contingent upon 550-msec UPs on a fixed ratio 3(FR₃) schedule (i.e., every third response was reinforced) in trials 3 to 12. In the case of the control groups, reinforcement was delivered on a VT schedule. No reinforcement was delivered in baseline trials (1 & 2) or in extinction trials (13 & 14).

After the final trial, Ss were interviewed to determine whether they had been aware of the experimental contingency. Their views about the experiment were also noted.

---

[3]Philip James, not the author.

TABLE 6.7

Number of UPs for Groups E₃ and C₃ (Reinforcement with Auditory Stimulus).

Group	Ss	Baseline				Trials Conditioning								Extinction	
		1	2	3	4	5	6	7	8	9	10	11	12	13	14
E₃	S₃₄	40	58	55	73	61	64	53	65	66	56	63	64	65	69
	S₃₅	61	60	72	53	59	51	59	56	50	43	36	35	54	47
	S₃₆	36	42	45	35	42	39	28	30	34	28	24	28	30	28
	S₃₇	55	64	57	63	52	60	60	51	61	61	65	61	66	65
	S₃₈	67	67	67	65	57	63	62	54	53	73	55	55	52	48
	S₃₉	52	52	57	50	57	49	53	51	55	54	52	54	50	57
	Mean	51.8	57.2	58.8	56.5	54.7	54.3	52.5	51.2	53.2	52.5	49.2	49.5	52.8	52.3
C₃	S₄₀	36	44	50	57	53	50	58	60	56	59	52	49	56	49
	S₄₁	57	56	56	59	64	64	58	65	61	47	50	63	58	50
	S₄₂	66	67	59	64	67	56	66	71	55	59	64	64	66	64
	S₄₃	58	51	51	42	37	38	30	40	38	35	27	39	28	37
	S₄₄	45	63	67	68	58	65	59	53	74	56	56	51	57	40
	S₄₅	64	59	59	63	67	61	65	63	59	66	67	57	62	61
	Mean	54.3	56.6	57.0	58.6	57.6	55.7	56.0	58.6	57.2	53.7	52.7	53.8	54.5	50.2

As in Study 1, judges rated the stories. However, there were a number of differences in this procedure. Two judges acting in collaboration were asked to rate stories on a scale from 0 to 21 and were provided with a series of guidelines; they were instructed to pay attention to the following aspects (in descending order of priority).

1. comprehensibility of speech
2. continuity
3. coherence
4. creativity   a. humor/interest
                         b. originality
                         c. complexity

Unlike Study 1, judges in this study actually listened to tapes of the stories, rather than reading transcripts.

Results

A. Reinforcement with Auditory Stimulus

Rate of Pausing. Table 6.7 shows the change in the rate of pausing across trials for groups E_3 and C_3. These changes are illustrated in Fig. 6.4, which shows the percentage change in pause rate across trials. An ANOVA was used to compare the rate of pausing in baseline trials (1 & 2), final conditioning trials (11 & 12), and extinction trials (13 & 14) for groups E_3 and C_3. The trials

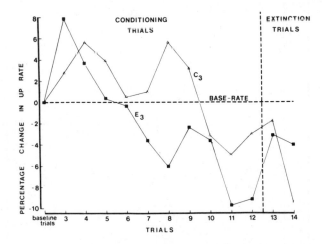

FIG. 6.4. Percentage change in unfilled-pause (UP) rate across trials for groups E_3 and C_3 (FR$_3$ schedule of auditory reinforcement, by E, of UPs in composition task).

TABLE 6.8
Number of UPs for Groups E₄ and C₄ (Reinforcement with Visual Stimulus).

Trials

Group	Ss	Baseline					Conditioning							Extinction	
		1	2	3	4	5	6	7	8	9	10	11	12	13	14
E₄	S₄₆	59	63	70	62	60	70	60	64	67	58	64	75	72	55
	S₄₇	43	44	45	46	49	46	52	48	55	51	50	52	51	53
	S₄₈	61	56	65	58	55	62	63	63	68	58	68	62	57	64
	S₄₉	52	60	66	60	57	57	51	61	58	57	54	63	59	64
	S₅₀	47	43	35	47	44	58	55	45	57	54	53	52	48	44
	S₅₁	48	50	61	53	72	62	65	64	54	67	70	59	51	54
	Mean	51.6	52.6	57.0	54.3	56.2	59.2	57.7	57.2	59.8	57.2	59.8	60.5	56.3	56.7
C₄	S₅₂	50	56	49	49	55	56	48	50	47	57	43	49	48	49
	S₅₃	52	53	55	55	55	58	59	47	53	51	61	52	50	47
	S₅₄	47	34	34	35	41	43	34	47	44	42	42	37	41	39
	S₅₅	64	53	63	62	64	63	67	66	43	60	63	66	68	62
	S₅₆	57	53	60	61	53	58	54	52	46	68	62	66	60	66
	S₅₇	43	36	33	33	46	34	32	36	40	45	36	38	50	44
	Mean	52.0	47.3	49.0	49.2	52.3	52.0	49.0	49.7	45.5	53.8	51.2	51.3	52.8	51.2

effect (MS = 166.194, df = 2, F = .291, ns), the groups effect (MS = 58.777, df = 1, F = .103, ns), and the groups × trials interaction effect (MS = 75.695, df = 2, F = .132, ns) were all nonsignificant ($F\ MAX$ = 2.911, df = 5).

Judges' Ratings of Stories.   The mean combined ratings for stories in baseline trials (1 & 2) and final conditioning trials (11 & 12) for E_3 were 17.50 and 21.25 respectively; and for C_3, 23.50 and 24.75 respectively. There was no significant difference in judges' ratings across trials for either group: E_3 (Sign Test, x = 1, n = 5, p > .05); C_3 (Wilcoxon Matched-Pairs Signed-Ranks Test, T = 8½, n = 6, p > .05).

B.   Reinforcement with Visual Stimulus

Rate of Pausing.   Table 6.8 shows the change in the rate of pausing across trials for groups E_4 and C_4. These changes are illustrated in Fig. 6.5, which shows the percentage change in pause rate across trials. An ANOVA was used to compare the rate of pausing in baseline trials (1 & 2), final conditioning trials (11 & 12), and extinction trials (13 & 14) for groups E_4 and C_4. The trials effect (MS = 272.694, df = 2, F = .885, ns), and the groups × trials interaction effect (MS = 140.584, df = 2, F = .456, ns) were both clearly nonsignificant; whereas the groups effect just failed to reach the 5% level of significance (MS = 930.249, df = 1, F = 3.020, .05 < p < .10), ($F\ MAX$ =3 .125, df = 5). However, a Wilcoxon Matched-Pairs Signed-Ranks Test

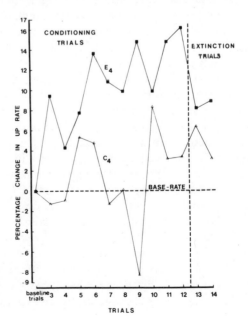

FIG. 6.5. Percentage change in unfilled-pause (UP) rate across trials for groups E_4 and C_4 (FR$_3$ schedule of visual reinforcement, by E, of UPs in composition task).

revealed that the rate of pausing significantly increased from baseline trials (1 & 2) to final conditioning trials (11 & 12) for E_4 ($T = 0$, $n = 6$, $p < .025$, one-tail), but not for C_4 ($T = 8$, $n = 6$, $p > .05$, one-tail). A Wilcoxon Matched-Pairs Signed-Ranks Test also revealed that rate of pausing was significantly higher in the extinction trials than in the baseline trials for group E_4 ($T = 0$, $n = 6$, $p < .05$, two-tail), which suggests that extinction is not as rapid as in Studies 1 and 2.

Judges' Ratings of Stories.   The mean combined ratings for stories in baseline trials (1 & 2) and final conditioning trials (11 & 12) for E_4 were 18.58 and 24.25 respectively, and for C_4, 23.25 and 26.33 respectively. There was no significant difference in judges' ratings across trials for either group: E_4 (Wilcoxon Matched-Pairs Signed-Ranks Test, $T = 1$, $n = 6$, $p > .05$, two-tail); C_4 (Wilcoxon Matched-Pairs Signed-Ranks Test, $T = 5$, $n = 6$, $p > .05$, two-tail). Although there was no significant difference in judges' ratings across trials, it is evident that all four groups tended to produce stories in the final conditioning trials that were rated higher by judges than those produced in baseline trials. These combined results were tested but were found to be nonsignificant ($\chi^2 = 10.595$, $df = 8$, $p > .05$; Jones & Fiske, 1953).

Discussion

This study demonstrated that reinforcement of UPs on an FR_3 schedule, in an interpersonal situation, resulted in a significant increase in pause rate with visual, but not with auditory, reinforcement. This seemed to occur without significant change in the judged content of utterances and without the conscious awareness of subjects. However, perhaps the most striking feature of this study is the large intertrial variability in pause rate displayed by C_4 (see Fig. 6.5). This variability may be attributed to the difficulty E found in generating purely random reinforcement in this condition; various patterns and contingencies may have developed (and changed) during the course of the experiment. One feature of the study was that a number of subjects in E_4, characterized by an almost total lack of direct gaze at the experimenter, nevertheless displayed significant changes in pause behavior as a result of reinforcement. One potentially important factor was that the signficance of E's head-nods was explicitly mentioned in the instructions to subjects to counteract the ambiguity of such cues observed by Mandler and Kaplan (1956). Apart from nodding occasionally, E remained as stationary as possible. Thus subjects simply had to detect movement in order to receive reinforcement. Human peripheral vision is of course designed to detect such movement, and thus direct gaze may not have been necessary. Studies of natural interaction, on the other hand, have revealed that movements of the same basic forms (e.g., head-nods), when executed differently, have different "meanings" and produce different effects on the speaker (Birdwhistell, 1970). Thus in natural interaction, not only has movement to be detected, but fine pattern discriminations have to be made and their specific meaning decoded. Such decoding presumably requires central vision. Thus in verbal conditioning studies in which movements are not explicitly defined, or in natural interactions, such influence in the abscence of direct gaze is considerably less likely.

GENERAL DISCUSSION AND CONCLUSIONS

This series of studies demonstrated that the temporal structure of spontaneous speech can be significantly modified through reinforcement and punishment of UPs of a preselected duration, with visual stimuli defined in particular ways. These changes apparently occurred in the absence of subjects' awareness of the experimental contingencies. There has been considerable debate over the possibility of effective conditioning without subjects' awareness (see Williams, 1977). Evidence currently suggests that with a sufficiently difficult task (like the free operant ones used in this series of studies) (Oakes, 1967), or with a sufficiently complex reinforcement schedule (Williams, 1977), conditioning without awareness can take place, since subjects have too little time or are simply unable to work out the contingencies.

Reinforcement and punishment of UPs in speech did not seem to significantly affect the absolute amount of pausing in speech, since speech rate was not significantly affected by the experimental contingency in any of the case studies. In Study 1, punishment of UPs did, however, result in substantial increase in speech rate (22.2% from baseline trials [1 & 2] to punishment trials [6 & 7]), but a significant increase in the amount of filled hesitation, particularly in speech repetition, was observed. These results do not therefore support the hypothesis that there is a class of noncognitive pauses in spontaneous monologue. They do, however, suggest that a speaker might be able to adapt to different conversational contexts by changing the overall temporal organization of speech and even the type of hesitation used for cognitive planning; and they highlight the necessity of considering different forms of hesitation, particularly repetition, in any studies of cognitive planning in speech. The results of the present studies suggest that the differences reported by Ramsay (1966, 1968) in pause behavior between introverts and exraverts may not have been reflected differences in "thoughtfulness" between these groups but rather "preferences" for different categories of hesitation. The low unfilled-pause rate in extraverts may have been compensated for by higher filled hesitation rates. This hypothesis is consonant with the observations that extraverts attempt to talk for longer periods of time in conversation than do introverts (Carment, Miles, & Cervin, 1965) and that speakers, when attempting to hold the floor in conversation, do use certain types of filled hesitation to prevent interruption (Beattie, 1977a). Thus, over time, extraverts may adopt characteristically higher levels of filled hesitations than introverts as a general conversational strategy. This hypothesis can easily be tested.

Unfilled Pauses and Filled Hesitations

It was discovered in Study 1 that when UP rate declined as a result of punishment, there was a significant increase in the amount of filled hesitation in speech, largely accounted for by a 104% increase in amount of repetition from baseline trials (1 & 2) to punishment trials (6 & 7). There was no tendency for filled pauses (FPs) or parenthetic remarks to increase in usage, however. The correlation between the percentage decrease in UP rate and the increase in amount of repetition failed to reach significance ($r_s = .700$, $p > .05$), suggesting that other filled hesitations, like false starts, are important in the case of some subjects.

These results are rather surprising. There is evidence of a similarity in function between UPs and FPs; they tend to occur in the same speech locations (Boomer, 1965; Cook, 1969; Tannenbaum, Williams, & Hillier, 1965), and a positive correlation has been reported between FPs (or vocal segregates) and short UPs (or zero segregates, UPs ≤ 1 sec), at least in one speech context (Levin & Silverman, 1965). There is considerably less evidence for a similarity in function between UPs and repetition, although it must be added that repetitions have not been investigated as much as either of the other two phenomena. Maclay and Osgood (1959) observed that UPs and repetitions were distributed similarly with respect to content and function words; there was a significant tendency for both to precede the relatively more unpredictable content words. Tannenbaum et al. (1965), however, using a measure of transitional probability, obtained different results. Repetitions were thought to follow rather than precede the most unpredictable words, and Tannenbaum et al. concluded that repetitions and pauses reflected different types of psychological process. However, if one considers the exact replacement measure of transitional probability (which is the most commonly used index in the literature), then the word subsequent to a repetition is found to be more unpredictable than a word occurring in a fluent context. This is exactly the observation that has been made with UPs (Goldman-Eisler, 1958a, 1958b). Moreover, Lay and Paivio (1969) demonstrated that repetition rate (number of repetitions/number of words) increased with task difficulty as did the total duration of unfilled pauses (and FP and false start rate).

Correlational studies have failed to find any significant relationship between UPs and repetition (Levin & Silverman, 1965; Maclay & Osgood,

1959). Thus it appears that in any given situation, these categories of hesitation are independent; only when the social context and contingencies are systematically changed do we detect possible functional dependencies between these variables. This result highlights the necessity of considering different categories of hesitation, particularly UPs and repetitions, in studies of the planning of speech.

The conclusions about the possible functional similarity of UPs and repetitions rest on the demonstration that judged content did not significantly change when the punishment manipulation effected a change in the predominant category of hesitation. The rating method employed is necessarily subjective, but no suitable objective procedure is currently available. A measure of the syntactic complexity of speech as an index of cognitive planning cannot be used, since evidence suggests that syntactic operations are noncognitive skills (Goldman-Eisler, 1968, p. 79). A measure of lexical unpredictability such as the Cloze procedure has been shown not to differentiate fluent and disrupted speech (as characterized by a high proportion of Mahl's [1956] "non-ah" speech disturbances; Feldstein, Rogalski, & Jaffe, 1966). Furthermore, since it appears that a larger proportion of pause time in speech is devoted to ideational planning than to lexical search (Butterworth, 1975, 1976), it follows that measures of semantic content should be more sensitive to deviations in planning time underlying speech than should measures of lexical unpredictability. Some recent research (Beattie, 1977b) has explored the relationship between aspects of temporal structure and objective measures of suprasentential organization such as degree of textual cohesion. Until such objective indices of speech planning and organization have been perfected, ratings of semantic content—although fundamentally subjective—are likely to prove the most sensitive indices of planning and speech.

The analysis of pause location in Study 1 failed to uncover any systematic trend in the effects of the punishment manipulation on the proportion of pauses at grammatical junctures, which suggests either that in monologue, a speaker is aware of all time available for planning (including the time invested at grammatical junctures) and actually uses it for planning, contrary to Barik's (1968) hypothesis; or alternatively, that grammatical junctures are not used for cognitive planning, but that substitution of filled hesitation provides an easier adaptive strategy.

Task Differences

Study 2 demonstrated that reinforcement of pauses in two types of speech (spontaneous composition and story repetition) produces disparate effects. In the repetition task, reinforcement of pauses led to an immediate increase in their emission rate (31.79% in the first conditioning trial), whereas in the case of the composition task, rate of change of pause rate was much slower (6.42%

in the first conditioning trial). Furthermore, reinforcement of pauses in the repetition task produced a greater effect overall (pause rate increased by a maximum of 42.66% in the repetition task, compared with 26.20% in the composition task). Extinction for both groups was rapid. However, since reinforcement produced greater effects in the repetition task, extinction was much more precipitous in this case.

Thus, the temporal organization of speech involving repetition appears to be more susceptible to change than that involving spontaneous composition, although it is interesting to note that there was no difference in baseline pause rate in these two speech tasks (mean 600-msec UP rate: 85.9 in repetition task, 84.0 in composition task, Mann–Whitney U test, $U = 63$, $p > .05$). Future research needs to test the generality of this effect; for example, it would be interesting to determine if adults' speech to children displayed different forms of temporal organization depending upon the specific cognitive operations underlying the speech. When adults spontaneously compose stories for children, they may be less sensitive to any social contingencies than when they repeat familiar stories, and consequently they may not structure the speech in the manner most appropriate for the given context (one may speculate that the tendency of adults to choose familiar stories for telling to children may be related to the greater susceptibility to change of the temporal structure of speech that involves story repetition). Task differences may be partly responsible for the variation in the modifiability of temporal structure of speech observed in natural interactions. For example, the comparative rigidity of the temporal structure of the psychiatrists' speech with respect to that of the patients in the Goldman-Eisler (1952) study may have been due to the nature of the psychiatric interview, which required the generation of new ideas by the psychiatrists in an attempt to arrive at a diagnosis, but which required the discussion of familiar problems by the patients. If the psychiatrists were involved in spontaneous planning, we may expect any feedback to be a less crucial influence on their speech than on that of the patients. Future research must pay more attention to the cognitive demands of speech in the investigation of the modifiability of its temporal structure.

Some Processes Considered

These studies demonstrated that immediate reinforcement of UPs on a full schedule produced rapid changes in pause rate, in both a composition and repetition task. In a composition task, visual reinforcement delivered on a partial schedule by E produced a significant, but much slower, effect. In an identical situation, auditory reinforcement produced no discernible effect. How then are we to interpret these results? The rapidity of behavior change in Studies 1 and 2 seems to be indicative of a "prepared" association between pausing and visual contingencies (cf. Seligman, 1970) and, therefore, one that is likely to operate in natural conversation. The fact that behavior change was much slower in the more "natural" interpersonal paradigm employed in Study 3 need not necessarily weaken such an interpretation; conversation is a process characterized by precision timing, and the paradigm used in Study 3 might not have captured this element. The preciseness of conversational timing has been demonstrated in a number of studies. Beattie (1978a) found that 31.1% of all speaker switches in natural conversation were immediate, i.e., with a latency ≤200 msec; 50.3% of all switches had a latency ≤500 msec. Morris (1969, cited by Meltzer, Morris, & Hayes, 1971) observed that auditory signals of attention, inserted by the listener during speaker pauses, rarely overlapped with actual phonation. The precision timing of natural conversation presumably depends on the ability of the participants to predict suitable response locations on the basis of a combination of semantic, syntactic, and prosodic cues (cf. Sacks, Schegloff, & Jefferson, 1974). In Study 3, as E did not attend to the content of the speech but rather to the (random) tones generated on his headphones, such predictive cues would not have been operative, and therefore E's reaction times to the tones must be considered as disruptive of the (precisely timed) conversational processes that this study attempted to reflect. Loeb and Schmidt (1963) found that RTs to random tones in the same decibel range as those used in Study 3 tend to be between 400 and 470 msec. Analyses of pause duration in Study 3 revealed that the mean duration over the criterion value (550 msec) varied across trials, between 627 msec (trial 13, Group E_3) and 1093 msec (Trial 2, Group E_4). In the case of some subjects, the mean duration over the criterion level was as low as 231 msec (S_2, Trial 12, E_3). Therefore, on a number of occasions in Study 3, reinforcement must have been delivered during actual phonation, since E's RT must often have exceeded pause duration over the criterion before phonation was resumed. This factor may thus be responsible for the tardiness of behavior change in Study 3.

Even given the relative ineffectiveness of the procedure used in Study 3, differences in the efficacy of the two types of reinforcement were observed. Visual reinforcement had a significant effect on pause rate, whereas auditory reinforcement had no discernible effect. This was probably not an artifact of differences in E's RTs in the two conditions, since there is greater S–R compatibility between a tone and an auditory response than between a tone and a head movement; and it has been demonstrated that the greater the compatibility, the shorter the RT (Fitts & Seeger, 1953). Similarly, it is probably not the case that this discrepancy is due to any natural tendency of one stimulus, but not the other, to occur during pauses in conversation. Recent evidence has suggested that in conversation, both auditory (mm-hmm) and visual (head-nod) cues tend to occur most frequently in exactly the same locations—during pauses (see Tables 11.6A and 11.6B, Duncan & Fiske, 1977). A more plausible explanation can be found in the actual cognitive processes of the speaker. Subjects in these studies had to plan, produce, and monitor their speech (to appreciate the importance of such monitoring, consider the effects of delayed auditory feedback on speech performances; see Smith, 1962) and, in addition, attend to either auditory or visual feedback stimuli. Shadowing experiments, in which subjects listen to and repeat a message while simultaneously performing a second task, have revealed that if the subsidiary task is also auditory, performance is very poor (Moray [1959] demonstrated that subjects often failed to recognize any elements of a short list of simple words repeated many times when it was presented simultaneously with the main shadowing taks.) However, Allport, Antonis, and Reynolds (1972) have shown that if the subsidiary task involves attention to visual rather than auditory stimuli, performance is much better. In one experiment, they demonstrated that auditory speech shadowing and playing the piano from a score could be performed simultaneously with little or no loss of efficiency in either task. In Study 3, therefore, subjects engaged in speaking (which is primarily auditory) may have found it easier to divide attention between this task and the simultaneous recognition and decoding of visual rather than auditory stimuli and consequently, may have been more influenced by the visual stimuli.

Directions for Future Research

The present series of studies have left a number of questions unanswered. For example, the effects of automatic reinforcement of pauses on a partial schedule were not investigated. Similarly, the efficacy of different types of stimuli as punishers of pauses was not considered. Visual stimuli might again prove more effective here, since there is evidence that a series of listener movements (again visually perceived cues) precede listener attempts to take the floor in conversation (Kendon, 1972)—the most likely punisher of pauses in natural conversation. The present series of studies also gives rise to a number of testable predictions concerning conversational interaction. For example, they suggest that in telephone conversation, where visual signals are necessarily excluded, the susceptibility to change of the temporal structure of speech should be reduced. It would also be interesting to determine if adults' speech to children over the telephone would be more "adultlike" in terms of its temporal structure. As already discussed, Study 2 predicts that speech on familiar topics should be more sensitive to change than spontaneous compositional speech.

The most striking implication of these studies is that in conversation, when listeners attend to what is said and signal their continued attention and interest therein, they may, unwittingly, and unbeknown to the speaker, be partially determining the temporal organization of the spoken message.

ACKNOWLEDGMENTS

I wish to thank Carol A. Beattie for invaluable criticism of earlier drafts of this paper and Dr. R. J. Bradbury for guidance during the execution of the earlier studies and for subsequent useful discussion. I also wish to extend thanks to Philip James for running Experiment 3, and Dr. B. Butterworth for his help. Part of this research, carried out at the University of Cambridge, was financed by a Northern Ireland Research Studentship (1974–1977), for which I am most grateful. I also wish to thank the Journal of Psycholinguistic Research for their permission to reproduce part of an article currently in press with them, and specifically Tables 6.1, 6.2, and 6.3 and Figs. 6.1 and 6.2.

REFERENCES

Allport, D. A., Antonis, B., & Reynolds, P. On the division of attention: A disproof of the single channel hypothesis. *Quarterly Journal of Experimental Psychology*, 1972, *24*, 225–235.

Argyle, M. *Social interaction*. London: Methuen, 1969.

Argyle, M., & Kendon, A. The experimental analysis of social performance. In L. Berkowitz (Ed.), *Advances in experimental social psychology* (Vol. 3). New York: Academic Press, 1967.

Barik, H. C. On defining juncture pauses: A note on Boomer's "Hesitation and grammatical encoding." *Language and Speech*, 1968, *11*, 156–159.

Beattie, G. W. The dynamics of interruption and the filled pause. *British Journal of Social and Clinical Psychology*, 1977, *16*, 283–284. (a)

Beattie, G. W. *The textual cohesion of spoken dialogue*. Unpublished paper, University of Cambridge, 1977. (b)

Beattie, G. W. Floor apportionment and gaze in conversational dyads. *British Journal of Social and Clinical Psychology*, 1978, *17*, 7–15. (a)

Beattie, G. W. Sequential temporal patterns of speech and gaze in dialogue. *Semiotica*, 1978, *23*, 29–52. (b)

Beattie, G. W. The role of language production processes in the organization of behavior in face-to-face interaction. In B. Butterworth (Ed.), *Language production*. London: Academic Press, in press.

Beattie, G. W., & Bradbury, R. J. An experimental investigation of the modifiability of the temporal structure of spontaneous speech. *Journal of Psycholinguistic Research*, in press.

Birdwhistell, R. L. *Kinesics and context: Essays on body-motion communication*. Harmondsworth: Penguin, 1970.

Boomer, D. S. Hesitation and grammatical encoding. *Language and Speech*, 1965 *8*, 148–158.

Butterworth, B. L. *Semantic analysis of the phasing of fluency in spontaneous speech*. Unpublished Ph.D. dissertation, University College, London, 1972.

Butterworth, B. Hesitation and semantic planning in speech. *Journal of Psycholinguistic Research*, 1975, *1*, 75–78.

Butterworth, B. *Semantic planning, lexical choice and syntactic organization in spontaneous speech*. Unpublished paper, University of Cambridge, 1976.

Butterworth, B., & Beattie, G. W. Gesture and silence as indicators of planning in speech. In R. N. Campbell & P. T. Smith (Eds.), *Recent advances in the psychology of language: Formal and experimental approaches*. New York: Plenum, 1978.

Carment, D. W., Miles, C. S., & Cervin, V. B. Persuasiveness and persuasibility as related to intelligence and extraversion. *British Journal of Social and Clinical Psychology*, 1965, *4*, 1–7.

Colton, C. C. *Lacon*. London: Longman, Rees, Orme, Brown, and Green, 1826.

Cook, M. Transition probabilities and the incidence of filled pauses. *Psychonomic Science*, 1969, *16*, 191.

Dale, P. S. Hesitations in maternal speech. *Language and Speech*, 1974, *17*, 174–181.

Dittmann, A. T., & Llewellyn, L. G. The phonemic clause as a unit of speech decoding. *Journal of Personality and Social Psychology*, 1967, *6*, 341–349.

Dittmann, A. T., & Llewellyn, L. G. Relationship between vocalization and head nods as listener responses. *Journal of Personality and Social Psychology*, 1968, *11*, 98–106.

Duncan, S., Jr. On the structure of speaker–auditor interaction during speaking turns. *Language in Society*, 1974, *2*, 161–180.

Duncan, S., Jr., & Fiske, D. W. *Face-to-face interaction: Research, methods and theory*. Hillsdale, N.J.: Lawrence Erlbaum Associates, 1977.

Eysenck, H. J. A dynamic theory of anxiety and hysteria. *Journal of Mental Science*, 1955, *101*, 28–51.

Eysenck, H. J. *An experimental application of modern learning theory to psychiatry*. London: Routledge & Kegan Paul, 1957.

Feldstein, S., Rogalski, G., & Jaffe, J. Predictability and disruption of spontaneous speech. *Language and Speech*, 1966, *9*, 137–152.

Fielding, G. *Participation in conversation: The phenomenon of response matching*. Paper presented at the annual meeting of the Social Psychology Section of the British Psychological Society, Brighton, 1972.

Fitts, P. M., & Seeger, C. M. S–R compatibility: Spatial characteristics of stimulus and response codes. *Journal of Experimental Psychology*, 1953, *46*, 199–210.

Garnica, O. K. Some prosodic and paralinguistic features of speech to young children. In C. E. Snow & C. A. Ferguson (Eds.), *Talking to children: Language input and acquisition*. Cambridge: Cambridge University Press, 1977.

Gleason, J. B. Talking to children: Some notes on feedback. In C. E. Snow & C. A. Ferguson (Eds.), *Talking to children: Language input and acquisition*. Cambridge: Cambridge University Press, 1977.

Goldman-Eisler, F. Individual differences between interviewers and their effects on interviewee's conversational behavior. *Journal of Mental Science*, 1952, *98*, 660–671.

Goldman-Eisler, F. The determinants of the rate of speech output and their mutual relations. *Journal of Psychosomatic Research*, 1956, *1*, 137–143.

Goldman-Eisler, F. Speech production and the predictability of words in context. *Quarterly Journal of Experimental Psychology*, 1958, *10*, 96–106. (a)

Goldman-Eisler, F. The predictability of words in context and the length of pauses in speech. *Language and Speech*, 1958, *1*, 226–231. (b)

Goldman-Eisler, F. The distribution of pause durations in speech. *Language and Speech*, 1961, *4*, 232–237. (a)

Goldman-Eisler, F. The significance of changes in the rate of articulation. *Language and Speech*, 1961, *4*, 171–174. (b)

Goldman-Eisler, F. Sequential temporal patterns and cognitive processes in speech. *Language and Speech*, 1967, *10*, 122–132.

Goldman-Eisler, F. *Psycholinguistics: Experiments in spontaneous speech*. London: Academic Press, 1968.

Goldman-Eisler, F. Pauses, clauses, sentences. *Language and Speech*, 1972, *15*, 103–113.

Henderson, A., Goldman-Eisler, F., & Skarbek, A. Sequential temporal patterns in spontaneous speech. *Language and Speech*, 1966, *9*, 207–216.

Jaffe, J. & Feldstein, S. *Rhythms of dialogue*. New York: Academic Press, 1970.

Jawanda, J. S. Personality and verbal conditioning. *Indian Journal of Experimental Psychology*, 1970, *4*, 22–24.

Jones, L. V., & Fiske, D. W. Models for testing the significance of combined results. *Psychological Bulletin*, 1953, *50*, 375–382.

Kendon, A. Some functions of gaze direction in social interaction. *Acta Psychologica*, 1967, *26*, 1–47.

Kendon, A. Some relationships between body motion and speech. An analysis of an example. In A. W. Siegman & B. Pope (Eds.), *Studies in dyadic communication*. New York: Pergamon, 1972.

Lay, C. H., & Paivio, A. The effects of task difficulty and anxiety on hesitations in speech. *Canadian Journal of Behavioral Science*, 1969, *1*, 25–37.

Lennard, H. L., & Bernstein, A. Interdependence of therapist and patient verbal behaviour. In J. A. Fishman (Ed.), *Readings in the sociology of language*. The Hague: Mouton, 1960.

Levin, H., & Silverman, I. Hesitation phenomena in children's speech. *Language and Speech*, 1965, *8*, 67–85.

Levin, H., Silverman, I., & Ford, B. L. Hesitations in children's speech during explanation and description. *Journal of Verbal Learning and Verbal Behavior*, 1967, *6*, 560–564.

Libby, W. L. Eye contact and direction of looking as stable individual differences. *Journal of Experimental Research in Personality*, 1970, *4*, 303–312.

Loeb, M., & Schmidt, E. A. A comparison of the effects of different kinds of information in maintaining efficiency on an auditory vigilance task. *Ergonomics*, 1963, *6*, 75–81.

Lounsbury, F. G. Transitional probability, linguistic structure and systems of habit-family hierarchies. In C. E. Osgood & T. A. Sebeok (Eds.), *Psycholinguistics: A survey of theory and research problems*. Baltimore, Indiana: Indiana University Press, 1954.

Maclay, H., & Osgood, C. E. Hesitation phenomena in English speech. *Word*, 1959, *15*, 19–44.

Mahl, G. F. Disturbances and silences in the patient's speech in psychotherapy. *Journal of Abnormal Social Psychology*, 1956, *53*, 1–15.

Mandler, G., & Kaplan, W. K. Subjective evaluation and reinforcing effect of a verbal stimulus. *Science*, 1956, *124*, 582–583.

Matarazzo, J. D. Psychotherapeutic processes. *Annual Review of Psychology*, 1965, *16*, 181–224.

McNair, D. M. Reinforcement of verbal behavior. *Journal of Experimental Psychology*, 1957, *53*, 40–46

Meltzer, L., Morris, W. N., & Hayes, D. P. Interruption outcomes and vocal amplitude: Explorations in social psychophysics. *Journal of Personality and Social Psychology*, 1971, *18*, 392–402.

Moray, N. Attention in dichotic listening: Affective cues and the influence of instructions. *Quarterly Journal of Experimental Psychology*, 1959, *11*, 56–60.

Morris, W. N. *The insertion of supportive bursts during dyadic communication*. Unpublished pilot study, 1969.

Oakes, W. F. Verbal operant conditioning, intertrial activity, awareness, and the extended interview. *Journal of Personality and Social Psychology*, 1967, *6*, 198–202.

Oakes, W. F., Droge, A. E., & August, B. Reinforcement effects on participation in group discussion. *Psychological Reports*, 1960, *7*, 503–514.

Pope, B., & Siegman, A. W. Relationship and verbal behavior in the initial interview. In A. W. Siegman & B. Pope (Eds.), *Studies in dyadic communication*. New York: Pergamon, 1972.

Ramsay, R. W. Personality and speech. *Journal of Personality and Social Psychology*, 1966, *4*, 116–118.

Ramsay, R. W. Speech patterns and personality. *Language and Speech*, 1968, *11*, 52–63.

Reynolds, A., & Paivio, A. Cognitive and emotional determinants of speech. *Canadian Journal of Psychology*, 1968, *22*, 164–175.

Rochester, S. R. The significance of pauses in spontaneous speech. *Journal of Psycholinguistic Research*, 1973, *2*, 51–81.

Sachs, J., Brown, R., & Salerno, R. Adult speech to children. In W. Von Raffler-Engel & Y. Lebrun (Eds.), *Baby talk and infant speech*. Amsterdam: Swets & Zeitlinger B. V., 1976.

Sacks, H., Schegloff, E. A., & Jefferson, G. A. A simplest systematics for the organization of turn-taking for conversation. *Language*, 1974, *50*, 697–735.

Scheflen, A. E. *Stream and structure of communicational behavior*. Philadelphia: Commonwealth Mental Health Research Foundation, 1965.

Seligman, M. E. P. On the generality of the laws of learning. *Psychological Review*, 1970, *77*, 406–418.

Simkins, L. Modification of pausing behavior. *Journal of Verbal Learning and Verbal Behavior*, 1963, *2*, 462–469.

Smith, K. U. *Delayed sensory feedback and behavior*. Philadelphia: Holt-Saunders, 1962.

Stern, H., & Grosz, H. J. Personality correlates of high and low interactors in group psychotherapy. *Psychological Reports*, 1966, *18*, 411–414. (a)

Stern, H., & Grosz, H. J. Visual interactions in group psychotherapy between patients with similar and with dissimilar personalities. *Psychological Reports*, 1966, *19*, 1111–1114. (b)

Taffel, C. Anxiety and the conditioning of verbal behavior. *Journal of Abnormal and Social Psychology*, 1955, *51*, 496–501.

Tannenbaum, P. H., Williams, F., & Hillier, C. S. Word predictability in the environments of hesitations. *Journal of Verbal Learning and Verbal Behavior*, 1965, *4*, 134–140.

Taylor, I. Content and structure in sentence production. *Journal of Verbal Learning and Verbal Behavior*, 1969, *8*, 170–175.

Webb, J. T. Interview synchrony: An investigation of two speech rate measures. In A. W. Siegman & B. Pope (Eds.), *Studies in dyadic communication*. New York: Pergamon, 1972.

Welkowitz, J., & Feldstein, S. Dyadic interaction and induced differences in perceived similarity. *Proceedings of the 77th Annual Convention of the American Psychological Association,* 1969.

Williams, B. W. Verbal operant conditioning without subjects' awareness of reinforcement contingencies. *Canadian Journal of Psychology*, 1977, *31*, 90–101.

III HESITATION, COGNITION, AND SPEECH PRODUCTION

7

Cognition and Hesitation in Speech

Aron Wolfe Siegman
University of Maryland Baltimore County

> ... *God spoke these words*
> *to your assemblage on the mountain*
> *amidst the fire, the cloud, and the darkness,*
> *with a strong voice without resumptions.*
> —Deuteronomy (5:19)

Rashi (1040-1105), a leading medieval commentator on the Bible, notes: "Onkelos translates *lo yosef* without resumptions. It is the nature of man that he cannot speak many words in a single breath. Not so the Almighty. He does not need to pause, and since He does not pause, His speech is without resumptions."

Human speech, unlike divine pronouncements, is far from the smooth, uninterrupted flow of words that it often appears to be to the naive listener. Instead, spontaneous speech is typically fragmented by silent pauses of varying durations. Some of these pauses, particularly the very brief ones, are undoubtedly necessary for the physical articulation of words. However, a simple comparison of silent pausing in reading and speaking will demonstrate that this explanation leaves unaccounted for a good deal of the variance of pauses in everyday speech. The function and meaning of these "surplus" pauses have become the subject of theoretical speculation as well as empirical research. Some authors have conceptualized these pauses in affective-motivational terms. For example, in one of the first empirical studies of silent pauses in interviewees' speech, Mahl (1956) attributes such pauses to the disruptive effect of anxiety arousal. Siegman and his associates, on the other hand, present evidence that suggests that anxiety arousal per se has an activating effect on speech that tends to reduce the frequency and duration of silent pauses, unless the anxiety gives rise to resistance and other defensive operations (Pope, Blass, Siegman, & Raher, 1970; Siegman, 1978a; Siegman, 1978b; Siegman & Pope, 1965, 1972). Other investigators, however, have conceptualized the meaning of silent pauses in speech in cognitive terms— specifically, as evidence of information processing that is taking place at the time of the pausing. This approach is reflected in Maclay and Osgood's (1959) work on the relationship between different classes of words and hesitation pauses. A strong cognitive interpretation of silent pauses would lead to the claim that all such pauses reflect cognitive decision making. In line with this position, a recent paper by the author of this chapter (Siegman, 1978a; Chapter 5, this volume) attempts to reinterpret the findings on the relationship between anxiety arousal and resistance on one hand and silent pauses on the other hand, within an information-processing framework.

A good deal of credit for the shift in emphasis from affective to cognitive factors, as far as silent pausing is concerned, must go to the work of Goldman-Eisler (1968). In a study frequently cited in support of the information-processing interpretation of silent pausing, she used a guessing technique in order to determine the predictability of words following hesitation pauses in a speaker's communication (Goldman-Eisler, 1958a, 1958b). She found that "... where guessers found themselves at a loss for predicting the next word as spoken originally... the original speaker also seemed to have been at a loss for the next word, for it was at these points that he tended to hesitate" (Goldman-Eisler, 1968, p. 42). On the basis of these findings, Goldman-Eisler concluded that hesitation pauses in speech reflect the speaker's lexical decision-making process, that is, his or her word choices. This experiment has been carefully scrutinized in a review article by Boomer (1970), in which he raises a number of methodological caveats. However, Goldman-Eisler's general position that silent pausing in speech reflects cognitive processes that are taking place at the time of the pausing is not based on the results of this study alone.

In another frequently cited experiment, Goldman-Eisler (1961a, 1961b) compared the ratios of silent pauses in speech associated with tasks of varying levels of difficulty, specifically, in the mere description of a series of cartoons versus their interpretation. She found that the cartoon interpretations were associated with longer silent pauses than the descriptions, a finding that she attributed to the more complex level of information processing that is required from the subject in the interpretation task than in the description task. Since the first study to be reported in this chapter is essentially a replication and extension of Goldman-Eisler's second experiment, its procedure and findings are presented in some detail.

Each subject who participated in that experiment was given the following instructions (Goldman-Eisler, 1968):

You will be shown a series of cartoon stories with no verbal captions. You are asked to have a good look at them. As soon as you have got the point, say "got it" and proceed to describe the content of the story as depicted in the pictures before you; conclude by formulating the general point, meaning, or moral of the story in as concise a form as you can...[pp. 51–52].

A comparison of the descriptions and the interpretations showed that the latter were associated with a significantly higher silent-pause ratio, but not filled-pause ratio,[1] than the former. This was true not only for the group as a whole but for every subject as well. Although the initial delays (i.e., latencies or reaction times) for the descriptions (the period from when the subject said "got it" to the first word of the description) were roughly the same as the initial delays for the interpretations, Goldman-Eisler argues that it took subjects proportionally more time to plan and to organize the interpretations than the descriptions, since the former contained fewer words than the latter (fewer than a third). This argument is based on the assumption that everything else being equal, there should be a positive correlation between RT and subsequent productivity. Goldman-Eisler views these findings as confirming the assumption that "hesitation pauses in speech are the delays due to processes taking place in the brain whenever speech ceases to be the automatic vocalization of learned sequences, whether occasioned by choice of an individual word, by construction of syntax, or by conception of content..." (Goldman-Eisler, 1968, p. 58). It should be noted that in addition to the higher silent-pause ratios associated with the interpretation task than with the description task, Goldman-Eisler (1968) found that (a) the words in the sentences used to interpret the cartoons were less predictable than the words in the sentences used to describe the cartoons, and that (b) the interpretations were syntactically more complex than the descriptions.

There have been several studies, the results of which could be considered conceptual replications of Goldman-Eisler's original findings. Reynolds and Paivio (1968) asked subjects to define a series of abstract and concrete words. On the assumption that the definition of abstract words is a more complex task and involves more encoding transformations than the definition of concrete words, they expected and found that the former task was associated with more frequent silent pauses (number of unfilled pauses exceeding 1.5 sec, divided by total word output) than the latter task. The definitions of the abstract words were also associated with significantly more filled pauses ("ah's" and similar expressions) than the definitions of concrete words. Levin, Silverman, and Ford (1967) asked a group of children ranging in age from 5 to

---

[1]The filled-pause ratio consists of the total number of "ah's" and similar expressions in a response, adjusted for productivity.

12 to describe and then to explain a series of demonstrations that were shown to each child on an individual basis. In one such demonstration, two colorless liquids were presented in separate beakers. They were then mixed together, and the result was a magenta-colored liquid. The children were asked to describe what they witnessed and then to explain the results. The children's explanations were associated with more frequent silent pauses (adjusted for productivity) and with longer pauses than their descriptions. Levin and his associates also looked at their subjects' filled pauses, although these were not looked at separately but were part of a broader category of speech disruptions. This ratio too was significantly higher in the children's explanations than in their descriptions. Finally, there is a study by Lay and Paivio (1969) on the effects of task difficulty on hesitation in speech. Male college students were asked: (a) to respond to questions of the kind usually found on application forms (e.g., name, address, and date of birth); (b) to describe a series of cartoons; and (c) to interpret and evaluate a series of proverbs. Presumably, the cartoon task was more difficult than the self-description task, and the proverb task more difficult than the cartoon task. These authors also found an increase in subjects' silent-pause ratios and in other hesitation indices as a function of task difficulty. One problem about this study is that the tasks varied not only in difficulty but also in content or subject matter and, as pointed out by the authors, in the anxiety level that the different tasks aroused in the participants—each of which can be a factor in speech fluency (Siegman, 1978a; 1978b).

In contrast to these studies, the results of which are certainly consistent with Goldman-Eisler's conclusion that silent or unfilled hesitation pauses are behavioral manifestations of cognitive processes, the results of a more recent investigation—one that perhaps comes closest to an actual replication of Goldman-Eisler's original study—are wholly negative. In this study (Rochester, Thurston, & Rupp, 1977), the subjects were asked to describe a series of humorous cartoons and then to explain why the cartoons were funny. The subjects' descriptions were associated with signficantly more pausing (silent pauses exceeding 250 msec, adjusted for speaking time) than their explanations, which is the exact opposite of Goldman-Eisler's central finding. One possible explanation for these unexpected results may be that since in this study the descriptions always preceded the explanations, subjects may have started to think about why the cartoons were funny while they were still describing them. But, then, a similar confounding between the experimental task (description vs. explanation) and task sequence also characterized Goldman-Eisler's original study, as well as the study by Levin and his associates (Levin, Silverman, & Ford, 1967).

There is yet another, and probably more serious, confounding that took place in Goldman-Eisler's original study. In that study, the subjects were instructed to formulate their explanations of the cartoons in as *concise* a form as possible, something that they were not specifically told to do in the description task. Goldman-Eisler herself cites evidence that the attempt to eliminate redundancy and to formulate concise responses is associated with an increase in silent, or unfilled, hesitation pauses. Specifically, she found that in subjects' interpretations, there was a positive correlation between conciseness (brevity of responses) and silent-pause ratio (1968, pp. 62–64). It is conceivable, therefore, that the higher pause ratio associated with the interpretations than with the descriptions in the Goldman-Eisler study reflects the differential instructions regarding conciseness rather than differences in task complexity. Considering the important implications of Goldman-Eisler's findings, a replication of this study without the confounding of its major experimental manipulation would seem very much in order. This, then, was the major purpose of the first in a series of studies reported in this chapter.

STUDY 1: A REPLICATION AND EXTENSION OF GOLDMAN-EISLER'S CARTOON STUDY

In addition to replicating Goldman-Eisler's cartoon study and to comparing the subjects' pausing behavior in TAT descriptions versus TAT stories, the present study also experimentally manipulated the speech conciseness variable. If a concise speech style, in contrast to a redundant and verbose one, is in fact associated with more hesitant speech, it would indeed constitute a conceptual replication of the basic hypothesis that the more complex the encoding process, the less fluent the speech process. However, the data cited by Goldman-Eisler in support of such an inverse relationship between conciseness and fluency are subject to an alternate explanation. The data are correlational in nature. Longer and more verbose interpretations were associated with lower pause ratios, both within subjects and between subjects. Short and concise interpretations, however, may reflect the fact that the subject found these particular cartoons difficult to interpret, in contrast to long and verbose interpretations, which may indicate that the subject had no such difficulty. In other words, it is suggested that the critical mediating variable may be task difficulty, which influences both productivity and fluency, rather than conciseness per se. In the present study, therefore, we attempted a direct manipulation of the conciseness variable by specifically instructing some subjects, but not others (the control group), to eliminate redundancies and to formulate their thoughts in as concise a manner as possible.

Hypotheses

Hypothesis 1.   Cartoon interpretations are associated with longer initial delays and with more frequent and/or longer silent pauses than cartoon descriptions.

Hypothesis 2.   TAT stories are associated with longer initial delays and more frequent and/or longer silent pauses than descriptions of TAT cards.

Hypothesis 3.   Subjects instructed to speak concisely demonstrate longer initial delays and more frequent and/or longer silent pauses than subjects not so instructed.

Subjects

The subjects for this study were 12 male and 12 female undergraduate volunteers. They were assigned to the various experimental conditions on a random basis.

Procedure

Each subject was asked to *describe* four cartoons and two TAT cards, to *interpret* the meaning of another four cartoons, and to *make up a story* about another two TAT cards. For one-half of the subjects, the description task preceded the interpretation and story-making tasks. The two sets of stimuli were counterbalanced between the two tasks. Furthermore, the order of the cards within each task was reversed for half of the subjects.

The following are the instructions that were given to the subjects who started on the description task.

> This study consists of two parts. In the first part, you will be shown a series of cartoon series with no verbal captions. Look at each card, consisting of one or more cartoon panels, and in your own words describe to me what you see. There are two pictures which are not cartoons but more like photographs. In relation to these two, I want you to describe what you see in each photograph. As I hand each card to you, I will say a number. I want you to repeat that number before you start with your description. This number simply indicates the position of the card in the series. When you are finished with your description, please indicate this to me by saying "finished." Do you have any questions?

The completion of the first part of the experiment was followed by a brief break, after which the experimenter continued with the following instructions.

> This is the second part of the experiment. Again, I will show you a series of cartoons. Each of these cartoons, consisting of one or more panels, is trying to make a point or a moral. This time, I don't want you to simply describe what you see. Instead, look at each panel or set of panels and tell me, in your own words, what you think the meaning or the moral of the cartoon is. You will also be shown two pictures that are not cartoons but photographs. In relation to these, I want you to make up a story—a complete story, with a beginning, a middle, and

an end. Again, you are to repeat the number of the card as I hand it to you. When you are finished with a card, please indicate this to me by saying "finished." Do you have any questions?

One-half of the subjects were given the additional instruction—both before the description task and before the interpretation and story-making task—to formulate their responses in as concise a manner as possible.

Dependent Variables.   The present study included the following four temporal hesitation indices: initial delay or reaction time (RT), pause duration ratio (PDR), average pause duraction (APD), and pause frequency ratio (PFR). RT represents the period between the presentation of a stimulus card to the subject and the subject's first word in response to the card. It should be pointed out that this index is not identical to Goldman-Eisler's "initial delay" (1968, pp. 54–55), since the latter excludes the period of time it takes the subject to get the "point" of the card. The PDR is procedurally equivalent to Goldman-Eisler's within-sentence hesitancy ratio (1968, p. 56).[2] It is obtained by summating the duration of the subject's silent pauses within the subject's response to a card (which is measured from the time the subject says the first word and lasts until the subject says "finished") and dividing it by the summed duration of the subject's vocalizations. The only difference between the two studies is that we used a .300-sec cutoff point for measuring the silent pauses, and Goldman-Eisler used a .250-sec cutoff point. The rationale for expressing this index as a ratio of pauses to vocalizations is that the summed duration of pauses tends to increase as a function of the summed duration of vocalizations. However, this particular method of adjusting for response productivity has been criticized on a variety of methodological grounds (Marsden, Kalter, & Ericson, 1974), which has prompted the addition of yet another index of subject's within-response silent pauses. The APD is simply the mean duration of subject's within-response pauses. It is immune to the criticisms that have been made against measures that include an adjustment for response productivity. Finally, the PFR is obtained by dividing the total number of pauses exceeding .300 sec by the summed duration of subject's vocalizations. We included this ratio, because we wanted some indication of the effect of the experimental manipulations on pause frequency, even though the measure is subject to methodological objections because it adjusts for response productivity.

This study included two additional measures, which were used primarily as manipulation checks (in relation to the conciseness manipulation): pro-

---

[2]This index includes all silent pauses within subjects' descriptions or interpretations, be they within-sentence pauses or between-sentence pauses. Consequently, Goldman-Eisler's designation of this measure as an index of within-sentence pauses is something of a misnomer.

ductivity and average duration of vocalizations (ADV). Productivity was obtained by summating the duration of subject's vocalizations within a response. The correlation between this temporal index of productivity and more conventional indices, such as word or clause counts, is .90 or higher (Siegman & Pope, 1972). The ADV refers to the mean duration of subject's vocalizations within a response (with a vocalization defined as a segment of sound bounded by pauses).

Results

The data were analyzed twice, once in an overall analysis of variance design for repeated measurements, which included both the cartoon and TAT data, and then again separately for the cartoons and the TAT cards. Separate analyses are justified, because the difficulty or complexity manipulation for the two sets of stimuli was not identical (description versus interpretation for the cartoons and description versus story telling for the TAT cards); and conceivably, this may have had different effects. We first present the results of the overall analysis of variance (Table 7.1) and then present a more detailed discussion of the findings based on the two separate analyses (Tables 7.2, 7.3, 7.4, and 7.5).

TABLE 7.1
Analysis of Variance Results:
Combined Cartoon and TAT Data.

		Mean Squares					
Source of Variance	df	RT^a	APD	PDR	PFR	Productivity	ADV
Conciseness (A)	1	.389	.00	.000	.0079	875	5.64
Ss within groups (error A)	22	4.373	4.51	.852	.0139	321	3.70
Task difficulty (B)	1	9.780**	58.84**	5.092**	.0004	41	.55
AB	1	.474	3.16	.327	.0002	445*	.66
Ss × B (error B)	22	.363	3.21	.635	.0060	91	.54
Cartoons vs. TATs (C)	1	25.380**	6.29	.067	.0194*	149	4.71*
AC	1	1.580*	1.78	.052	.0089	3	1.53
Ss × C (error C)	22	.382	2.06	.336	.0031	64	.63
BC	1	.059	15.47*	.852	.0008	1563**	1.85
ABC	1	.384	1.08	.014	.0002	139	.00
Ss × BC (error BC)	22	.264	2.45	.225	.0023	103	.26

*$p < .05$
**$p < .01$
[a]Based on logarithmic transformation of data.

TABLE 7.2
Analysis of Variance Results for Cartoon Data.

| Source of Variance | df | Mean Squares | | | |
		RT^a	APD	PDR	PFR^b
Conciseness (A)	1	.200	3.22	.020	16.936†
Task order (B)	1	14.37*	5.67	.010	1.730
A × B	1	.728	5.44	.068	2.884
Ss within groups (between error)	20	1.83	16.65	.453	5.087
Task difficulty (C)	1	5.68**	224.46**	5.05**	1.344
AC	1	.862*	13.26	.101	.022
BC	1	.177	1.63	.002	4.392
ABC	1	2.38**	2.91	.466	10.169*
Ss × C (within error)	20	.191	16.71	.495	2.336

$*p < .05, **p < .01, + .05 > p < .10$
^{a}Based on logarithmic transformation of data.
^{b}All the original values for this variable were multiplied by 1,000.

TABLE 7.3
Mean and SD (Standard Deviation) of Subjects' Scores
on Dependent Variables in Two Cartoon Tasks.

| Variables | Tasks | | | |
| | Description | | Interpretation | |
	Mean	SD	Mean	SD
RT^a	5.284	5.275	9.478	6.332
APD^a	.876	.247	2.174	1.635
PDR	.603	.274	1.252	.882
PFR	.196	.067	.186	.058

^{a}The statistics for this variable are expressed in seconds.

Description versus Interpretation of New Yorker Cartoons. Task difficulty, i.e., description versus interpretation, was a highly significant source of variance in relation to all the pausing indices except the one measuring pause frequency (PFR) (Table 7.2). As hypothesized, the interpretations were associated with longer RTs and with more within-response pausing (as measured by the APD and PDR indices) than the descriptions (Table 7.3). The order or sequence of the tasks, i.e., description first versus interpretation first, had no significant effect on the above results except in relation to RT (Table 7.2). However, task difficulty interacted with task order and conciseness. Task difficulty had no significant effect on the

TABLE 7.4
Analysis of Variance Results for TAT Data.

Source of Variance	df	RT^a	APD	PDR	PFR^b
		Mean Squares			
Conciseness (A)	1	1.76	2.74	.033	.074
Task order (B)	1	8.25*	2.41	.004	5.692
A × B	1	3.14	2.19	.007	.9891
Ss within groups (between error)	20	2.07	6.68	.848	13.360
Task difficulty (C)	1	4.15*	23.28*	.888	.093
AC	1	.039	.91	.240	.401
BC	1	.005	2.14	.246	4.403
ABC	1	.777	.06	.221	1.907
Ss × C (within error)	20	.329	3.74	.404	5.549

$*p < .05, + .05 < p < .10$
[a]Based on logarithmic transformation of data.
[b]All the original values for this variable were multiplied by 1,000.

subject's RTs unless they were in the interpretation-first sequence or unless they were instructed to be concise.

Description versus Story Making for TAT Stimuli.   Task difficulty was a significant source of variance in relation to RT and APD, with subjects obtaining longer RTs and longer APDs on the story telling than on the description task (Tables 7.4 and 7.5), but not in relation to the PDR and the PFR indices. Task order did not interact significantly with task difficulty in relation to any of the variables (Table 7.4).

TABLE 7.5
Mean and *SD* (Standard Deviation) of Subjects' Scores
on Dependent Variables in Two TAT Tasks.

Variables	Description		Stories	
	Mean	SD	Mean	SD
	Tasks			
RT^a	3.533	3.887	5.294	7.106
APD^a	1.036	.373	1.453	.847
PDR	.844	.666	1.116	.823
PFR	.219	.107	.220	.075

[a]The statistics for this variable are expressed in seconds.

It should be pointed out, however, that although task difficulty was a significant source of variance in relation to both RT and APD, it accounted for less of the within-subjects variance of these variables when the stimuli involved TAT cards than when the stimuli involved *New Yorker* cartoons (36% versus 44% in relation to RT, and 23% versus 39% in relation to APD).

The Conciseness Manipulation. Another major hypothesis of this study concerned the effect of the conciseness manipulation on subject's response latency and within-response pausing. It was expected that the subjects who were instructed to formulate their thoughts as concisely as possible would evidence longer response latencies and more within-response pausing than the control subjects. However, before discussing the findings for these variables, it is first necessary to demonstrate that the manipulation was indeed effective, in the sense of reducing subjects' excess verbiage. If the conciseness manipulation was effective, it should reduce the subjects' productivity level—i.e., the summed duration of subjects' vocalizations per stimulus card. We also were interested in seeing whether the conciseness manipulation reduced the average duration of the subjects' within-response vocalizations.

Although the conciseness manipulation did not significantly influence subjects' overall productivity level, the interaction between conciseness and task difficulty was significant (Table 7.1). This interaction reflects the fact that the subjects who were instructed to be concise were in fact less productive than the control subjects, but only for the cartoon interpretation and TAT story-making tasks ($t(11) = 2.309, p < .01$), not in relation to the description tasks. Finally, the conciseness manipulation had no clearly significant effect on the average duration of the subjects' within-response vocalizations (Table 7.1).

The conciseness manipulation was not a significant source of variance in subjects' response latency scores, nor in their within-response pausing indices. However, the interaction between conciseness and task difficulty as well as the triple interaction between conciseness, task difficulty, and task sequence were significant sources of variance in the subjects' RT scores, but only for the *New Yorker* cartoons (Tables 7.2 and 7.4). As noted earlier, these interactions reflect the fact that subjects who followed a description–interpretation sequence showed a significant increase in RT in the interpretation task as compared to the description task only if they were under the additional constraint of formulating their thoughts in a concise manner ($t(5)=5.272, p < .01$). The conciseness manipulation also had a borderline effect on the subjects' pause frequencies as measured by the PFR, but again only in relation to the cartoons but not the TAT cards (Tables 7.2 and 7.4). Although the conciseness manipulation reduced the productivity levels of the subjects' TAT stories ($t(22) = 2.11, p < .05$), there was no corresponding change in their response latencies or in their within-response pausing behavior.

Discussion

Goldman-Eisler's finding that cartoon interpretations are associated with longer within-response pausing than cartoon descriptions was clearly replicated by the results of the present study, both when using her method of measuring such pauses (the PDR) and when using a measure that is independent of subject's productivity level (the APD). In fact, the PDR values associated with the description and the interpretation tasks in the Goldman-Eisler study approximate fairly closely the values for these two tasks obtained in the present study (.82 versus 1.32 in the Goldman-Eisler study and .60 versus 1.25 in the present study).

The results of the present study are less conclusive as far as the subjects' initial delays (RTs) are concerned. The cartoon interpretation task was associated with significantly longer RTs than the cartoon description task, but only when the interpretation task preceded the description task or when subjects were under the additional pressure of formulating their responses in a concise manner. Subjects who followed a description–interpretation sequence and were not instructed to be concise obtained shorter RTs on the interpretation task than on the description task, although this difference was not significant. It should be pointed out that in Goldman-Eisler's original study, subjects' initial delays to the two tasks were roughly the same. Nevertheless, Goldman-Eisler takes the position that it took subjects proportionately more time to plan and to organize the interpretations than the descriptions, since the former contained significantly fewer words than the latter. As has been pointed out earlier, this argument is based on the assumption that everything else being equal, we should expect a positive correlation between RT and subsequent productivity. We have not found this to be the case in our laboratory, whether using between-subjects or within-subjects comparisons. At any rate, it is possible to adjust subjects' RT values for subsequent productivity level. Making such an adjustment in the present study (by dividing subjects' RTs by their subsequent productivity levels) does not change the finding that subjects who followed a description–interpretation sequence and who were not instructed to be concise obtained shorter RTs in the interpretation than in the description condition. As a final comment on this issue, the reader should be reminded that the RT measure used in the present study is not identical with Goldman-Eisler's "initial delay," which does not include the time it takes the subject to get the point of the card.

Turning now to the TAT data, we found that the description versus stories manipulation (task difficulty) was a significant source of variance in subjects' RT scores and in their within-response pausing scores, but only when such pausing was measured by the APD index (not when it was measured by the PDR index, which was used by Goldman-Eisler in her study). The findings suggest that task difficulty was a more potent source of variance (both in terms of significance level and the amount of variance accounted for) in subjects' verbal behavior when the stimuli involved cartoons rather than TAT cards. However, before reaching such a conclusion and speculating about the reasons for it, we first need to determine whether the different results obtained with the *New Yorker* cartoons than with the TAT cards are indeed reliable. Such a determination is made necessary by the fact that only four TAT cards were used in order to determine the effects of card description versus story telling (two cards for each task), in contrast to the eight stimuli that were used to compare the effects of cartoon description versus cartoon interpretation. The next study reported in this chapter was designed to assess the effects of task difficulty in the TAT, on the basis of a broad sampling of TAT cards.

Conciseness and Hesitation in Speech. The conciseness instruction apparently had the intended effect on subjects' cartoon interpretations and on their TAT stories, i.e., a reduction in subjects' verbosity. Nevertheless, this manipulation only had a minimal effect on the hesitation indices in subjects' cartoon interpretations and no significant effect at all on the hesitation indices in subjects' TAT stories. It is of interest to note that as with the task difficulty manipulation, the effects of the conciseness manipulation also were more apparent in subjects' cartoon interpretations than in their TAT stories; but even in the former case, the effects were quite minimal. On the assumption that a concise style, in contrast to a verbose and redundant style, reflects a more complex encoding process involving both semantic and syntactic decisions, the results of the present study would suggest that such an increment in the complexity of the encoding process can take place without being clearly manifested in subjects' within-response pausing behavior or in their initial delays. Stated somewhat differently, the results of the present study suggest that certain kinds of cognitive decision making, such as those involved in producing concisely formulated statements, can take place at the same time that the person is engaged in speech production, even if the latter is as complex as the cartoon interpretation task. It could be, however, that the minimal effects of the conciseness manipulation in the present study reflect the fact that this manipulation involved a between-subjects comparison in contrast to the task difficulty manipulation, which involved a within-subjects comparison, which is much more likely to yield significant differences on variables with large between-subjects variability. What is needed, then, is a study on the effects of conciseness using a within-subjects paradigm. The last study reported in this chapter uses a within-subjects paradigm to assess the effects of economy or conciseness in speech on hesitation phenomena.

STUDY 2: A COMPARISON OF
TAT DESCRIPTIONS AND TAT STORIES

The major purpose of this second study was to assess the effects of task complexity on hesitation in speech, by comparing response latencies and the within-response pauses in subjects' descriptions of TAT cards as compared to the subjects' TAT stories. In contrast to the previous study, the present investigation was based on a broad sampling of TAT cards.

Method and Procedure

Thirty-two female undergraduate students participated in this study. As in the previous study, each subject described one set of TAT cards and made up stories about another set of cards. Each set consisted of nine cards.[3] One-half of the subjects were assigned to a descriptions–stories sequence, the others to a stories–descriptions sequence. The two sets of cards were counterbalanced between the two tasks. Furthermore, the order of the cards within each task was reversed for half of the subjects.

The dependent variables included RT, APD, PDR, and productivity, all of which have been defined earlier in this chapter, plus the following additional indices that were not used in the previous study: speech rate, filled-pause (FP) ratio, and Mahl's (1956) speech disturbance (SD) ratio. In the present study, speech rate was defined as the number of words per response divided by total response time, excluding all silent pauses 2 sec and over. The FP ratio was obtained by dividing the total number of "ah's" and similar expressions in a response by the total number of words in that response. Finally, Mahl's SD ratio consists of the total number of "speech disruptions" per response, such as word repetitions, corrections, incomplete sentences, stutters, etc., divided by the total number of words per response.

There is evidence that a slowing down of speech rate or an increase in filled pauses, like an increase in silent pauses, reflects cognitive decision making and information processing. Ambiguous interviewer questions that create interviewee uncertainty have been found to be associated with an increase in interviewees' filled pauses and a slowing down of their speech rate (Siegman, 1978b; Siegman & Pope, 1965, 1972).

Speech disruptions, on the other hand, tend to be associated with anxiety arousal rather than with cognitive decision making (Siegman & Pope, 1972). Yet, the evidence is not unambiguous. For example, Brenner, Feldstein, and Jaffe (1965) conclude that both anxiety and uncertainty play a role in the SD ratio. This conclusion, as far as the contribution of uncertainty is concerned, is based on the finding that when subjects read passages that have a low approximation to English, they evidence more speech disturbances than when they read passages that have a high approximation to English. Of course, the finding that the reading of strange and unfamiliar words produces speech disturbances may not generalize to other kinds of information processing. More evidence should be obtained concerning the role of

---

[3]One set of TAT stimuli consisted of the following cards: 13B, 13G, 13MF, 17GF, 3GF, 8BM, 12BG, 20, and 18BM. The other set consisted of the following cards: 17BM, 8GF, 9BM, 7GF, 3BM, 2, 1, 12M, and 6BM.

uncertainty and cognitive decision making in the SD ratio. In the present study, therefore, which is concerned with the effects of task complexity on speech, we looked not only at the changes in subjects' silent pauses, filled pauses, and speech rates, but also at their SD ratios.

Results

Neither task complexity nor the interaction between task complexity and task sequence were significant sources of variance in the subjects' APD and PDR scores (Table 7.7). In contrast, task complexity clearly influenced subjects' RT scores: Every subject in the group obtained higher RT scores for the stories than for the descriptions! The only other significant finding

TABLE 7.6
Mean and SD (Standard Deviation) of Subjects'
Scores on Hesitation Indices in Second TAT
Study as a Function of Task Difficulty.

	Tasks			
	Description		Stories	
Variables	Mean	SD	Mean	SD
RT^a	4.29	2.12	15.18	14.50
APD^a	1.087	.305	1.148	.325
PDR	.818	.411	.794	.330
PFR	.795	.335	.812	.426
Speech rate	2.77	.338	2.82	.320
FPR	.0264	.0242	.0295	.024
SDR	.0323	.0178	.0378	.0216

TABLE 7.7
Analysis of Variance Results of TAT Data in Second Study.

Source of Variance	df	Mean-Square						
		RT^a	APD	PDR	PFR	SR	FPR	SDR
Task order (A)	1	2.43	.06	15.66	9.23	18.73	.008	.090
Ss withing groups (between error)	30	1.81	145.82	17.58	19.10	11.42	.073	.449
Descriptions vs. stories (B)	1	19.55**	1.78	.743	.37	1.39	.001	.303*
AB	1	.17	.207	1.58	.81	.28	.001	.039
Ss × B (within error)	30	.151	1.31	5.13	5.18	2.39	.014	.066

^{a}ANOVA results based on logarithmic transformation of data.
*$p < .05$; **$p < .01$.

involves the SD ratio, with the subjects' stories being associated with higher ratios than the descriptions (Tables 7.6 and 7.7). A discussion of these findings is deferred until after the presentation of the next study.

STUDY 3: ECONOMY AND HESITATION IN SPEECH

The major purpose of this study was to obtain further evidence regarding the hypothesis that subjects who are asked to speak concisely and economically will evidence a relatively high level of silent pauses and/or other manifestations of hesitation than subjects who are not so instructed. The major difference between the first study and the present one is that the present study used a within-subjects comparison paradigm rather than a between-subjects paradigm.

Subjects and Procedure

The subjects consisted of 32 undergraduate students, with an equal number of males and females. Subjects were asked to formulate the meaning or moral of two sets of *New Yorker* cartoons, each set consisting of six cartoons. There was a brief break between the two sets of cartoons. Before they started on their second set, the subjects who comprised the experimental group were told to formulate their thoughts as concisely and as economically as possible. No such instructions were given to the subjects who comprised the control group.

The dependent variables were: RT, APD, PDR, PFR, productivity, and average duration of vocalizations (ADV), with the latter two functioning primarily as manipulation checks. One other measure, not used in the two previous studies, is the PC_v/PC_p ratio.

In a recent paper, Feldstein (1976) proposed this index, which is based on automatically measured sound–silence sequences, as an adequate estimate of speech rate. Specifically, this index consists of the proportionality constant of a speaker's vocalizations divided by the proportionality constant of the speaker's pauses. The proportionality constant is identical with the probability of continuing the event in question, be it a vocalization or a pause. In a previous study on the effects of interviewer warmth on interviewee's verbal behavior, the correlations (r) between this ratio and subjects' speech rates, based on actual word counts, in four experimental conditions were .793, .694, .840, and .752. Furthermore, the PC_v/PC_p ratio discriminated between the warm and reserved interview conditions somewhat better than the conventional but more laborious speech rate measure (Siegman, Chapter 5, this volume).

Results

Subjects' productivity scores (summed duration of vocalizations) and their average duration of vocalization scores indicate that the conciseness manipulation was indeed effective. In the control group, there was a slight but nonsignificant increase from the first to the second session in relation to subjects' productivity scores and their duration of vocalization scores ($t(15) = .171$ and $.795$, respectively). In the experimental group, however, there was a significant decrease on both indices as a function of the experimenter's instructions that subjects speak concisely and economically ($t(15) = 5.127$ and 2.566, respectively). The interaction between sequence and conciseness was clearly a significant source of variance in relation to both of these manipulation-check variables (Table 7.9). The interaction between sequence and conciseness was also a significant source of variance in subjects' APD and PDR scores (Table 7.9), reflecting the fact that the subjects who were instructed to speak concisely showed an increase in the duration of their within-response pauses as measured by the APD and PDR indices ($t(15) = 2.249$ and 2.261, respectively), whereas the subjects who were not given such instructions showed a slight but nonsignificant decrease on both indices ($t(15) = 1.188$ and 1.326, respectively). This decrease occurred in the transformed means and is not reflected in Table 7.8, which presents the untransformed means. It should be noted that the logarithmic transformations of the subjects' PDR scores actually changed the rank ordering of the subjects' mean scores in the various conditions. The mean values of the transformed PDR scores were 1.420 and 1.231 for the two sessions in the control condition and 1.578 and 2.051 for the two sessions in the experimental

TABLE 7.8
Subjects Mean and SD (Standard Deviation) Scores
on Dependent Variables in Conciseness Study.

	Control Group				Experimental Group			
	First Session		Second Session		First Session		Second Session	
Variables	Mean	SD	Mean	SD	Mean	SD	Mean	SD
Productivity	12.89	9.04	13.39	8.55	16.93	9.43	7.29	4.66
ADV	1.485	.405	1.569	.367	1.437	.384	1.155	.244
RT	14.81	8.24	19.15	22.04	17.53	12.55	25.80	13.44
APD	1.51	.83	1.51	1.85	2.02	2.00	2.79	1.66
PDR	.981	.597	1.097	1.925	.978	.514	1.017	.889
PFR	.176	.033	.176	.046	.197	.034	.241	.077
PC_v/PC_p	1.108	.271	.992	.188	1.216	.369	1.155	.196

TABLE 7.9
Analysis of Variance Results
of Conciseness Study.

Source of Variance	df	Produc-tivity^a	Mean Squares					
			ADV	RT^a	APD^a	PDR^a	PFR	PC$_v$/PC$_p$
Groups (A)	1	.265	14.20*	1.525	2.468	3.819*	.750**	7.339
Ss within groups (error A)	30	.836	2.90	.424	.623	.854	.055	2.734
Sequence (B)	1	2.413**	2.61	.970*	.215	.323	.187	3.094
A × B	1	2.692**	8.93*	.456	1.182*	1.752*	.198	.307
Ss × B (error B)	30	.158	1.31	.216	.187	.257	.076	.819

^{a}Based on logarithmic transformations of data.
*$p < .05$; **$p < .01$.

condition. No such reordering was produced by the transformations of subjects' APD scores or by the other transformations cited in this paper. This finding, plus the fact that the significance levels associated with the APD index tend to be higher than those associated with the PDR index, plus the various methodological criticisms that have been directed against the PDR, all combine to give a clear-cut edge to the APD over the PDR as a measure of within-response pausing.

The interaction between sequence and conciseness, which is of course the proper source of variance for evaluating the effects of the conciseness manipulation, was not significantly related to subjects' RT scores, their PC$_v$/PC$_p$ ratios, or their PFR scores (Table 7.9).

Discussion

The results of this study, which used a within-subject comparison design, were different from those obtained in the first study, which used a between-subjects comparison design. First, in the present study, unlike in the first study, there is no ambiguity about the effectiveness of the conciseness manipulation, which was clearly reflected in subjects' productivity scores and in their average duration of vocalization scores. Second, there is no evidence in the results obtained in the present study that the conciseness manipulation affected either subjects' latencies or their pause frequencies. Instead, the results indicate that when individuals attempt to speak economically and concisely, they manifest longer within-response silent pauses. Although this was true of most subjects in this study, there were exceptions. Five subjects in the experimental group, all of whom spoke concisely and economically when told to do so, showed no concomitant increase on any of their hesitation indices.

GENERAL DISCUSSION

The first of the three studies reported in this chapter, at least that part of the study that used *New Yorker* cartoons as stimuli, had as its major objective to replicate Goldman-Eisler's "cartoon study," the results of which are frequently invoked in support of the general hypothesis that cognitive planning and information processing are associated with hesistant speech—specifically, with increased within-response pausing. In fact, six out of the eight cartoons that were used here were also used by Goldman-Eisler in her original study. Although there are several procedural differences between Goldman-Eisler's original study and the present one, all of which were introduced in order to rule out the confounding influence of sequence effects and of the instructions to speak concisely, the results of the present study confirm Goldman-Eisler's original findings. The cartoon interpretations were associated with significantly longer within-response silent pauses than the cartoon descriptions. Using the APD score as an index of within-response pausing, 20 out of the 24 subjects exhibited more pausing during their cartoon interpretations than during their descriptions. However, the results with regard to response latency as a function of cartoon description versus cartoon interpretation are somewhat ambiguous. The hypothesized effect was obtained only in the interpretation–description sequence, or if the subjects were under the additional constraint of having to speak economically and concisely.

That part of the first study in which TAT cards were used as stimuli and all of the second study represent attempts to test the generality of the findings obtained with the *New Yorker* cartoons. The difference is not only in the nature of the stimuli, but also in the nature of the task manipulation: description versus interpretation in the case of cartoons and description versus story telling in the case of the TAT cards. In the story-telling task, once the subject has decided on a theme, he or she is free to proceed with the story with few additional restrictions imposed by the nature of the stimulus. There are no correct or incorrect stories. With the cartoons, however, there is, at least implicitly if not explicitly, a single correct interpretation. It can be argued, therefore, that the cartoon interpretations present the subject with a more difficult task, with more uncertainty, and with a greater load of information processing than the TAT stories.

In the first study, the TAT stories were associated with longer response latencies than the TAT descriptions. The findings with regard to within-response pausing are somewhat ambiguous. The TAT stories were associated with longer within-response pauses than the TAT descriptions only when such pausing was measured by the APD index, but not when it was measured by the PDR. Furthermore, the task manipulation accounted for a greater portion of the variance in subjects' RT scores than of the variance in their APD scores (36% versus 23%). It would seem, then, that with the TAT cards, the task manipulation clearly affected subjects' response latencies and somewhat less so their within-response pauses, with precisely the reverse pattern obtaining with the *New Yorker* cartoons. However, the reliability of this finding may be attenuated by the fact that in the first study there was a broader sampling of *New Yorker* cartoons than of TAT cards (8 versus 4). This problem prompted the second study, which was based on 18 TAT cards. The results of this study confirm and sharpen the conclusion that the specific effects of description of TAT cards versus story telling are different from those of cartoon description versus interpretation. In fact, the differences seem to be even greater than was suggested by the results of the first study. In the second study, the TAT stories were associated with longer response latencies than the TAT descriptions, and this was true for every subject in the group; but there was no evidence that the two tasks differentially affected subjects' within-response pausing behavior.

One can only speculate as to why task complexity in the cartoon study had different effects on subjects' hesitation behavior than task complexity in the TAT study. One possibility is that in the TAT story-telling task, as opposed to the cartoon interpretation task, subjects felt freer to take their time and to do all the information processing and encoding that they needed to do during the RT period. By way of contrast, in the cartoon interpretation task, where subjects were likely to assume that there was only one correct response, subjects may have experienced greater evaluation apprehension and greater pressure to respond promptly. Subjects' RT scores for the TAT stories in the second study were in fact significantly longer than their RT scores for the cartoon interpretations in the first study ($t(54) = 2.296$, $p < .05$). Furthermore, subjects' RT scores for the TAT stories of the secoond study were significantly longer than their RT scores for the TAT stories of the first study ($t(54) = 3.728$, $p < .01$). It would seem that the set that was created by the cartoon interpretation task in the first study carried over to the TAT stories, and subjects continued to respond quickly, i.e., with relatively brief initial delays. This may explain why in the first study the TAT stories, in contrast to the TAT descriptions, were associated not only with longer RTs but also with longer within-response pauses, at least as measured by the APD index. Subjects simply may not have had enough time to do all the information processing they needed to do during the latency period and may have felt compelled to continue the process as they were telling their stories.

There is yet another possible explanation for the different effects of the task-complexity manipulation on subjects' hesitation behavior in the cartoon study than in the TAT study—at least in the second TAT study. As pointed out earlier, the decision-making and encoding process associated with cartoon interpretations may be more complex than that associated with TAT stories. In the latter case, once the subject has decided on a theme, he or she is subject to few additional constraints. There are no incorrect stories. By way of contrast, in the cartoon-interpretation task, subjects are likely to assume that there is only one correct response. Subjects may continue to assess the adequacy of their responses even as they formulate them. This is, of course, a somewhat speculative, if not post-hoc, explanation. It is, however, rather difficult to identify the number of encoding operations and to specify the difficulty level associated with each of the two tasks.

Let us now turn to the effects of the conciseness manipulation on hesitation indices in subjects' speech. This issue was investigated in the first study on the basis of between-subjects comparisons and in the third study on the basis of within-subjects comparisons. The major objective of this manipulation, too, was to assess the generality of Goldman-Eisler's position that information processing is associated with hesitant speech, specifically, with relatively long within-response silent pauses. The advantage of the conciseness manipulation, as compared to the task complexity manipulations in the cartoon and TAT studies, is that in this case we can identify the precise additional encoding operations that are associated with the more complex of the two tasks—i.e., additional semantic and lexical decisions or choices.

In the first study, the conciseness manipulation had only a barely noticeable effect on two hesitation indices, RT and PFR. In the third study, however, its effects were unambiguous: When subjects were instructed to speak concisely, they evidenced a clear-cut increase in within-response silent pausing, as measured by both the APD and the PDR index. The difference between the two studies undoubtedly reflects the greater power of within-subjects comparisons over between-subjects comparisons, especially in relation to measures on which there is considerable between-subjects variability. Most of the indices used in the present studies—especially RT, productivity, and APD (in that order)—have such variability. Therefore, within-subjects comparisons are indicated whenever they are possible.

The results of the conciseness study also have implications for the functional meaning of initial delays and of within-response pauses. Goldman-Eisler (1958a, 1958b, 1968) takes the position that within-response pauses reflect primarily lexical decision making. Boomer (1970), on the other hand, argues that such pauses reflect primarily structural and syntactic decisions. As to the latter, Goldman-Eisler has suggested two possibilities. One is that syntax is a matter of habit or skill rather than of cognitive planning (Goldman-Eisler (1968):

> The examination of sentence structure in the light of the concomitant hesitation pauses showing an absence of any relationship between the two indicates that the hierarchical structuring of sentences and embedding of clauses is more a matter of linguistic skill than of planning. Syntactical operations had all the appearance of proficient behavior as distinct from the volitional aspect of lexical and semantic operations [p. 80].

Elsewhere, however, Goldman-Eisler suggests that syntax may involve cognitive decision making and that such decisions take place during the period referred to by her as initial delays. In discussing the functional meaning of the latter category, she writes (1968): "Judging from their position in relation to the whole sentence, they should be much more heavily weighted with the activity of generating content and organizing grammatical structure than the within-sentence pauses which one would expect to be concerned more with lexical decisions [p. 62]."

The results of the conciseness manipulation suggest that to the extent that concise formulations involve both lexical and syntactic decision making, such decisions are reflected in longer within-response pauses rather than in longer initial delays. Subjects who are asked to speak concisely and to avoid using unnecessary words clearly have to make lexical decisions. The fact that the conciseness manipulation affected only subjects' within-response pauses and not their RT scores indicates that such decisions are made as the subjects formulate their responses rather than during the initial delays. However, Goldman-Eisler (1968) reports that concise formulations are also syntactically more complex than redundant ones. If so, it would appear that syntactic decisions, too, to the extent that syntax involves planning and decision making, occur within the response rather than during the RT period, the latter being devoted primarily to generating content.

A comparison of the effects of task complexity in the first study—which involved cartoon descriptions versus cartoon interpretations—with the effects of task complexity in the third study—which involved spontaneous speech versus concisely formulated speech—indicates that the specific manifestations of task complexity vary as a function of the decisions that are involved in the complex as opposed to the simple task. In the first study, i.e., the cartoon study, the task manipulation affected not only subjects' within-response pauses but also their RT scores, with subjects responding with longer RTs in the interpretation task than in the description task (provided that they were under pressure to speak concisely or were in the group that followed an interpretation–description sequence). However, in the third study, i.e., the conciseness study, task complexity had no significant effect on subjects' RT scores. The variable effects of different decision-making processes on the subjects' speech are even clearer if we compare the effects of task complexity in the second study, i.e., TAT descriptions versus TAT stories, with the effects of task complexity in the third study. In the second study, task complexity affected subjects' RT scores but not their within-response pauses, with the precise reverse pattern occurring in the third study. Thus, although all three studies involve a manipulation of task complexity, they each involve different types of complexity that apparently manifest themselves in different hesitation patterns.

In the context of the argument that different types of cognitive decisions are associated with different patterns of hesitation phenomena, we now turn to a finding that was noted in the second study, the significantly higher rate of speech disturbances associated with subjects' TAT stories than with their TAT descriptions. As pointed out earlier, the weight of prior evidence does not support the hypothesis that speech disruptions, as measured by Mahl's SD ratio, are a manifestation of cognitive decision making. Instead, that evidence suggests that such disruptions are a manifestation of anxiety-arousal (Siegman & Pope, 1965, 1972). Thus in a series of studies on the initial interview it was noted that, depending on the interview conditions, ambiguous interviewer probes—in contrast to specific ones—are associated with a higher rate of filled pauses and with a slower speech rate in interviewees' responses or with longer latencies and within-response silent pauses, but not with speech disruptions. The latter appear instead to be associated with the anxiety-arousing potential of the interviewer's questions (Pope, Blass, Bradford, & Siegman, 1971; Siegman, 1978b; Siegman & Pope, 1965, 1972). Also, in the Reynolds and Paivio (1968) study which was cited earlier, subjects' definitions of abstract nouns were associated with higher filled pauses ratios, longer RTs and higher silent pause ratios than their definitions of concrete nouns, with no significant effect noted in relation to subjects' SD ratios. It is of interest to note, therefore, that in the second TAT study, subjects' TAT stories were associated with higher SD ratios than their TAT descriptions. Further evidence that cognitive decision making can take the form of an increase in the speaker's SD ratio is provided by the results of a study (Siegman & Pope, 1966) that investigated the effects of stimulus ambiguity in the TAT on hesitation phenomena in subjects' stories. Stimulus ambiguity was defined in terms of variability of themes evoked by the different TAT cards. In this study, stimulus ambiguity was associated not only with an increase in the various hesitation indices discussed earlier, such as RT, filled-pause ratio, and speech rate, but also with an increase in subjects' SD ratios. On the other hand, in this study, stimulus ambiguity had no significant influence on subjects' silent-pause ratios. An important feature of this study was the attempt to partial out the effects of the anxiety-arousing potential of the cards (as projected in the subjects' stories).

If we accept the proposition that speech disruptions, as measured by the SD ratio, can be a manifestation of speaker uncertainty, we are in a position to reinterpret the widely noted positive correlation between anxiety arousal and speech disruptions (Siegman, 1978b) in cognitive terms. Anxiety tends to have a distracting effect, which is likely to make the speaker's task—especially if it involves cognitive choices and decision making—more difficult than otherwise; hence the increase in the SD ratio. A cognitive interpretation of the effects of anxiety arousal on speech is discussed in greater detail elsewhere (Siegman, 1978a; Chapter 5, this volume).

The data discussed thus far strongly suggest that information processing and cognitive decision making are manifested by a variety of hesitation phenomena, depending on the nature of the encoding task. Interviewee uncertainty that is a result of ambiguous interviewer remarks is associated with a different pattern of hesitation phenomena than lexical decision making, which in turn produces different forms of hesitation than those produced by thematic decision making. Of course, in real life, different kinds of decision making are frequently confounded. Thus, TAT stories involve not only more complex thematic choices than TAT descriptions, but they probably also require more complex lexical and syntactic decision making.

There are indications that the same cognitive activity may be associated with different hesitation indices, depending on the social–interpersonal and other contextual factors. As was mentioned earlier, ambiguous interviewer probes, in contrast to specific ones, produce interviewee uncertainty and are associated with hesitantly articulated interviewee responses. However, the specific manifestations of this hesitation seem to be a function of the interview conditions. Under the usual interview conditions, this hesitation will take the form of an increased number of filled pauses ("ah's") and a slower speech rate. If, however, the interviewees do not have to fear that by prolonging their initial responses or within-response silent pauses they may lose the floor (which can be achieved by letting the interviewee control the duration of his or her responses), then this hesitation will take the form of relatively long initial delays and within-response silent pauses (Siegman, 1978b; Siegman & Pope, 1972). In dyadic conversations, prolonged silences carry the risk of losing one's speaking turn. Consequently, uncertainty and cognitive decision making are likely to manifest themselves in forms other than prolonged initial delays and within-response silent pauses.

That the hesitation manifestations of specific cognitive activities tend to vary as a function of contextual factors that are independent of the task-complexity dimension per se is also illustrated by some of the studies reported in this chapter. For example, cartoon interpretations were associated with longer RTs than cartoon descriptions only if the interpretation task preceded the description task. If, however, the description task preceded the interpretation task, this difference was completely washed out (unless subjects were under the additional pressure to speak concisely), presumably because the subjects' relatively short RTs during the description task created a set to respond promptly. Under these conditions, i.e., the description-interpretation sequence, the extra load of information processing that is involved in the interpretation task manifested itself in some form of hesitant speech other than long RTs. Finally, as has been pointed out earlier, contextual factors unrelated to the task-complexity manipulation per se may also account for the finding that the TAT story-making task was associated with a different pattern of hesitation phenomena in the first study than in the second study.

CONCLUSIONS AND IMPLICATIONS

1. The results of the three studies reported in this chapter—i.e., the study on cartoon interpretations versus descriptions, the study on TAT stories versus TAT descriptions, and the study on economy in speech—are consistent with the general hypothesis that cognitive decision making is associated with hesitant speech. However, the specific manifestations of a speaker's hesitations vary as a function of the decisions that the speaker has to make.

2. Goldman-Eisler's (1968) study, in which she found that cartoon interpretations are associated with longer within-response silent pauses than cartoon descriptions, is typically cited in support of the general hypothesis stated in the first paragraph. The finding, that cartoon interpretations are associated with longer within-response silent pauses than cartoon descriptions, was replicated in a study that corrected several methodological shortcomings of the original Goldman-Eisler study. In light of these replicated findings, we need to address ourselves to the study by Rochester, Thurston, and Rupp (1977), who used a very similar task—i.e., describing versus interpreting a series of humorous cartoons—and yet failed to obtain the expected results. In order to resolve this inconsistency, it is suggested that for an increase in task difficulty to produce hesitation pauses, the subject must be operating at or near his or her information-processing capacity. If, however, the two tasks—i.e., the easier of the two and the more difficult one— are both relatively undemanding, the experimental manipulation may have no significant effect on subjects' pausing ratio or other hesitation indices. It is suggested that such a situation obtained in the study by Rochester et al. (1977). This is supported by the fact that the within-response pausing values for both the description and the interpretation tasks were extremely low (less than one-third of the magnitude obtained by Goldman-Eisler).

A similar rationale may account for the finding that in the first study the conciseness manipulation had no effect whatsoever on subjects' hesitation indices in the TAT story-telling task, even though the subjects who were instructed to formulate their thoughts concisely did in fact produce more concise stories than the subjects in the control group. The story-telling task may provide subjects with sufficient "slack" to absorb the additional cognitive load associated with concise speech.

3. Even the identical task from the point of view of the nature of the decisions that are involved may be associated with different hesitation phenomena, depending on social–interpersonal and other contextual factors. For example, if by lapsing into a relatively long silent pause, a speaker risks losing his or her turn, the speaker may instead resort to filled pauses or may reduce his or her speech rate. If in a particular study, the manipulation of task complexity is not associated with changes in a specific hesitation index, this

does not necessarily mean that the manipulation did not produce hesitant speech. Only a broad sampling of hesitation indices would allow for such a conclusion.

4. Although it is proposed that hesitation in speech is an indication that information processing is taking place at the time of the hesitation, it is not suggested that fluent speech is necessarily an indication that no complex decision making is taking place at that time. In the conciseness study, five subjects—all of whom responded to the experimental manipulation by speaking more concisely and economically than in the control condition—showed no corresponding increase on any of the hesitation indices. Apparently they engaged in the additional encoding required by the conciseness manipulation as they were generating their cartoon interpretations, even though the latter required them to generate new and complex speech sequences. One of these five subjects spoke very hesitantly, i.e., with frequent and long silent pauses, even before he was instructed to speak concisely. It can be argued that in his case there was enough "slack" in his speech to absorb the additional cognitive load that was placed upon him by the conciseness manipulation. However, at least two other subjects were very fluent to begin with (they were among the four most fluent speakers in the group), and yet they, too, were able to absorb the additional cognitive load required of them by the conciseness manipulation without any reduction in their fluency.

5. Elsewhere (Siegman, 1978b), it has been suggested that the study of silent pauses in speech (pausology) may have implications for the diagnosis of clinical disorders. For example, there is evidence that an increase in silent pauses accompanies the aging process. Subtle changes in pausing behavior may very well precede the more obvious indications of senility.

An analysis of pausing behavior and of other hesitation indices may also be helpful in assessing the effects of drugs on cognitive efficiency. For example, in a study on the effects of alcohol on speech (Siegman & Pope, 1967), it was found that even relatively small dosages of alcohol (about 4 oz. adjusted for body weight) were associated with an increase in the subjects' silent-pause ratios and in other hesitation indices. The significant finding, however, was that the level of interference of alcohol with cognitive efficiency, as measured by the silent-pause ratio, did not correspond with blood alcohol levels. The maximum interference with cognitive efficiency occurred about 30 minutes after drinking, but the blood alcohol levels did not reach their highest concentration until about 60 minutes later, by which time all subjects demonstrated—at least on the behavioral level—an adaptatin to the alcohol in their blood. This, of course, has important practical implications.

There are yet other ways in which an analysis of silent pausing and of other hesitation indices may have psychodiagnostic implications. A comparison of youngsters who have been identified as having specific learning disabilities in the verbal area with adequate control subjects in relation to pausing and other hesitation indices may contribute to a better understanding of the former. It was pointed out earlier that people do engage in cognitive decision making even while they are talking, provided that they are not operating at or near their information-processing capacity. This is illustrated by subjects' performance in the Rochester et al. study (1977). Similarly, the conciseness manipulation in our first study did not produce an increase in hesitation in the story-telling task. It would be useful to see how individuals with a diagnosis of specific learning disabilities in the verbal area would do on such tasks. More significantly, by analyzing the pausing and hesitation behavior on the part of learning disabled subjects and controls on tasks varying in specific encoding operations—i.e., lexical, syntactic, or abstracting—we may be better able to identify the precise nature of their learning disabilities. If it is true that silent pauses and other hesitation indices in speech provide us with a window to the brain—i.e., with an indirect measure of the cognitive operations taking place in the brain—they should represent an as yet untapped but potentially powerful psychodiagnostic tool.

ACKNOWLEDGMENTS

The author is very much indebted to his colleagues, Dr. Marilyn Wang for her thorough critique of an earlier draft of this chapter and Dr. Stanley Feldstein for his many helpful editorial comments.

Mark Reynolds, a student at the University of Maryland Baltimore County, is responsible for the computational aspects of the research program reported in this paper. The author is most grateful to him for his unstinting help

REFERENCES

Boomer, D. S. Review of F. Goldman-Eisler, Psycholinguistics: Experiments in spontaneous speech. *Lingua*, 1970, *25*, 152–164.

Brenner, M. S., Feldstein, S., & Jaffe, J. The contribution of statistical uncertainty and task anxiety to speech disruption. *Journal of Verbal Learning and Verbal Behavior*, 1965, *4*, 300–305.

Feldstein, S. Rate estimates of sound–silence sequences in speech. *Journal of the Acoustical Society of America*, 1976, *60* (Supplement No. 1), 546. (Abstract)

Goldman-Eisler, F. Speech production and the predictability of words in context. *Quarterly Journal of Experimental Psychology*, 1958, *10*, 96–106. (a)

Goldman-Eisler, F. The predictability of words in context and the length of pauses in speech. *Language and Speech*, 1958, *1*, 226–231. (b)

Goldman-Eisler, F. Hesitation and information in speech. In C. Cherry (Ed.), *Information theory*. London: Butterworth, 1961. (a)

Goldman-Eisler, F. A comparative study of two hesitation phenomena. *Language and Speech*, 1961, *4*, 18–26.(b)

Goldman-Eisler, F. *Psycholinguistics: Experiments in spontaneous speech*. New York: Academic Press, 1968.

Lay, C. H., & Paivio, A. The effects of task difficulty and anxiety on hesitation in speech. *Canadian Journal of Behavioral Science,* 1969, *1,* 25–37.

Levin, H., Silverman, I., & Ford, B. L. Hesitations in children's speech during explanation and description. *Journal of Verbal Learning and Verbal Behavior,* 1967, *6,* 560–564.

Maclay, H., & Osgood, C. E. Hesitation phenomena in spontaneous English speech. *Word,* 1959, *15,* 19–44.

Mahl, G. F. Disturbances and silences in the patient's speech in psychotherapy. *Journal of Abnormal and Social Psychology,* 1956, *53,* 1–15.

Mardsen, G., Kalter, N., & Ericson, W. A. Response productivity: A methodological problem in content analysis studies in psychotherapy. *Journal of Consulting and Clinical Psychology,* 1974, *42,* 224–230.

Pope, B., Blass, T., Bradford, N. H., & Siegman, A. W. Interviewer specificity in seminaturalistic interviews. *Journal of Consulting and Clinical Psychology,* 1971, *36,* 152.

Pope, B., Blass, T., Siegman, A. W., & Raher, J. Anxiety and depression in speech. *Journal of Consulting and Clinical Psychology,* 1970, *35,* 128–133.

Reynolds, A., & Paivio, A. Cognitive and emotional deteminants of speech. *Canadian Journal of Psychology,* 1968, *22,* 164–175.

Rochester, S. R., Thurston, S., & Rupp, J. Hesitation as clues to failures in coherence: A study of the thought-disordered speaker. In S. Rosenberg (Ed.), *Sentence production: Developments in theory and research.* Hillsdale, N.J.: Lawrence Erlbaum Associates, 1977.

Siegman, A. W. The meaning of silent pauses in the initial interview. *Journal of Mental and Nervous Disease,* 1978, *166,* 642–654. (a)

Siegman, A. W. The telltale voice: Nonverbal messages of verbal communication. In A. W. Siegman & S. Feldstein (Eds.), *Nonverbal behavior and communication.* Hillsdale, N.J.: Lawrence Erlbaum Associates, 1978. (b)

Siegman, A. W., & Pope, B. Effects of question specificity and anxiety-producing messages on verbal fluency in the initial interview. *Journal of Personality and Social Psychology,* 1965, *4,* 188–192.

Siegman, A. W., & Pope, B. Ambiguity and verbal fluency in the TAT. *Journal for Consulting Psychology,* 1966, *30,* 239–245.

Siegman, A. W., & Pope, B. *The effects of alcohol on verbal productivity and fluency.* Paper presented at the annual meetings of the Eastern Psychological Association, Boston, April 1967.

Siegman, A. W., & Pope, B. The effects of ambiguity and anxiety on interviewee verbal behavior. In A. W. Siegman & B. Pope (Eds.), *Studies in dyadic communication.* New York: Pergamon Press, 1972.

8

Speaking and Not Speaking: Processes for Translating Ideas into Speech

Patricia Brotherton
University of Melbourne

INTRODUCTION

Performance models of speech production have been slow to develop for at least two reasons. The first is that many of the relevant empirical variables are considered to lie outside mainstream psycholinguistics and are labeled as "extralinguistic." One example is the lip service that has been paid to the role of hesitation phenomena as indicative of central planning processes (Fillenbaum, 1971); yet the empirical work has taken considerable time to capture the interest of more than a few workers. Related theoretical conclusions, too, are underdeveloped (O'Connell & Kowal, 1972).

The second reason is the heavy concentration in psycholinguistics on acquisition and comprehension studies to the point where a recent reviewer of psycholinguistic research asserts that "the fundamental problem in psycho-linguistics is simple to formulate: what happens when we understand sentences?" (Johnson-Laird, 1974, p. 135). This neglect of speech production has led one group of researchers to claim that: "Practically anything that one can say about speech production must be considered speculative even by the standards current in psycholinguistics" (Fodor, Bever, & Garrett, 1974, p. 29).

Although this comment seems unduly pessimistic, it is true that the central theoretical and empirical issue in speech production studies has proved intractable to solution, despite recurrent references to it in psychological studies of language since the 19th century (Blumenthal, 1970). That issue is: What are the processes and structures that enable "thoughts" or "ideas" to be realized in overt speech acts?

Vocalizing and pausing are complementary aspects of the process of spontaneous speech production that are related conceptually to the aforementioned issue in the following way. Ideas to be expressed require encoding in structural form, and semantic, syntactic, and phonological features of language realize this translation process. In the research literature, there is a strong assumption that encoding requires some real time for resolution and that pausing is a behavioral indicator of the encoding process. In this chapter, investigation of the patterning and distribution of pauses within speech sequences is regarded as one important method of studying the process of speech production and the nature of the planning decisions required of speakers when they are talking spontaneously. The method is one that tests the empirical fit between the location of pauses and selected structural features of the speech product.

It is also argued that knowledge about the process of speech planning is facilitated when attention is paid to the social origins of speakers. The concept of social class rests on the assumption that the substructures of a given society operate as relatively closed systems, producing in their members class-associated behaviors. The study of contrasting social class groups should indicate whether variations in speech-pause patterns are so dissimilar amongst different groups that alternative speaker models are necessary to account for these effects.

The link between social class and the process of speech production was conceptualized in terms of verbal planning strategies, a concept first proposed by Goldman-Eisler and later developed by Bernstein. In a larger study from which the present report is drawn (Brotherton, 1976), a detailed investigation of pauses, speech disruptions, and redundancies in speech was made, together with an account of their relationship to syntactic and lexical aspects of speech samples. However, the focus of this chapter is confined to a discussion of the role of unfilled and filled pauses in spontaneous speech and their relationship to the process of verbal planning.

SUMMARY OF SELECTED EMPIRICAL STUDIES

Previous work on pausing and vocalizing has been reviewed and summarized in detail by Brotherton (1976) and Rochester (1973). For present purposes, only the major conclusions from two selected sets of studies are presented here. These were conducted by Goldman-Eisler (1968) and Bernstein (1962a, 1962b), the former concerned with regularities and the latter with variations in speech-pause patterns.

The literature on pausing reveals a distinction between the vocalized (filled) pause and the unvocalized (silent) pause. Although Goldman-Eisler gave some attention to the filled pause, both Bernstein and Goldman-Eisler concentrated almost exclusively on unfilled-pause analysis. Both are considered in the present study.

Goldman-Eisler

Goldman-Eisler presented no systematic theory of speech production, the summary of her work (Goldman-Eisler, 1968) consisting of a post-hoc account of the theoretical implications of a number of experimental studies that spanned a 17-year period. In brief, her major propositions can be summarized as follows.

1. Between the idea to be expressed and the related speech act is the central act of encoding what one intends to say.
2. Concurrently with the act of planning, there is a delay (pause) that is indicative of that act of central planning. Specifically, pauses are "synchronous with and indicative of encoding processes responsible for generation of information" (Goldman-Eisler, 1968, p. 51).
3. With the exception of over-learned or familiar speech sequences, speech must be suspended to enable planning to occur: "the delay is a total one, the time is unfilled, emptied of peripheral verbal behaviour; it is a time of external inactivity and requires an ability to postpone verbal activity altogether" (Goldman-Eisler, 1968, p. 126). It follows that one cannot encode and speak concurrently.
4. Time is required for encoding general content and for lexical decisions, syntactic formulation requiring no extra pause time.
5. The frequency and length of pause increases as encoding difficulty increases.

Two research problems are suggested from the above summary but have not been answered by Goldman-Eisler's empirical work. First, can there be planning without pausing? Pausing may be a function of planning, but does planning *necessarily* entail pausing, as Goldman-Eisler has claimed? Second, what are the functional properties of different types of pauses in different locations, and what is the nature of the unit(s) in which speakers encode their intentions?

Bernstein

Bernstein proposed a verbal planning hypothesis based on Goldman-Eisler's work; using pausing as an index of verbal planning, he claimed that frequency of pausing was indicative of self-monitoring in spontaneous speech (Bernstein, 1961, 1962a). Duration or length of pausing was assumed to be related to: (a) the relative difficulty in selecting the next sequence; (b) the ability to tolerate delay and the associated tension arising from encoding difficulty; and (c) the production of better organized speech sequences. In his general theory of the sociolinguistic codes, elaborated code speech (largely middle class) was regarded as relatively hesitant, whereas restricted code speech (largely lower working class) was fast and fluent (Bernstein, 1962a).

Bernstein (1962a) found that the proportion of pauses amongst middle-class subjects was significantly greater than amongst lower working-class subjects. Although he claimed to have measured mean duration of pauses, in fact this measure was the inverse of his proportion (frequency) measure. His conclusions on pausing, therefore, rest on the single finding of a greater *frequency* of pausing among middle-class subjects.

The unresolved research problem arising from Bernstein's pausing studies is the question of whether social class differences in speech-pause patterns reflect fundamentally different strategies of verbal planning.

LOCATION ANALYSIS OF PAUSES

Retardation of theoretical developments in the field of pausing and speech production is due to at least three methodological factors:

1. Criteria for and methods of measuring pauses vary widely.
2. Filled and unfilled pauses are not always conceptually distinguished and/or separately measured.
3. Detailed analysis of the location at which pauses fall within speech sequences is not often attempted.

In the present chapter, the latter issue occupies a central place for the following reasons. First, a number of studies have implied or assumed that filled and unfilled pauses are functionally equivalent (e.g., Cook, 1969; Fodor, Bever, & Garrett, 1974). If this assumption is correct, it might be expected that the location in which each is found would be similar. Second, the meaning of any class differences in pausing would be unclear, unless the location at which those differences were most apparent was also known.

Where location analyses have been attempted previously, there is little consensus as to which locations should be used, thus compounding the problem of the function served by pauses. Three pause positions have been most commonly identified: in relation to content and function words (e.g., Martin & Strange, 1968; O'Connell, Kowal, & Hörmann, 1969); in relation to variously defined "syntactic" or "grammatical" units (e.g., Lalljee & Cook, 1972; Martin, 1967; Rochester & Gill, 1973); and by phonemic clause analysis (e.g., Boomer, 1965). Furthermore, in most studies it is common for researchers to eliminate much of the data in order to facilitate coding of "messy" speech output (e.g., Goldman-Eisler, 1958), or to concentrate only on lengthy, sustained utterances (e.g., Bernstein, 1962a; Maclay & Osgood, 1959).

In the studies of particular interest here, both Bernstein and Goldman-Eisler adopted a criterion of .250 sec for measuring unfilled pauses, but filled pauses were largely ignored. Some work on location was undertaken by Goldman-Eisler (1958) and by Henderson, Goldman-Eisler, and Skarbek (1966), but a conceptual distinction made by Goldman-Eisler that pauses falling at major grammatical boundaries should be separated from other within-utterance pauses was not maintained in most of her work. Generally, pauses of .250 sec and longer were measured and summed to give an account of total pause time per subject. Goldman-Eisler (1961) distinguished between "initial delay" pauses in dialogues and "within-sentence" pauses, a sentence being defined as the period of speech from the time the subject commenced speaking until the last word was uttered. In summarizing her position concerning the role of unfilled pauses in spontaneous speech, Goldman-Eisler (1968) argued that initial delay pauses represented points of planning the content of whole speech sequences, whereas the remaining within-utterance hesitations were assumed to be related to difficulties in lexical choice. However, since the range of sentence lengths on which she based this conclusion extended from 16.900 to 75.500 sec (Goldman-Eisler, 1968, pp. 55–56), and no further within-sentence analysis was attempted, it is highly improbable that none of the within-sentence pauses fell at grammatical boundaries.

THE PRESENT STUDY

Design and Procedure

Data consisted of two 10-minute samples of spontaneous speech selected from interviews with 10 middle-aged female subjects engaged in discussing their child-rearing practices. Interviews were conducted by one interviewer in the subjects' own homes.

Two groups of subjects were selected, five in each of two strongly contrasting class groups. Class position was determined on the basis of a social class index involving education and occupation with built-in cross-generational stability, therefore producing relatively "pure" upper middle-class (MC) and lower working-class (WC) groups (Brotherton, 1976).

All interviews were tape-recorded, and transcripts made of them. Two 10-minute time samples consisting of the first 10 and middle 10 minutes of the interviews were selected, thus enabling application of a repeated measures 2 × 2 analysis of variance design on the data (i.e., time samples × class).

Interruptions and periods of simultaneous speaking were infrequent and do not affect the results reported here.

All unfilled pauses were measured from oscillogram records and later matched to and inserted in the transcripts at the exact point of occurrence. In the absence of strong evidence that pauses of less than .200 to .250 sec are other than phonational gaps, the .250-sec criterion was used for the purpose of comparability with relevant other studies. No a priori decision to label some pauses as "juncture" and others as "genuine hesitations" (Boomer, 1965) on the combined criteria of length and location was made. Filled pauses were identified on oscillogram records and subsequently inserted into the transcripts, but they were not measured for length.

Definition and Measurement of Variables

Interviewer and Subject Utterances

Interviewer and subject speech units were defined as follows:
1. *Subject utterance.* A period of time incorporating both speech and silence that lasted from the conclusion of a question or comment by the interviewer to the conclusion of vocalizing by the subject.
2. *Interviewer utterance.* A period of time incorporating both speech and silence that lasted from the commencement of interviewer vocalizing to the end of the interviewer's question or comment.

Dialogue Pauses

Two types of pause, peculiar to the dialogue situation, were identified:
1. *Initial response pauses.* Periods of silence from the end of the interviewer's question or comment until the subject began vocalizing. These pauses were included as part of the subject's total pausing time.
2. *Interface pauses.* Periods of silence from the end of subject vocalizing to the commencement of the interviewer's next comment or question. These pauses are ambiguous in that the interviewer may be waiting for the subject to say more or may be searching for the next most appropriate question (cf. Jaffe & Feldstein, 1970). Ambiguity is not present in the case of initial response pauses; once the interviewer has asked a question, the next move is clearly up to the speaker.

Other Pause Measures

1. *Proportion of unfilled pauses.* The number of unfilled pauses of .250 sec or longer was expressed as a proportion of number of words, to control for subject productivity.
2. *Mean length of unfilled pauses.* The average length of unfilled pauses

for each subject was determined by expressing the total amount of pausing in seconds, as a function of the number of unfilled pauses.
3. *Filled-pause ratio*. The number of filled pauses was expressed as a proportion of number of words.

In all statistical analyses, scores were routinely transformed by methods appropriate to the type of raw score involved. Untransformed values are presented in all tables to facilitate interpretation of results.

Units of Analysis for Location Purposes

The surface structure clause was selected as an appropriate unit for location analysis, partly on the basis of work by Valian (1971) that suggested that such clauses are primary speech-encoding units. A surface structure clause was defined as a stretch of speech consisting of subject and predicate, where the predicate involved a finite verb or participle. Various subcategories of the clause were separately defined, to allow for the coding of all vocalizations including casual, unfinished, and disrupted speech, but these are not of direct relevance here. Content/function word analyses were based on traditional grammatical categories (Nesfield & Wood, 1964).

Locations Within Speech Sequences

Three major locations were distinguished to enable precise identification of pauses within speech sequences.

1. *Initial response position*. Pauses at the beginning of utterances that followed an interviewer question or comment and that preceded commencement of speaking by the subject were labeled as initial response pauses.
2. *Clause-boundary position*. Pauses between clauses were labeled as clause-boundary pauses. Such pauses have often been regarded in functional terms as "conventional pauses" or pauses "for the speaker."
3. *Within-clause position*. Any pause that was not in either of the above two positions was by definition a within-clause pause.

Location of Within-Clause Pauses

The claim in previous research that within-clause pauses are related to difficulty of lexical selection required identification of the items following those pauses. Rather than coding these initially as content or function words, lexical items following within-clause pauses were carefully examined and a finer set of mutually exclusive categories developed. A brief definition of these within-clause positions follows.

1. *At major surface-structure phrase boundaries.*
   a. *Major phrase boundary.* The phrase was defined as a series of words with no main verb that functioned as a substitute for other parts of speech.
   b. *Implicit clause boundary.* This position was effectively equivalent to a clause boundary, where simple statements of affirmation or negation were attached to whole clauses or where automatisms (e.g., "You know") were attached to the whole clauses. Pauses marked the point of attachment.
2. *Interrupting major surface-structure phrase boundaries.*
   a. *NP # VP.* The position marked # indicated a pause between a noun phrase and a verb phrase.
   b. *NP VP # NP.* The position marked # indicated a pause within a larger phrase unit, falling between a verb phrase and a second noun phrase.
   c. *# AJ NU.* Pauses in the position marked # preceded an adjective–noun pair.
   d. *AJ # NU.* Pauses in the position marked # interrupted an adjective–noun pair.
   e. *Within a verb (predicate) phrase.* Pauses falling at any point within a verb phrase were assigned to this category.
   f. *Other.* This was a residual category where finer classification seemed neither necessary nor obvious.
3. *Associated with speech disturbances.* Pauses at any point within a clause that were preceded and/or followed by a speech disturbance were assigned to this category. The system devised by Kasl and Mahl (1965) was used to identify speech disturbances.

Preliminary Analysis of Interviewer Effects and Task Demands

There were two preliminary analyses. Matarazzo, Hess, and Saslow (1962); Matarazzo and Wiens (1967), and Webb (1969) have indicated that interviewer pause patterns can affect subject pausing behavior. Interviewer behavior on the following three measures did not differ significantly between class groups: amount of interview time occupied by the interviewer; amount of interface pausing (see p. 184); and total amount of within-utterance interviewer pausing.

Secondly, because exact comparability of content could not be assumed due to the method of selecting the two time samples of speech, a content analysis of task demands implicit in the interviewer's questions was applied to those questions. At three levels of increasing task difficulty, no significant differences were found in the proportion of questions of each type administered to the two groups. Task difficulty was therefore considered to have been adequately controlled.

RESULTS AND DISCUSSION

Results and discussion have been interwoven to facilitate a sequential, developing exposition of results. Since the present chapter is principally concerned with the function of pauses, social class differences are discussed only where they bear directly on the location analyses. There were no significant class × time-interaction effects in any of the results presented hereafter.

Unfilled Pauses

For the sample as a whole, subjects were silent for 26.7% of the total time, confirming the claim that pausing is a common feature of temporal speech acts (Goldman-Eisler, 1968). The percentage of what have been called "pauses for effect" or "pauses of unusual length" was very small, with over three-quarters of all unfilled pauses being accounted for by those of up to 1 sec in length.

Location Analysis: Proportion of Unfilled Pauses

Table 8.1 sets out the distribution of unfilled pauses according to the three locations listed previously. The results indicate that 64.9% of all unfilled pauses fell at structural boundaries. (In these data, there was only one instance of a criterial pause interrupting a word.)

With initial response pauses removed, recalculated figures approximate more closely the monologue situation and enable comparisons to be made with other studies. Table 8.2 sets out the results. The overall mean values were

TABLE 8.1
Distribution of Unfilled Pauses Within
Utterances, in Three Locations.

		At Beginning of Utterance (Initial Response Pauses)	At Clause Boundary (Clause-Boundary Pauses)	Within Clause (Within-Clause Pauses)	Total
MC	N	324	562	592	1,478
	%	21.9	38.0	40.1	100.0
WC	N	412	435	367	1,214
	%	33.9	35.9	30.2	100.0

TABLE 8.2
Percentage Distribution of Unfilled Pauses Within
Utterances, in Two Locations.

	At Clause Boundary	Within-Clause	Total
MC	48.7	51.3	100.0
WC	54.2	45.8	100.0
Mean	51.5	48.5	100.0

found to be similar to the monologue distributions reported by Henderson, Goldman-Eisler, and Skarbek (1966) and by Maclay and Osgood (1959). Comparison of the results in Tables 8.1 and 8.2 indicates the necessity for initial response pauses to be distinguished from clause-boundary pauses in dialogue situations.

The Concept of Potential Pause Positions

The only significant effect for proportion of pauses produced was a main effect for class (F = 12.411, df = 1, 8, $p < .01$), due to an anticipated higher proportion of unfilled pauses produced by middle-class subjects. The results in Table 8.1 suggested that this class difference lay at the initial response position and the within-clause position. However, a test of *where* the difference between groups was most marked required some control for the relative potential opportunities to pause in each location by subjects in each group. The concept of "potential pause positions" was therefore used as a control factor, and location analyses were conducted on the following basis.

Since a speaker potentially can pause on each occasion that a new utterance is produced, the number of potential pause positions in the utterance-initial position will be equal to the number of utterances produced. In the case of clause boundaries, a speaker potentially can pause on each occasion that a clause is produced. After adjustment for clauses classified in the utterance-initial position, the number of potential pause positions will be equal to the number of clauses minus the number of utterances produced. A speaker also potentially can pause between each word of a clause: The number of such potential pauses will only be limited by the number pauses that occur at clause boundaries. Hence, the number of within-clause potential pause positions is equal to the number of words produced minus the number of clauses.

The number of unfilled pauses produced in each location was thus expressed as a ratio of number of potential pause positions in each location, for each subject. Table 8.3 sets out the group mean values derived from the

TABLE 8.3
Means and Standard Deviations—Distribution of
Unfilled Pauses as a Ratio of Potential Pause Positions
in Each of Two Social Class Groups.

		At Beginning of Utterance	Location At Clause Boundary	Within- Clause
MC	Mean	.689	.398	.076
	Standard deviation	.097	.063	.018
WC	Mean	.619	.244	.040
	Standard deviation	.096	.035	.011

treatment of subjects' data in this way. T tests were chosen to test for differences between groups at each location, due to the skewed distribution of pauses across locations. In all three positions, the MC utilized the unfilled pause to a greater extent than the WC, although the effect was significant in only two of the three positions: at clause boundaries ($t = 4.302, 8\, df, p < .005$, one-tailed), and within clauses ($t = 3.288$, 8 df, $p < .01$, one-tailed). The clause-boundary results are interesting in view of the fact that the WC subjects actually produced significantly more clauses than the MC ($F = 22.936$, $df = 1, 8, p < .001$), and therefore had more positions to utilize. However, the MC used 40% of these potential pause positions compared with only 24% by the WC.

Location Analysis: Length of Unfilled Pauses

The second aspect of unfilled pausing concerned the relationship between the location and length of pauses. All unfilled pauses of .250 sec or longer were grouped in one of the three locations, and mean values were determined on the basis of the number of pauses of varying lengths in each position. Table 8.4 sets out the means and standard deviations on which the t tests were based.

Mean values for pause length in each of three locations showed that initial response pauses were longer than clause-boundary pauses, which in turn were longer than pauses occurring within clauses. This strong general effect was found in the scores of all 10 subjects and must therefore be regarded as a systematic "length by location" factor where unfilled pauses are measured under spontaneous speech conditions.

There were no significant class differences in the length of unfilled pauses in the initial response position, but significant differences were found at the clause-boundary position ($t = 2.556$, 8 df, $p < .025$, one-tailed) and within-clause position ($t = 2.413$, 8 df, $p < .025$, one-tailed).

The pause length measure used here is the one that was presumably intended but not measured by Bernstein (1962a). In his theoretical work, it

TABLE 8.4
Means and Standard Deviations—Length of
Unfilled Pauses (in Seconds)—in Three Locations.

		At Beginning of Utterance	Location At Clause Boundary	Within-Clause
MC	Mean	1.204	.854	.647
	Standard deviation	.475	.181	.098
WC	Mean	.939	.605	.527
	Standard deviation	.162	.070	.049

was linked to his claim that middle-class subjects had greater ability to tolerate delay of speech output and the resulting tension associated with coding difficulty. However, any differences in toleration for delay of speech would be more likely to become apparent in the case of exceptionally long pauses, of which there were relatively few in these data.

Linking the pause length results with the results for proportion of pauses, the MC not only paused significantly more often than the WC in relation to their potential to do so (both at clause boundaries and within clauses), but they also paused for significantly longer. A significant effect was not found at the beginning of utterances for either the length of, or the proportion of, unfilled pauses.

Pauses Present and Absent

Initial Response Pauses. The finding that 34.5% of utterances commenced without an unfilled pause (Table 8.3) raises the central issue of the role of these pauses in planning speech sequences. Goldman-Eisler (1968, p. 62) argued that initial delay pauses (approximately equivalent to the initial response pauses in the present study) enabled generation of the content of utterances. Since she also argued that suspension of speech was a necessary condition for formulating ideas, the absence of initial response pauses in over one-third of these utterances is an important observeration. If these utterances were very short, then it could be argued that one or two word responses could quickly be encoded and produced. All initial response pauses for each subject were therefore categorized according to whether they were longer or shorter than the subject's mean length of pause and whether they preceded an utterance that was longer or shorter than that subject's mean length of utterance.

Even when utterances exceeded the group mean utterance length, 8.1% of all utterances commenced without an unfilled pause; expressed as a percentage of relatively long utterances only, 24.6% of long utterances commenced without an unfilled pause. Since the latter were, on average, 22 words long, it is unlikely they were composed only of simple or automatic phrases. The results indicate clearly that subjects launched into sustained passages of speech without pausing initially and that this was the case in about one-quarter of all long utterances produced.

By contrast, 17.5% of all initial response pauses were found to be longer than average, yet in utterances that were shorter than average. An example of such a response follows:

S1 (MC)
Q.   What was his birth weight?
A.   (Pause 7.125 sec) Oh about six and a half pounds.

This is a syntactically simple yet novel utterance where delay of speech action is, relatively speaking, exceptionally long and where pausing appears to be related to memory search. Such unpredictably long pauses in response to apparently straightforward questions would have contributed to the larger standard deviations in both groups for initial response pauses (Table 8.4).

Utterances Without Pauses. A number of utterances were also found to have no measured pauses of any kind (filled or unfilled) before *or* within them. This is a result that has not been reported previously and is crucial to the arguments made by Goldman-Eisler (1968) that pausing is essential for verbal planning. Though all these were short, relative to the mean length of utterance, exhaustive analysis indicated that each one provided new information that was not predictable from the prior context of the utterance in question. An example follows:

S5 (WC Group)
Q. Were you able to put him to the breast right away on that first day, do you remember?
A. No, I couldn't feed him. I had inverted nipples, so he was always a bottle baby.

Two other types of utterance were also identified that had no associated pauses of any kind. The first consisted of simple affirmation/negation, and the second of a small set of simple restatements or elaborations by the subject of the interviewer's own words or phrases. It seems reasonable that these would require little real time for formulating a response, but the fact remains that many instances were found of whole utterances that produced apparently nonautomatic and novel information and that not only had no initial response pause but had no other criterial pause associated with them.

It would be premature to draw the conclusion that unfilled pausing is not, after all, a systematic accompaniment of speech, for there were only five instances of complete utterances consisting of *three or more* clauses in length, *and* where no pauses of any kind were present. This strongly suggests that there is some limit to the number of clauses that can be produced as a complete utterance unit without benefit of pauses.

The foregoing analysis reinforces the claim that initial response pausing does not appear to be essential for planning the overall content of utterances, whether those utterances are long or short, and that pausing is not essential for planning short utterances up to three surface structure clauses in length.

Fluent Speech Runs Within Utterances. The fact that utterances longer than three surface structure clauses without pauses were rarely found in these data does not apply in the same way to longer utterances. A number of instances were located of speech sequences of up to six or seven surface structure clauses within longer utterances and where no pause of any kind was present in that sequence. Pauses were, however, present elsewhere in the utterance. For the MC, there were 36 fluent speech runs, ranging from three to eight clauses in length and representing 6.8% of the total number of MC surface structure clauses. Corresponding figures for the WC were 112 fluent runs representing 17.1% of the WC clauses. When these longer speech runs were analyzed, it was found that they were commonly descriptive in nature, and the lengthier ones often included reports of direct speech. Their anecdotal quality suggests that they are examples of the type of speech Goldman-Eisler (1968) referred to as "well-organized" or "well-learned" and that Bernstein (1962a, 1962b) associated particularly with the speech of lower working-class subjects. In this situation, there was considerably more descriptive, narrative style speech amongst the WC than the MC subjects.

Linking these results with those in the previous section, where only five utterances of three or more clauses in length were found without pauses of any kind, indicates that runs of three to four surface structure clauses without a pause of some kind are extremely rare in sustained conversational speech and that such long runs are only possible where the speech product appears to require little cognitive effort. The first question suggested by these findings is whether initial response pauses serve as general planning pauses, as both Bernstein and Goldman-Eisler have suggested.

The Role of the Initial Response Pauses

The length of the initial response pauses relative to pause lengths in other locations suggests that some time is required for decoding the interviewer's question. Since the standard deviations for the mean length of initial response pauses were much larger than in other positions, and since task difficulty was relatively constant, this variation appears to reflect the idiosyncratic nature of pauses in the initial response position.

For Goldman-Eisler, absence of initial delay pauses was an indication that an utterance was not a semantically novel one, since delay of speech action was regarded as essential to the planning of novel utterances. Because utterances without pauses were not considered to constitute cases of novel utterances, it was possible for Goldman-Eisler—in her later formulations—to argue a distal theory for pauses in relation to planning; i.e., a nonhesitant (fluent) speech phase could be planned at some earlier point in the utterance, and a distal pause was the indicator of that point of planning for the later sequence. That instances do occur of fluent runs with pauses at some distal point is apparent from these data; however, they are not only unusual in an absolute sense but also represent only one of several types of pause–speech patterns that have been identified. In particular, whole utterances were found where there were no pauses present at all. Even where subjects' responses were syntactically simple, these utterances went beyond exclamations and clichés. How and where were they planned, if pauses are the sine qua non of speaking, as Goldman-Eisler proposed?

It is possible, of course, that the cutoff point for unfilled pauses was too great. It is also probable that formulating an utterance can at least commence while the other person is still speaking. Where the social context is shared and is mutually intelligible to both speakers, some anticipatory planning can be expected. However, for this to serve as a general explanation, it would have to be argued that in *all* instances where there was no initial response pause the meaning of the interviewer's question was understood by the speaker before the interviewer completed speaking. Such an explanation is improbable. It is more likely that speakers commenced speaking without extensive forward planning and that within the limits described earlier, a planning pause inevitably followed.

Goldman-Eisler (1961, 1968) also observed that initial delay pauses did not vary as a function of length of utterance in the two conditions of her widely cited cartoon experiment. She concluded that since it took about the same amount of time to organize the long (descriptive) and short (interpretative) utterances, it must be the case that "lexical choice becomes more difficult in proportion to the increase in complexity of general planning" (Goldman-Eisler, 1968, p. 62).

In Goldman-Eisler's data as well as in the present data, short *or* long initial delay pauses could be followed by either short *or* long utterances. Goldman-Eisler explicitly claimed that initial pauses of whatever length were for planning overall content, that all other within-utterance pauses were for lexical choice, and that this was the case irrespective of the length of those utterances. In the present data, most utterances consisted of several clauses, and many pauses occurred at clause boundaries, an observation that was not available to Goldman-Eisler, since she did not perform the necessary analyses. Therefore, the proposal that initial response pauses are for the general planning of content, irrespective of utterance length, and that all other pauses are lexical choice pauses does not appear to be a valid one.

It is clear that initial response pauses show a variable pattern. Although a definite answer to their function cannot be determined exactly from these data, the following conclusions are consistent with the obtained results.

1. The fact that initial response pauses differed in length from other pauses suggests that this particular type of pause has a joint decoding/encoding function in dialogue.

2. The proposal by Goldman-Eisler that the initial response pause has a single function, i.e., the planning of overall content of a response, *cannot* be correct due to: (a) the absence of initial response pauses in some utterances,

including approximately one-quarter of very long utterances; (b) the frequency of clause-boundary pauses within utterances that—by virtue of their location—cannot by assigned a purely lexical function, as Goldman-Eisler suggested.

3. Although initial response pausing was present in the majority of cases of sustained speech, it was not an *invariable* accompaniment of speech. This in turn means that the suspension of speech is not a *necessary* condition for the planning of speech sequences in the way envisaged by Goldman-Eisler.

The Role of Clause-Boundary Pauses

The demonstration that whole utterances can be produced without pauses of any kind can now be extended to the role of clause-boundary pauses. Results showed that 68.0% of all clause transitions were fluent. Expressed in terms of the frequency of clause-boundary pausing, the MC was found to pause on average once in every 2.6 clauses and the WC once in every 4.1 clauses where utterances were longer than a single clause. It is therefore an overwhelmingly strong effect in these data that production of a single clause does not require an attendant clause-boundary pause. This finding is one that previously has not been investigated in detail, largely due to the selected speech data used for analysis. For example, Boomer (1965) assumed that planning decisions were made at the beginning of clauses and that the decision-making task was directly reflected in pausing. (Boomer's unit of analysis was the phonemic clause; there is evidence of correspondence between the phonemic clause and the surface structure clause—e.g., Dittmann & Llewellyn, 1967; Halliday, 1970.)

Boomer assumed that planning and speaking must be concurrent operations in the case of clauses without pauses but in so doing begged the question of why some clause transitions were fluent whereas others were not. Boomer also considered that semantic intentions were in some way represented in the structural unit of the clause, that pauses indicated planning, and that the clause was the primary unit of encoding. It is therefore an important finding that there are so many instances of clauses without prior pauses. That the way we speak can be characterized in terms of clause structure is demonstrably true, and that speakers' pauses sometimes coincide with those structural boundaries is also true; but any suggestion of isomorphism between the clause and the pause should be abandoned. Once all spontaneous speech data in a corpus are included in analysis, far too many within-clause pauses and far too many clauses without detectable pauses are found for this to be a sensible construction.

If the connection between pausing and particular structural units of a specified length and form is not productive, what other explanation can be given for the presence and patterns of clause-boundary pauses in spontaneous speech?

The point has been made that some whole utterances were without pauses of any kind. The corollary is that some planning of speech intentions must have been carried out simultaneously with the act of speaking. However, in relation to the large amount of data analyzed, the number of utterances without pauses was very small. A fair summary of the data would be that utterances longer than three surface structure clauses in length were not found without a pause in some position and that the majority of utterances that had no initial response pause and no other pause were either short, single-word utterances, or were longer, descriptive, or anecdotal utterances.

By contrast, very long utterances can be *commenced* without an initial response pause but not *sustained* without clause-boundary pauses. It is in this context that a claim that pausing is a necessary accompaniment of speech can now be validly argued. It is not that each clause "requires" a pause but that sequences of speech cannot be sustained without them. This means that speaking spontaneously is dependent on pausing but not in the manner suggested in previous research. It also provides the basis for a strong argument that clause-boundary pauses serve a planning function related to the semantic intentions of the speaker for the following reasons.

As Goldman-Eisler suggested, it appears that speakers must suspend vocal activity frequently in sustained speech. But since the location analysis showed that the length of speech sequences between those intervals did not correspond to a known, specified structural unit, such pauses most likely indicate points of thinking about what it is the speaker wishes to say and perhaps reflecting upon what she or he has already said, rather than of planning to say it in a specific structural form. Obviously, speech can be characterized as structurally regular, and it is not surprising that pauses often relate to such regularities. However, the point at issue is whether production of pauses is determined by something in the nature of the grammar or whether the pause reflects some superordinate, semantic planning operation that is then translated into an appropriate structural form. A third possibility is a simultaneous assembling of form and meaning. Although the present data do not allow resolution of this problem, it seems more likely that structural factors play a relatively minor role, in temporal terms, in speech production. It does not appear from these data that speakers "think in clauses" but rather that an idea is formulated and then rapidly assembled into units of about three to four clauses that conform to the structural constraints of the language.

This suggested explanation for clause-boundary pauses does not account for all the data. Some long, fluent runs within utterances were also located and some novel utterances found that had no pauses at all. This strongly confirms Boomer's (1965) suggestion that planning and speaking can operate simultaneously in speech production. However, the fact that in the former case the material produced was relatively simple conceptually and that in the latter case the utterances were all very short suggests that there are marked constraints in the degree to which multiple processing could determine the outcome of the speech-production process without the concurrent contribution of unfilled pauses.

The foregoing conclusions should not be taken to mean that there are no other possible functions for such pauses. For example, the question of whether syntactic planning takes up a proportion of pause time is not answered from these data. However, if this is the case, the fact that there is no one–to–one correspondence between the clause and pause suggests that the syntactic features of a number of clauses can be quickly assembled. It also seems likely that because speaking is a highly developed skill by middle age, adults have developed some implicit rules concerning the timing of speech in dialogue situations. Though it is impossible to speak for longer than a few seconds without pausing, some clause-boundary pauses may be "for the speaker" in the above sense. This would explain why clause-boundary pauses still occur in tasks that involve reading prepared material, even though within-clause pauses do not. Even if some proportion of clause-boundary pauses were taken up by some or all of these additional functions, this would further reinforce the claim that the remaining pauses serve a general planning function; i.e., the proportion of planning pauses coincident with clause boundaries would be further reduced, and the ratio of pauses to number of clauses would increase.

A brief comment is necessary on the class differences, which were found to be most pronounced *after* speakers had commenced an utterance. Brotherton (1976) has shown that these middle-class speakers produced more elaborated, complex and less redundant responses than the working-class subjects. The location analysis of clause-boundary pauses tends to confirm the view that planning sustained speech sequences is a skill that is significantly class related. This can in turn be linked with the fact that 17% of all WC clauses consisted of fluent speech runs, compared with 7% of the MC, and that these were associated with more descriptive material. That MC subjects may elaborate beyond what the situation requires is entirely possible, but the results suggest that the type of material they produced required more planning breaks than that of the WC. These data indicate the process by which clause-boundary breaks in the stream of speech can be used to organize and maintain a more elaborated and less redundant form of conversational speech.

Filled Pauses

Location Analysis: Proportion of Filled Pauses

The procedure followed for analyzing filled pauses was the same as for unfilled pauses. Table 8.5 sets out the distribution of filled pauses in three locations; 41.1% of all filled pauses fell at structural boundaries.

TABLE 8.5
Distribution of Filled Pauses Within Utterances, in Three Locations.

		At Beginning of Utterance	At Clause Boundary	Within Clause	Total
MC	N	58	110	302	470
	%	12.3	23.4	64.3	100.0
WC	N	37	52	103	192
	%	19.3	27.1	53.6	100.0

The theoretical question at issue is whether the filled pause can be regarded as functionally equivalent to the unfilled pause. Even if the two are related, there was clearly a strong "preference" for the use of the unfilled pause, occurrence rates being three times as great for the MC compared with the filled pauses and four times as great for the WC; the relative occurrence rate between the two types of pause was sustained by both groups and by all 10 subjects across both time samples.

Some indirect evidence on the functional equivalence hypothesis comes from the finding that in the case of the filled pause measure, there was a significant main effect for the two time samples ($F = 14.985$, $df = 1, 8, p < .01$), with significantly more filled pauses being produced in the first 10 minutes of the interview, the decrease in the middle phase of the interview being apparent in 9 out of 10 subjects. The effect was independent of the class grouping of subjects as indicated by a nonsignificant interaction term. This result suggests that some differential situational factor was operating with respect to the two time samples to which only one of the pause measures was responsive.

Applying the concept of potential pause positions, a comparison was made of opportunities to pause at potential pause positions with the actual distribution of filled pauses. Table 8.6 sets out results.

TABLE 8.6
Means and Standard Deviations—Distribution of
Filled Pauses as a Ratio of Potential Pause Positions.

		At Beginning of Utterance	Location At Clause Boundary	Within- Clause
HG	Mean	.127	.073	.036
	Standard deviation	.059	.037	.019
LG	Mean	.055	.029	.011
	Standard deviation	.050	.016	.005

TABLE 8.7
Percentage Distribution of Filled Pauses Within Utterances,
in Three Locations and Across Two Time Samples.

		At Beginning of Utterance	At Clause Boundary	Within-Clause	Total
MC	Time 1	9.1	11.7	34.3	55.1
	Time 2	3.2	11.7	30.0	44.9
					100.0
WC	Time 1	16.1	15.6	35.4	67.2
	Time 2	3.1	11.5	18.3	32.8
					100.0

In all positions, the MC utilized the filled pause considerably more than the WC, with differences between the groups being most stable in the within-clause position ($t = 3.25$, 8 df, $p < .01$, one-tailed). By contrast with the unfilled-pause results, the MC paused significantly more often in the initial response position ($t = 1.96$, 8 df, $p < .05$, one-tailed), utilizing 13% of potential pause positions compared with 6% by the WC. Clause–to–clause transitions were again more fluently made by the WC than the MC, but differences were not significant.

Because of a significant time sample effect on this measure, the distribution of filled pauses according to location in each of the two time samples was determined, and results are set out in Table 8.7. The relative percentage of filled pauses in the clause-boundary position did not alter markedly for either group across the two time samples, but a sharp reduction in filled pauses in the second time sample was found in the initial response position.

Co-Occurrence of Filled and Unfilled Pauses

It was suggested earlier that the function of filled pauses may be related to difficulty in word selection. An alternative explanation was offered by Maclay and Osgood (1959), who argued that the filled pause may function as a signal to the listener that the speaker has not finished what she or he wishes to say and that the filled pause might therefore be expected to be especially prominent following an unfilled pause.

Boomer (1965) found that only 28% of filled pauses were preceded by an unfilled pause and that most of these unfilled pauses were relatively short. By contrast, O'Connell, Kowal, and Hörmann (1969) found that 73% of filled pauses were preceded by an unfilled pause but in later work found that a higher proportion of filled pauses were followed by unfilled pauses (O'Connell & Kowal, 1973). O'Connell, Kowal, and Hörmann (1969)

TABLE 8.8
Percentage of Filled Pauses Preceded by Unfilled
Pauses of Varying Lengths

	MC + WC
Preceded by an unfilled Pause	
(a) longer than average length unfilled pause	13.5
(b) less than average length unfilled pause	24.1
	37.6
Not preceded by an unfilled pause	62.4
	100.0

indicated that the filled pause was followed by an unfilled pause in about 47 to 50% of instances.

Table 8.8 sets out sequence results for the total sample. It excludes cases where a pause of either type was interrupted by a speech disturbance or automatic phrase. Figures are also given for the average length of these unfilled pauses that preceded filled pauses. The figures supported Boomer's (1965) claim that filled pauses are generally not preceded by an unfilled pause and certainly provide no strong backing for the claim that the filled pause is a response to the speaker's own silence. The majority of filled pauses were not preceded by an unfilled pause at all, and where they were, those unfilled pauses tended to be shorter on average than the mean pause length for the group in question.

All instances where filled pauses were *followed* by unfilled pauses were also counted and converted to percentages, and these were found to approximate the figures given by O'Connell, Kowal, and Hörmann (1969); the filled pause was followed by an unfilled pause in 51.8% of cases. The two sets of results together indicate that it is more common for the filled pause to be followed by an unfilled pause than to be preceded by one. The difference in percentages is not large, but the figures clearly fail to support Maclay and Osgood's argument concerning the role of the filled pause as a response to one's own silence. When the filled pause is preceded by an unfilled pause, those unfilled pauses are shorter than subjects' mean pause lengths, contradicting Maclay and Osgood's (1959) suggestion that the critical factor in producing a filled pause is the duration of the nonspeech interval.

The Role of Filled Pauses

Maclay and Osgood (1959) proposed that in dialogue situations, the filled pause indicates that the speaker wishes to retain control of the floor and that filled pauses therefore tend to prevent interruption by others. This social-psychological perspective on the function of filled pauses might appear to be at variance with the earlier suggestion that filled pauses occur at points of encoding difficulty. But it now is argued that the filled pause has a dual function: It is an interpersonal signal, produced in social situations, that is used where some processing difficulty or uncertainty is being experienced.

Although a dual role for filled pauses has been proposed previously by other researchers, data analysis has often been dependent on correlational techniques, and the way in which that dual role was actually expressed in speech was not made clear.

The suggestion of a dual role for the filled pause arises from studying the distribution of filled pauses shown in Table 8.7. The majority of filled pauses were found at the within-clause position, most probably indicating difficulties of lexical choice. Table 8.7 also indicated, however, that the time sample main effect for the filled pause measure was due to a marked fall in filled pauses by the middle of the interview and that the fall was most apparent in the initial response and within-clause positions. The higher proportion of initial response filled pauses in the first 10 minutes of the interview, compared with the middle phase, is most likely due to greater interpersonal stress and uncertainty during the establishment of a working relationship between the two parties in the interview situation. By contrast the reduction in filled pauses in the within-clause position later in the interview is probably related to a measured reduction in word complexity for both groups in that same period (Brotherton, 1976).

The fall in filled pauses in the initial response position in the second time sample reflects the fact that the interview was then well advanced. All interpersonal situations incorporate nonverbal signals of various kinds that assist in regulating social encounters; the vocalized hesitation or filled pause is, it is suggested, one such regulator that signals to the other speaker that some uncertainty about how to proceed is being experienced by the speaker but that she or he intends to continue speaking.

That so many filled pauses were found in the initial response position makes it extremely unlikely that the lexical choice hypothesis is a viable one for pauses in that position. When this effect is considered in conjunction with the significant fall in filled pauses by the middle of the interview, such pauses can fairly be regarded as part of a social signaling system that helps to regulate interpersonal conversation. When uncertain about how or in what way to respond, the filled pause in that position would indicate to the listener that the speaker has not finished and is uncertain about her or his next speech action. The results of the present study are consistent with those of Lalljee and Cook (1973), who found that filled-pause rates were much higher in the first 3 minutes of a 9 minute sequence but showed a marked and significant drop after the first 3 minutes. They concluded that uncertainty decreases as social interaction progresses, but the finer analysis performed on the present data suggests that this generalization is too sweeping. The majority of filled pauses are not accounted for in this way, and uncertainty concerning lexical choice is still a strong factor, as indicated by the large number of filled pauses in the within-clause position.

Finally, the data in Table 8.6 produced significant class effects due to proportionately more filled pauses by the MC in the initial response and within-clause positions. One of the most consistent effects noted for the filled pause in previous studies is its higher incidence amongst educated speakers, an effect that is strongly confirmed here. In view of the explanation that initial response pauses signal uncertainty in social situations, the only sensible conclusion is either that educated speakers are less certain and WC speakers more fluent, at least in this communicative situation, or that MC speakers signal uncertainty in ways that differ from those of WC speakers (Brotherton, 1976).

The Role of Within-Clause Pauses

The within-clause pause is often referred to as the "true hesitation pause," indicating a point of encoding difficulty with particular lexical items. However, the research literature has assumed rather than demonstrated that within-clause pauses indicate points at which single lexical items are being selected. Maclay and Osgood's (1959) partial analysis of within-clause pauses is the one report that showed that at least some pauses may be used for planning units larger than the word (e.g., phrases). For this reason, it was decided to categorize within-clause pauses initially according to the complexity of individual items. This would indicate whether within-clause pauses are primarily associated with single items in conversational speech.

An analysis of clause-initial lexical items that were followed by an unfilled or a filled pause was first undertaken on the basis of Boomer's (1965) argument that clause-initial items set strong structural constraints on the sequences that followed and that only final lexical selections are made during that pause period. Detailed results of this analysis are not presented here (see Brotherton, 1976), but it was found that these initial lexical items were accounted for in the following ways. For the unfilled pause, only 12.4% of such items were found to be items that set strong structural constraints. For the filled pause, all but 9.3% of total instances of filled pauses in that position were accounted for by items that set relatively trivial structural constraints (e.g., repetitive, simple conjunctions; automatisms; speech disruptions). Brotherton (1976) argued that such pauses could properly be regarded as functionally similar to clause-boundary pauses, thus eliminating the clustering effect noted by Boomer in the position following the first word of a clause.

Following the foregoing analysis, remaining within-clause pauses were analyzed on the basis of the coding system set out on p. 186.

TABLE 8.9
Percentage Distribution of the Location of Unfilled Pauses Within Clauses.

	MC		WC	
A. *At Major Surface-Structure*				
Phrase Boundaries				
1. Implicit clause boundary	3.6		7.5	
2. Major phrase boundary	21.4		22.1	
B. *Interrupting Major Surface*				
Structure Phrases				
3. NP # VP	8.3		8.9	
4. NP VP # NP	13.6		16.4	
5. # Adjective noun	8.1		4.9	
6. Adjective # noun	5.7		3.5	
7. Within a verb phrase	11.7		12.8	
8. Other	10.9		6.2	
C. *Associated with Speech*				
Disturbances	16.7		17.7	
D. *Total*	100.0	(420)	100.0	(226)

Unfilled Pauses

Table 8.9 sets out the distribution of the remaining within-clause unfilled pauses for each of the two social class groups. The figures in Category A showed that 27.3% of within-clause pauses were asociated not with particular lexical items but with the initiation of a phrase unit, most commonly a prepositional phrase. Categories B3 and B4 together show that 23.5% of breaks were within major surface structure phrases. Category C represented instances where a within-clause pause was associated with one of several speech disruption elements. For both groups, about half of these involved "sentence corrections" and "sentence incompletions," thus indicating some on-line correction to speech intentions. The next largest type of disruption involved repetition of a word or group of words, the majority of which consisted of repetition of a clause-initial noun phrase. Categories B3, B4, and C therefore indicate processing difficulties once a clause has been partially articulated and represent 40.8% of the total.

In the case of Categories B6 and B7, pauses were unequivocally and directly linked to a single lexical item, whereas Category B5 involved two lexical items. An analysis was not made of the verb-phrase component of Category B3 and the noun-phrase component in Category B4, but inspection suggested that the pause was typically followed by multiple rather than single items.

A breakdown of Category B8 revealed that approximately one-third of these pauses preceded items that in a context-free analysis would be classified as function words. For example: "He bought the car and the scooter with # his money"; "He would be away for # a month or so." In such cases, the immediately preceding pause clearly relates to the group and not to the function word in isolation. Once this was taken into account, only 4% of MC pauses in this category preceded function words, whereas there were no such instances for the WC.

Of the words included in Category B7 (Table 8.9) two-thirds of instances for both groups were content items. Hence, when Categories B3–8 were considered together, 50.5% of all within-clause pauses were found to be associated either with single content words or with short phrases where a content word was the key lexical item.

The importance of including all forms of vocalizing is demonstrated by the Category C results. In studies where "noise" of this type is eliminated, the associated pause is presumably attached to the immediately following item and the associated disruption ignored; where the focus is upon processing factors in production, this would represent a severe loss of information and would markedly distort the conclusions drawn from that type of analysis.

Filled Pauses

Table 8.10 sets out the distribution of within-clause filled pauses for each of the two class groups. One-third of all within-clause filled pauses were associated with speech disruptions, mostly accounted for by sentence correction, sentence incompletions, and repetition of a clause-initial noun phrase. Categories B3, B4, and C together accounted for 54.3% (MC) and 70.2% (WC) of all breaks, thereby indicating processing difficulties once a clause had been partially articulated.

Category B8 was analyzed in terms of the content–function word distinction; there were no instances at all of a filled pause preceding a single

TABLE 8.10
Percentage Distribution of the Location of Filled Pauses Within Clauses.

	MC		WC	
A. *At Major Surface-Structure Phrase Boundaries*				
1. Implicit clause boundary	1.0		0.0	
2. Major phrase boundary	12.2		10.5	
B. *Interrupting Major Surface Structure Phrases*				
3. NP # VP	8.6		10.5	
4. NP VP # NP	13.2		26.3	
5. # Adjective noun	8.1		0.0	
6. Adjective # noun	3.0		1.8	
7. Within a verb phrase	10.2		7.0	
8. Other	11.2		10.6	
C. *Associated with Speech Disturbances*	32.5		33.3	
D. *Total*	100.0	(197)	100.0	(57)

function word for either group, except for those few cases where the pause preceded an article or pronoun that in turn was immediately followed by a content item.

Of the items included in Category B7, all of the WC and three-quarters of the MC instances were content words. When Categories B3–8 were totaled, 53.2% of all within-clause pauses were found to be associated with content items.

Inspection of Tables 8.9 and 8.10 indicates that differences in the distribution of pauses *between* the two class groups were not large. Approximately half of both filled and unfilled pauses were associated directly with content items; elsewhere, the most striking difference between the two measures was the relatively stronger link of filled pauses with speech disruptions, which were also shown by Brotherton (1976) to reflect processing uncertainty in social situations.

To summarize the functions of within-clause pauses (in positions other than after the first word of a clause), there was an almost total absence of function words following within-clause pauses (apart from those initiating prepositional phrases, which reflect selection of a unit and not a single word). The pattern of results indicated that content words are considerably overrepresented relative to their occurrence in English. The concentration of pauses preceding content words is thus an unequivocal indication that such pauses reflect lexical choice processes for subjects in both class groups.

The location analysis also indicated that classifying pauses in relation only to immediately adjacent lexical items is likely to result in misleading conclusions. Had the occurrence of pauses prior to function words been taken at its face value, it would have obscured the fact that 20% of unfilled and 11% of filled pauses preceded whole phrases rather than single items. Interview transcripts indicated that these phrases represented the addition of information by tagging phrases onto main clauses. In context, pauses in this position cannot reasonably be considered as pauses for the selection of particular lexical items; the implication is that some processing of speech intentions involves units smaller than the clause but larger than the word. Tables 8.9 and 8.10 indicated that a number of within-clause pauses fell at deep structure boundaries (e.g., NP # VP), which further confirms the view that planning can take place at any one of several levels. This suggests that semantic intentions are not always fully known until the speaker has already begun speaking. Such a conclusion, of course, modifies the claim that within-clause pauses are primarily lexical choice pauses.

It was found that 32.9% of these filled pauses coincided with speech disruptions, especially sentence corrections and sentence incompletions. The disruption appears to indicate a "stop" mechanism on production of the clause in question, and the subsequent filled pause acts as an interpersonal signal to the hearer that the speaker is encountering a processing difficulty but intends to continue.

Tables 8.1 and 8.5 indicated substantially different distributions for filled and unfilled pauses; in the within-clause position, filled pauses appear to be related to interpersonal signaling of processing difficulties associated with lexical choice and choice of units smaller than the clause. However, it is not clear from these data why some processing difficulties are signaled vocally whereas others are not; a stronger methodology, and one that incorporates a wider range of signaling devices (vocal, verbal, and nonverbal), may indicate whether there is some functional independence of the two types of pause or whether the filled pause is simply a sociovocal overlay on an unfilled pause.

The unfilled pause in the within-clause position almost certainly indicates that (1) time is required for planning minor constituents and selecting lexical items (which together account for 77.8% of all instances); and that (2) the remainder follow speech disruptions and reflect planning points for reorganization or recommencement of a speech intention.

The significant class effect for both filled and unfilled pauses in the within-clause position was reflected most strongly in the greater amount of pausing before content words by the MC. Since content words tend to be longer than function words (Miller, Newman, & Friedman, 1958), the fact of these content word differences is consistent with other results in the larger study that indicated that the MC had a significantly greater proportion of multi-syllabic lexical items than the WC (Brotherton, 1976).

Finally, the conclusion from previous research (Rochester, 1973) that pauses that fall within clauses reflect difficulty in the choice of lexical items requires some modification. Once all vocalizations are included for analysis, within-clause pauses are seen to have multiple functions that would not become apparent where specially selected material is the datum. Furthermore, those multiple functions provide important information on the nature and form of the speech-production process under spontaneous conditions.

Summary

General Effects

The occurrence of initial response pauses, filled and unfilled, is a special feature of pausing in dialogue situations. Unfilled initial response pauses reflect both encoding and decoding processes but cannot be considered as pauses for planning the content of an utterance from its beginning to its end, as Goldman-Eisler (1968) claimed. Pauses were often found to be unnecessary for the production of short utterances where the content was descriptive and anecdotal. Initial response pauses are certainly not essential for the production of an utterance, even where the utterance is very long. However, the maintenance of sustained speech sequences, whether an initial response pause is present or not, is dependent on the introduction of clause-boundary pauses. This suggests that speaking "on one's feet" is a type of speech behavior where one idea succeeds another, with the person developing, sustaining, and elaborating speech intentions as she (or he) goes and utilizing pauses at intra-utterance points for the purpose of continuous planning. In that sense, pauses are an invariable and necessary accompaniment of speech. Although some planning in dialogue situations can probably be undertaken while the other person is speaking, the amount of anticipatory and concurrent planning appears to be severely limited unless there is concomitant use of within-utterance pauses.

The majority of clause transitions in sustained speech were found to be fluent, suggesting that the search for a strict correspondence simply between the pause and a specified syntactic unit is not the most useful way of conceptualizing the process of speech production. The data further suggested that unfilled pauses generally represent semantic planning points. Though the representation of meaning may be realized in segments that are shorter than the clause, they are most often realized in segments that are longer than the clause. This view could be said to place the major planning focus in speech production on "ideas" and the associated time required for their formulation.

The suggestion of the primacy of semantic factors in planning and of the association of pauses with semantic factors is very close to Goldman-Eisler's (1968) conclusions but is based on different empirical grounds. The location analysis in the present study has gone part of the way to tightening the empirical–theoretical relationships she proposed.

Within-clause pauses (other than those following the first word of a clause) were found to be related to lexical selection and to planning units intermediate in length between the clause and the word. The inclusion of all vocalizations also led to the conclusion that pauses in the within-clause position that are associated with speech disruptions are unlikely to be lexical choice pauses, but probably function as planning points for reconstructed and/or new clause runs.

Unfilled pauses were found to decrease in length as a function of location (i.e., initial response pauses > clause-boundary pauses > within-clause pauses). This is consistent with the functions proposed for unfilled pauses in each of the three positions and suggests that the various processing tasks involved in the foregoing positions may require successively less time for resolution.

The proposal that unfilled pauses serve a purely processing function can be contrasted with the dual function proposed for the filled pause. In the initial response and clause-boundary positions, the filled pause functions as a social-interpersonal signal that the speaker intends to continue but is uncertain about the content of the utterance; this is also true when the filled pause is associated with speech disruptions in the within-clause position. Other within-clause filled pauses precede more complex lexical items and probably serve as indicators of uncertainty about lexical decisions. The suggestion that the filled pause is a vocal overlay on an unfilled pause requires further investigation; if correct, the filled pause assumes relatively less significance than the unfilled pause in terms of describing the basic features of the speech-production process.

Class Effects

Middle-class subjects produced significantly more filled and unfilled pauses than working class subjects, and differences in all measured locations contributed to the main effect for class in the analysis-of-variance results. The length of unfilled pauses was found to be significant in the clause-boundary and within-clause positions, as was the proportion of pauses in those same locations. In sustained speech, class differences appear only after subjects have commenced speaking, the higher proportion of clause-boundary pauses enabling maintenance of speech in a more elaborated and less redundant form in the MC subjects. Class differences in both unfilled and filled pauses in the within-clause position appear to be related to the greater proportion of longer lexical items produced by MC subjects.

Filled pauses are significantly more common in the initial response and within-clause positions for the MC. The dual function of filled pauses is related to this finding, with pauses in the initial response position indicating a class-related tendency to signal uncertainty about how to continue the speech sequence. A similar function is also apparent in the within-clause position, class differences being especially related to the production of a greater proportion of complex lexical items and phrases amongst MC subjects.

The results suggest that MC subjects exercise more temporal control over their linguistic resources and that they have greater processing facility in manipulating those resources. However, the class differences clearly are relative: all subjects consistently displayed similar patterns and forms of speech behavior but to a greater or lesser extent, consistent with Bernstein's more recent statements on the sociolinguistic codes to the effect that code and class differences are differences of use and not of competence (Bernstein, 1973).

CONCLUSION

In the introduction to this chapter, it was asserted that performance models of speech production have been slow to develop. The present study allows the specification of some empirically derived speaker features that must be taken into account as part of that continous endeavor.

1. Speakers can plan and produce a speech sequence without any measurable time lag between those processes, but there are severe limitations on both the content and length of whole sequences that can be produced in this way.

2. Verbal planning and processing operate at very high speed.

3. In sustained speech, speakers *generally* produce sequences containing more than a single idea and in structural units larger than a single clause. There is no isomorphic relationship between the "idea" and the clause.

4. Speakers can nevertheless formulate speech sequences at any one of several structural levels: the word, phrase, single clause utterance, and multiple clause utterances.

5. Speakers can formulate and structure a new idea while another is being articulated.

6. A single model of the speech-production process can account for class differences in verbal planning strategies.

REFERENCES

Bernstein, B. Social class and linguistic development: A theory of social learning. In A. H. Halsey, J. Floud, & C. A. Anderson (Eds.), *Education, economy and society.* New York: Free Press, 1961.

Bernstein, B. Linguistic codes, hesitation phenomena and intelligence. *Language and Speech,* 1962, *5,* 31–46.(a)

Bernstein, B. Social class, linguistic codes and grammatical elements. *Language and Speech,* 1962, *5,* 221–240.(b)

Bernstein, B. Postscript to the Paladin edition of *Class, codes and control* (Vol. 1). St Albans, Hertfordshire: Paladin, 1973.

Blumenthal, A. L. *Language and psychology: Historical aspects of psycholinguistics.* New York: Wiley, 1970.

Boomer, D. S. Hesitation and grammatical encoding. *Language and Speech,* 1965, *8,* 148–158.

Brotherton, P. L. *Aspects of the relationship between speech production, hesitation behaviour, and social class.* Unpublished Ph.D. thesis, Department of Psychology, University of Melbourne, 1976.

Cook, M. Transition probabilities and the incidence of filled pauses. *Psychonomic Science,* 1969, *16,* 191–192.

Dittmann, A. T., & Llewellyn, L. G. The phonemic clause as a unit of speech decoding. *Journal of Personality and Social Psychology,* 1967, *6,* 341–349.

Fillenbaum, S. Psycholinguistics. *Annual Review of Psychology,* 1971, *22,* 251–308.

Fodor, J. A., Bever, T. G., & Garrett, M. F. *The psychology of language: An introduction to psycholinguistics and generative grammar.* New York: McGraw–Hill, 1974.

Goldman-Eisler, F. The predictability of words in context and the length of pauses in speech. *Language and Speech,* 1958, *1,* 226–231.

Goldman-Eisler, F. Hesitation and information in speech. In C. Cherry (Ed.), *Information theory.* London: Butterworth, 1961.

Goldman-Eisler, F. *Psycholinguistics: Experiments in spontaneous speech.* London: Academic Press, 1968.

Halliday, M. A. K. Language structure and language function. In J. Lyons (Ed.), *New horizons in linguistics.* Harmondsworth, England: Penguin, 1970.

Henderson, A., Goldman-Eisler, F., & Skarbek, A. Sequential temporal patterns in spontaneous speech. *Language and Speech,* 1966, *9,* 207–216.

Jaffe, J., & Feldstein, S. *Rhythms of dialogue.* New York: Academic Press, 1970.

Johnson–Laird, P. N. Experimental psycholinguistics. *Annual Review of Psychology*, 1974, *25*, 135–160.

Kasl, S. V., & Mahl, G. F. The relationship of disturbances and hesitations in spontaneous speech to anxiety. *Journal of Personality and Social Psychology*, 1965, *1*, 425–433.

Lalljee, M. G., & Cook, M. Anxiety and ritualized speech. *British Journal of Psychology*, 1975, *66*, 299–306.

Lalljee, M. G., & Cook, M. Uncertainty in first encounters. *Journal of Personality and Social Psychology*, 1973, *26*, 137–141.

Maclay, H., & Osgood, C. E. Hesitation phenomena in spontaneous English speech. *Word*, 1959, *15*, 19–44.

Martin, J. G. Hesitations in the speaker's product and listener's reproduction of utterances. *Journal of Verbal Learning and Verbal Behavior*, 1967, *6*, 903–909.

Martin, J. G., & Strange, W. Determinants of hesitations in spontaneous speech. *Journal of Experimental Psychology*, 1968, *76*, 474–479.

Matarazzo, J. D., Hess, H. F., & Saslow, G. Frequency and duration characteristics of speech and silence behavior during interviews. *Journal of Clinical Psychology*, 1962, *18*, 416–426.

Matarazzo, J. D., & Wiens, A. Interviewer influence on durations of interviewee silence. *Journal of Experimental Research in Personality*, 1967, *2*, 56–69.

Miller, G. A., Newman, E. B., & Friedman, E. A. Length–frequency statistics for written English. *Information and Control*, 1958, *1*, 370–398.

Nesfield, J. C., & Wood, F. T. *Manual of English grammar and composition*. London: Macmillan, 1964.

O'Connell, D. C., & Kowal, S. Cross-linguistic pause and rate phenomena in adults and adolescents. *Journal of Psycholinguistic Research*, 1972, *1*, 155–164.

O'Connell, D. C., & Kowal, S. *Time aspects and hesitation phenomena in spontaneous speech of children and adolescents.* Unpublished preliminary research report, presented at Midwestern Psychological Association meeting, Chicago, May 1973.

O'Connell, D. C., Kowal, S., & Hörmann, H. Semantic determinants of pauses. *Psychologische Forschung*, 1969, *33*, 50–67.

Rochester, S. R. The significance of pauses in spontaneous speech. *Journal of Psycholinguistic Research*, 1973, *2*, 51–81.

Rochester, S. R., & Gill, J. Production of complex sentences in monologues and dialogues. *Journal of Verbal Learning and Verbal Behavior*, 1973, *12*, 203–210.

Valian, V. V. *Talking, listening, and linguistic structure.* Unpublished Ph.D. thesis, Northwestern University, 1971.

Webb, J. T. Subject speech rates as a function of interviewer behaviour. *Language and Speech*, 1969, *12*, 54–67.

9 Recent Studies on Cognitive Rhythm

Brian Butterworth
University of Cambridge

Frieda Goldman-Eisler
University College, London

INTRODUCTION

The point in the language production process that has seemed the most mysterious, and the most intractable to experimental investigation, has been where what James (1890) has called "the intention of saying a thing [p. 253]" becomes transmuted into a specific plan for the actual linguistic output. Recent models of the process have tried to avoid the problem, though attentive critics like Jonckheere (1966) have been quick to spot the evasion: "The point that interests me about Wales and Marshall's scheme of linguistic performance is this: there is no input for producing. . . . presumably the input for production should be a little arrow at the top into the conceptual matrix— just a cloud above it with 'thinks' inside it [p. 89]!" Alas, Jonckheere does not go on to describe the nature of the conceptual rain that falls from the little cloud or how it might nourish the growth of linguistic trees below. We, of course, cannot really resolve these mysteries, either, but we can report some work that we and our colleagues have carried out that indicates in a general way how this transmutation might work.

The idea we wish to develop is that broadly, the transduction takes place in two identifiable stages. *Stage 1:* A plan is formulated that consists of a complex semantic specification of the shape of the clause or clauses to be output and of the lexical items required to fill slots in the clause structures. *Stage 2:* The plan is executed—realized as an ordered string of morphemes— and the next clause part that is fully realized as words in construction is output; where slots are still not filled by lexical items, the lexicon is searched for items matching the prior specification. The two stages will correspond to

211

temporal characteristics of the speech. Stage 1 will correspond to periods of relative hesitancy, and we shall call it the "planning phase" or "P-phase"; Stage 2 will correspond to periods of relative fluency—"Execution" or "Ex-phases." P- and Ex-phases will alternate such that a P-phase plus an immediately succeeding Ex-phase constitutes a "cycle"; and the regular alternation of planning and execution we shall call "cognitive rhythm." It will turn out that execution functions impinge upon P-phases, since speakers typically say something while planning ahead; and we offer some evidence as to how speakers manage planning and execution tasks at "the same time."

Since speaking typically occurs as part of an interaction between two or more people, the speaker has another task, which is to monitor and regulate the course of the interactional exchange. He may, therefore, have to "trade off" or otherwise arrange in time these planning and social tasks. Two aspects of conversational management have received considerable attention in the literature: first, how speaker turns are assigned in general (conversely, how interruptions are prevented), and second, what functions gaze has in turn assignment and in monitoring the listener. With few exceptions, these aspects have been treated separately from planning, but we examine how the speaker adapts to the competing demands of speech planning and conversational management.

HISTORY

The original observations were reported in 1966 (Henderson, Goldman-Eisler, & Skarbek). It was noticed that spontaneous speech shows a distinctive temporal patterning: Periods of relative hesitancy alternate with periods of relative fluency where both are defined in terms of a pause/phonation ratio, such that there was a constant ratio of silence in the hesitant phase to phonation in the immediately succeeding fluent phase. This mathematical dependency suggested a psychological dependency; the fluent phase is assumed to execute the Plans formulated in the preceding hesitant phase. That is to say, the temporal rhythm of speech reflects an underlying "cognitive rhythm"; the hesitant–fluent cycle (one hesitant phase plus the immediately succeeding fluent phase) reflects a planning–execution cycle.

Additional support for this idea was provided by further observations. Indications that speakers did not know what they were about to say were more marked in Planning phases than in Execution phases. For example, pauses not at grammatical boundaries constituted a higher proportion of pauses in the assumed Planning phases than in Execution phases (Henderson et al., 1966). Likewise, breathing pauses were more likely to fall at clause boundaries in Execution phases than in Planning phases, even taking into account the greater percentage of grammatical pauses in Execution phases (Goldman-Eisler, 1968, Chapter 7).

However, not all samples of spontaneous speech showed this rhythm, and the question arises: Why only some samples? In a subsequent study, we (Goldman-Eisler, 1967) found that there was a significant relationship between the occurrence of rhythm and speech samples containing more than 30% pausing; and we argued that cognitive rhythm is only employed in organizing speech output when the content is demanding enough in novelty or complexity to require a substantial proportion of pausing.

Historically, this paper turned out to be misleading. Jaffe, Breskin, and Gerstman (1972) reported that temporal patterns similar to these could be generated randomly and crucially were more likely to be identified when the percent pause parameter is fairly close to our criterial value and "cognitive rhythm" is thus artifactual. In the original study (Henderson et al., 1966), it was observed that reading, which presumably does not require this kind of cognitive organization, did not typically show temporal rhythm. Since readings are simply less hesitant than speech, the absence of rhythm may just be an artifact of the very low pause value (often below 20%) where, according to Jaffe et al. (1972), rhythm is unlikely to be randomly generated. A problem with the interpretation of the later study (Goldman-Eisler, 1967) is that data were pooled from readings, simultaneous translations, and spontaneous speech. The 30% criterion holds for the readings and translations, but not for the spontaneous speech samples. And indeed the absence of a criterial effect for a different set of spontaneous speech samples was subsequently confirmed (Butterworth, 1972). The occurrence of rhythm in readings and simultaneous translations can be seen as an indicator that the reader or translator is doing a good job; he or she is putting a lot of cognitive work into it and in the case of reading, perhaps is even trying to give the impression of spontaneous speech. As for the artifact hypothesis, it is only tenable if rhythmic phases fail to predict the behavior of other pertinent variables. We have already mentioned two pauses—grammatical and breathing— where rhythm is predictive, and others are described later.

A natural next step was to examine the semantic and structural properties of rhythmic cycles. A number of authors have suggested, not implausibly, that speakers plan out their utterances in terms of well-understood structural units—e.g., phonemic clauses or tone groups (Boomer, 1965; Boomer & Laver, 1968); (surface) sentences (Fodor, Bever, & Garrett, 1974; Fromkin, 1968, 1971; Miller, Galanter, & Pribram, 1960; Wundt, 1912). However, cycles tend to last on average between 10 sec and 18 sec but can be as long as 39 sec (Butterworth, 1975; Henderson et al., 1966), and although no one has reported the mean duration of a clause or sentence, these values are considerably longer than most single sentences found in our corpora. Since linguistics has not, traditionally, treated structures larger than the sentence, syntactic analysis of the speech within cycles could not provide adequate tools for this job. Moreover, it was semantic, rather than syntactic, factors that seem to contribute to the variation of pause time between speech samples

(Goldman-Eisler, 1968, Chapter 5), and it made sense, therefore, to look to semantic factors for an account of the pausal variation within samples.

In this study (reported in Butterworth, 1975), speech from unrehearsed and cognitively demanding conversations was analyzed for temporal rhythm and transcribed for syntactic and semantic analysis. Out of a total of 43 cycle transitions, 32 corresponded to the beginning of a new clause; however, there were 183 clauses in all, so cycles would comprise on average about 4.5 clauses.

To get at the semantic structure, we asked eight judges (who were not the original speakers) to divide up a transcript—in normal orthography and punctuation, but with no additional temporal information marked—into "Ideas." Judges had to decide for themselves what these were and would presumably rely upon intuitions employed in marking a précis, taking notes of a lecture, or summarizing an argument. Where more than half the judges agreed on a location as a transition between one "Idea" and the next, we designated that location an "Idea division." Of 32 Ideas, 17 corresponded to cycle transitions. Since cycle transitions and Idea divisions could theoretically occur between any 2 of the 1,736 words (excluding those in nonrhythmic initial and terminal sections) in the three texts, the two categorizations were found to be reliably associated ($G = 42.23$, $p < .001$; G statistic in Sokal & Rohlf, 1973).

It should be noticed that all Idea divisions and all but 11 (out of 43) cycle starts coincided with clause starts; thus clausal boundaries appear roughly to be necessary, but not sufficient, for the occurrence of cycle and Idea boundaries. This syntactic feature is perhaps most usefully thought of as an output constraint on the product of higher planning processes that are semantic in nature.

LOCAL VS. FORWARD PLANNING

During a Planning phase, the speaker continues to speak, but more hesitantly; the speaker seems thus to carry out two cognitive tasks: the organization of the current output (local functions) and the output of the subsequent execution phase (nonlocal functions). One way of examining how the speaker can manage these dual tasks is to compare the kinds of pauses and their distributions in the Planning and Execution phases. We can identify two local functions that some pauses mediate—clause-boundary marking and choosing unpredictable lexical items (Butterworth, 1972; Goldman-Eisler, 1958). Now, if local and nonlocal functions have to be managed in planning phases, we expected that pause distribution would differ between phases in one or both of the following ways: Pauses at clause boundaries and before unpredictable lexical items would be longer; and/or there would be a larger proportion of pauses that could not be attributed to either local function.

For this study, the speech corpus described in Butterworth (1975) was used. It consisted of uninterrupted passages from spontaneous conversations where the speaker was arguing for a proposition he agreed with from a list of 16 propositions on social and moral issues. Four passages showing rhythm were selected, which comprised in total 15 min, 36.6 sec of speech, during which 2,010 words (excluding false starts and repeats) were uttered. Each word was assigned a predictability score on the basis of a preliminary study employing the "cloze" procedure. This method gives a measure broadly equivalent to Goldman-Eisler's (1958) method of estimating transitional probabilities (see Butterworth, 1972, 1976; Schiavetti & Burke, 1974). It was thus possible to classify each pause as 1, preceding an unpredictable item (defined here as a word that one or no judge guessed correctly); 2, marking a clause juncture; 3, preceding an unpredictable word at a clause boundary; 4, "other" pauses. We cross-classified according to whether the pause was in a Planning or Execution phase.

It will be noted (see Table 9.1) that mean pause duration is reliably longer in Planning phases than in Execution phases for: (1) lexical pauses by .32 sec; (2) at clause boundaries by .54 sec; and (3) at "other" pauses by .58 sec. The difference between means for lexical/clause pauses (Column 3) was .37 sec in the same direction but failed to reach significance because of the small number of P-phase exemplars and large variance. The "other" category is responsible for 49% of all pause time in Planning phases, but only 26% in Execution phases. Lexical pauses account for 11% of Planning phase pause time but 25.8% Execution phase pause time (both comparisons significant beyond the 1% level). Pauses associated with *false starts* (see Maclay & Osgood, 1959, for definition) are not included in Table 9.1 but turned out to be six times as great in planning phases (30.8 sec) as in execution phases (5.0 sec).

Given this data, we can estimate the proportion of pause time occupied by making lexical choices and planning ahead. We assume that the purest estimate of lexical choice time comes from non-clause-initial lexical pauses (where clause-marking effects will not be present) in Execution phases. From Table 9.1, we can see that this value for our sample is .57 sec. Therefore the total time will be equal to the number of lexical pauses including the potentially bifunctional clause-initial lexical pauses, multiplied by this value—i.e., $(62 + 38 + 15 + 9) \times .57 = 70.68$ sec, which represents 28% of total pause time.

Similarly, we can estimate the total pause time used for forward planning. This will include "other" pauses in Planning phases, plus for each pause category, the additional time that such pauses occupy when located in Planning phases. This assumes again that Execution phase pauses are the best estimates of pure clause marking and pure lexical choice and that, therefore, the additional time represents the forward planning function. The total, 80.17 sec, represents 31% of all pause time in our sample (see Table 9.2).

TABLE 9.1
Distribution of Pause Duration and Number of Pauses Associated with
Low Cloze Items, Clause Junctures, and Other Pauses in Planning and
Execution Phases in Four Samples of Spontaneous Speech.

		Preceding Low Cloze Items	At Clause Junctures	Pauses At Clause Junctures that Precede Low Cloze Items	Others	Total
P-phase	Pause time	13.3	35.4	11.1	58.1	117.9
	N	15	26	9	46	96
	Mean (in sec)	.89	1.36	1.23	1.26	
Ex-phase	Pause time	35.4	35.2	32.6	35.8	139
	N	62	43	38	52	195
	Mean (in sec)	.57	.82	.86	.69	
	Mean P-Mean Ex (in sec)	.32	.54	.37	.57	
	t-test	2.33	3.47	1.62	3.89	
	between P & Ex	< .025	< .001	< .10	< .001	

[a]From Butterworth, 1976.

TABLE 9.2
Estimate of Total Pause Time Used for Long-Range Planning (Formulating
and Idea).[a]

Additional Time in Each Pause Category of Planning Phase		Number	Total Time
1. Lexical pauses (preceding low cloze items)	(0.89 – .57) ×	15	4.80
2. Clause-boundary pauses	(1.36 – .82) ×	26	14.04
3. Clauses initiated by low cloze item	(1.23 – .86) ×	9	3.33
4. "Other"		46	58.10
		96	80.27

[a]From Butterworth, 1976.

The efficient speaker needs to arrange and organize his or her activities to make time available for a specific cognitive task, which Goldman-Eisler has called "time made"; the speaker may also make use of time made available for some other purpose—"time found" (Goldman-Eisler, 1968, pp.122–123).

In P-phases, the speaker cannot treat "time made" for clause-boundary marking and lexical choice as "time found" for forward planning; rather, the speaker has to make extra time by extending pauses at these locations (27% of the additional pause time in P-phases) and by further output delays at other locations ("other" pauses represent 73% of the additional time). At this stage, we can only present data on mean differences between phases, and thus we cannot identify which P-phase lexical and boundary pauses are bifunctional and whether there is systematic difference between those that are and those that are not.

Notice that only the addition of a forward planning function to "local" pauses shows an extra time requirement. The addition of the two local functions does not show this effect. Boundary pauses that mark clauses starting with an unpredictable lexical item are not longer than those that do not. Thus pauses marking clause boundaries represent "time found" that the speaker can use to make lexical choices (see Table 9.1).

GESTURAL ANALYSIS

Recently we have found a novel way of pinning down the processes of lexical choice and idea planning (Butterworth & Beattie, 1976). Spontaneous speech is typically accompanied by movements of hands and arms, and furthermore, it is a matter of common observation that many of these movements are related to what is being said at the time. Now body movements and gestures, including some mention of those accompanying speech, have been studied before, usually from a semiotic and social point of view (Critchley, 1939; Efron, 1941). But we know of only one previous study that has tried to relate them to cognitive processing, though this study pooled data from all movements of hands, arms, feet, etc. and not just those that were clearly speech related (what we call "speech-focused movements"). The results of that study were inconclusive (Dittmann, 1972).

Our study used judges to first define the class of speech-focused movements (SFMs) as those hand or arm movements that were timed with the stress pattern of the speech. This class, therefore, excludes self-touching movements like scratching, stroking, and rubbing (which would have been included in Dittmann's study). We then had judges break down the class of SFMs into two further subclasses:

1. "Emphatic" movements. These were batonic movements consisting of simple single or repeated movements in one plane.

2. "Gestures."   These were complex movements that seemed to bear an iconic relationship to the words spoken; e.g., the word *raise* was associated with the upward movement of the hand.

There was also a third class of movement, which we called "equilibrium changes." When a single emphatic movement or gesture or a succession of them has finished, the hands return to a rest or equilibrium position. From time to time, the position to which the hands return changes. For example, a speaker may have been returning each hand to one thigh; after the next gesture, he or she returns them instead in a clasp to the lap. Now a striking feature of these changes was that they were not distributed randomly with respect to the temporal and syntactic structure of the speech. Although, theoretically, the speaker could return his or her hands to a new equilibrium position at any time after an SFM, there was, in fact, in spite of the relatively small N in our corpus, a quite noticeable pattern. Out of 38 equilibrium changes, 24 occurred at the ends of clauses, and of these, 13 occurred at phase transitions (both distributions reliably nonchance at 0.1% level).

To go back to SFMs, the first interesting feature was that SFMs distributed differently with respect to Planning and Execution phases (see Table 9.3). We plotted movement type (gesture vs. emphatic movements) against phase (Planning vs. Execution) and against activity type (initiation of movement occurring on a phonation [S] vs. on a hesitation [H], per 1,000 sec. We tested data by analysis of variance on the rates in each category (see Table 9.4). It can be seen that Execution phases attracted more SFMs than Planning phases,

TABLE 9.3
The Rate of Production (per 1,000 Seconds) of SFMs, Gestures, and SFMs-Gestures During Pauses (H) and Phonations (S) In Planning (P) and Execution (Ex) Phases.

		H	*S*	*Mean Rate*
SFMs	P	118.4	191.9	153.0
	Ex	341.0	199.7	226.2
	Mean rate	196.5	197.5	
Gestures	P	59.2	44.3	52.2
	Ex	280.1	106.9	139.4
	Mean rate	136.7	89.6	
SFMs Gestures	P	59.2	147.6	100.9
	Ex	60.9	92.8	86.8
	Mean rate	59.8	107.9	

[a]From Butterworth & Beattie, 1976.

but more interestingly, there was an interaction between phase and activity such that SFMs tended to start on phonation in P-phases, but in hesitations in Ex-phases.

A further breakdown of the data shows that this interaction is due to the distribution of gestures—not emphatic movements, which do not themselves show this interaction.

Why should "gestures" be so distributed, and emphatic movements not? Emphatic movements will be closely linked with intonational emphasis; that is, we should expect the durations of the emphatic movement and of the syllable receiving nuclear stress to overlap. There is evidence from the study of speech errors that stress assignment and lexical selection take place independently, since when the to-be-stressed word is mislocated or transposed with another word, the stress pattern of the sentence is unaffected; the stress does not move with the word (Fromkin, 1971). It may, therefore, be the case that it is possible for the speaker to assign emphasis, knowing the syntactic structure but without having decided on the final lexical form of the thought he or she wishes to express. Incidentally, it should be noted that the distribution of emphatic movements is again reliably distinct from gestures (see Table 9.4).

On the other hand, we can usually detect an iconic relationship between gestures and lexical items. This would indicate a semantic characterization of some specificity at the moment the gesture begins. It is thus of particular

TABLE 9.4

Analysis of Variance of the Rates Per Unit Time (1,000 Seconds) of Speech-Focused Movements in Planning and Execution Phase (P, Ex) and by Activity Type—Hesitation (H) and Phonation (S) [a]

A. All Speech-Focused Movements				
Source	MS	df	F Ratio	P
Phase type (P/Ex)	68,121.00	1	8.65	$p < .05$
Activity type (H/S)	5,278.03	1	.67	NS
Phase × Activity	59,853.62	1	7.60	$p < .05$
Error	7,871.87	12	—	—

B. Gestures and SFMs-Gestures				
Source	MS	df	F Ratio	P
Movement type (Gesture/SFMs-Gestures)	10,639.76	1	1.30	NS
Location in rhythm (PH, PS, ExH, ExS)	22,205.17	3	2.71	NS
Movement type × Location in rhythm	25,751.75	3	3.15	$p < .05$
Error	8,186.28	24	—	—

[a]From Butterworth & Beattie, 1976.

TABLE 9.5
Mean Duration of the Delay Between Gestures and the
Associated Word, Analyzed by Syntactic Class, Clause Position,
and Clause Length.[a]

	A.	Syntactic Class				
	N	V	Adj.	Pron.	Prep.	Dem. Adj.
M_1	.915	.736	.747	1.20	2.33	1.06
M_2	.770	.661	.664	.905	.583	1.06

	B.	Clause Position (in Words)			
	1–2	3–4	5–6	7–8	8 +
M_1	1.29	.534	.881	1.82	.804
M_2	.737	.393	.672	1.22	.746

	C.	Clause Length (in Words)			
	1–4	5–8	9–12	13–16	17 +
M_1	.498	.868	.744	.810	1.26
M_2	.498	.706	.650	.540	.990

[a]From Butterworth & Beattie, 1976.
M_1 = all gestures that show some delay.
M_2 = M_1 + gestures that are initiated with or during the word.

interest that gestures are, first of all, most frequent in Ex-phases after a broad plan has been formulated. Second, the onset of a gesture precedes the word it is associated with, occasionally is synchronous with it, but never follows it (see Table 9.5). And, third, it should be recalled that there is an interaction between the phase factor and whether the gesture onsets in a hesitation or in a phonation (Tables 9.3 and 9.4).

It seems that the speaker has formulated semantic characterizations of the to-be-uttered lexical items by the time he or she embarks on the Ex-phase and simultaneously searches for the lexical realization of semantic characterization and a gesture. Since the ensemble of gestures is, of course, much smaller than that of the mental lexicon, search time will be shorter for gestures and hence will yield an asynchrony. Asynchronies, which show up in those gestures starting in hesitations, will then be proportionately less frequent in P-phases, since at points in the utterance where a lexical item is required, the semantic specification still needs to be formulated.

SOCIAL ADAPTATION TO COGNITIVE DEMANDS

In addition to planning output, the speaker in conversations has the task of managing the interactions. Not only does he or she talk, but must also monitor the effects of that talk on the listener or listeners and from time to time modify what is being said or how it is being said to achieve some desired effect. Listeners, of course, become speakers; and thus speakers may also need to fend off listeners' attempts to take the floor. How does the speaker manage these simultaneous task demands?

If the speaker has an Idea that he or she wishes to express uninterruptedly, then the greatest cognitive load will be carried by the P-phase. Therefore, the speaker should try to avoid in this phase the additional cognitive task of monitoring listener reaction.

Another ground for predicting that gaze will be averted from the listener during P-phases can be derived from what is known about turn-yielding cues in conversations. Silence is one such cue and indeed seems an almost (though not quite) necessary but not sufficient indication for speaker change. Listener-directed gaze and clause endings are two others. Combinations of these cues are potent listener-response elicitors (Duncan, 1972, 1973; Kendon, 1967). The speaker will thus be particularly vulnerable to interruption during periods when pauses are frequent and long. Therefore, he should try to avoid listener gaze during P-phase; especially gaze + clause ending + pause.

Geoffrey Beattie, a research student at Cambridge, has been carefully analyzing the pattern of gaze in relation to the distribution of pauses and clauses for the corpus used in the study of gestures described earlier. He plotted percentage listener-directed gaze (G_1) by their position in the clause. It can be seen from Table 9.6 that for all but two clause positions, G_1 is more probable in Ex-phases.

Beattie has also argued that gesture display may function to prevent interruption and that gesture termination may serve as a cue that the speaker is willing to yield the floor. It turns out that at the end of Ex-phases, there is a 10:1 preponderance of gesture termination over gesture display; whereas at the end of P-phases, the ratio is only 5:3. Thus both gaze and gesturing, which have an interactional, conversational management function, adapt to cognitive demand as indicated by phase pattern.

We hypothesized that one reason why gaze aversion would be more likely in P-phases is that the speaker would try to avoid taking on the additional

TABLE 9.6
Percentage of Locations in Surface Structure Clauses
Accompanied by Listener-Directed Gaze (G_1).[a]

Phase Type	Position in Clause											
	1	2	3	4	5	6	7	8	9	10	11	12
Planning	60.27	50.68	56.76	57.14	57.14	58.33	55.17	57.14	68.75	71.42	80.00	50.00
Execution	60.61	64.65	59.79	65.85	66.15	69.09	72.73	72.73	75.00	70.00	76.92	85.71
Both	60.47	58.72	58.15	63.55	64.83	68.49	62.96	66.00	73.53	70.70	77.50	75.00

[a]From Beattie, 1978.

cognitive load of monitoring the listener while carrying the major load of speech planning. Although in the corpus, the speaker almost never gazes at the listener in a P-phase without also doing so in the immediately succeeding Ex-phase, 11 out of 20 cycles show gaze dominating both phases—i.e., with more than 50% of each phase showing listener gaze (G_1). We would expect that in cycles of this type, the monitoring task would have some detrimental effect on the planning. Beattie has compared several indicators of planning failure in cycles with each phase dominated by listener gaze (G_1G_1) and in cycles with G_1 only in the Ex-phase (G_0G_1) (see Table 9.7).

False starts, which are perhaps the best indicators of a high-level planning failure, are reliably more frequent in G_1G_1 cycles, whether rate is measured against time or number of words. It should be noticed that the effect of G_1 in P-phases is spread across the whole cycle such that the effect is reliable whole cycles. The other measures do not show an effect of G_1 in P-phases, and there are independent grounds for ascribing other functions to filled pauses (Beattie, 1977; Cook & Lalljee, 1972; Goldman-Eisler, 1961); parenthetic remarks may, of course, be part of the Plan.

We think that this evidence of adaptation of interactional behavior to cognitive demands not only validates the notion of planning cycles but also provides an important corrective to views of conversational management that take no account of the cognitive tasks the speaker must undertake (as in Argyle & Cook, 1976).

TABLE 9.7
Mean Filled Hesitation Rate (Measured in Words) Per Phase and FH Rate Per Unit Word Spoken Within the Hesitant and Fluent Phases of Cycles with the H Phases Dominated by Gaze Aversion ($G_0 G_1$ Cycles) or Gaze ($G_1 G_1$ Cycles).

| | | Type of Cycle | | | | | |
| | Hesitation Type | $G_0 G_1$ ($n = 7$) | | | $G_1 G_1$ ($n = 11$) | | |
		H	F	Both	H	F	Both
Hesitation rate (in words)	False starts	1.28	0	1.28	3.64	1.45	5.09
	Parenthetic remarks	0.86	1.43	2.29	0.73	1.27	2.00
	Repeats	0.14	0.57	0.71	0.27	0.37	0.64
	Filled pauses	0.86	1.28	2.14	0.55	0.73	1.28
Hesitation rate, per unit word spoken	False starts	0.0689	0	0.0221	0.1558	0.0609	0.179
	Parenthetic remarks	0.0463	0.0364	0.0396	0.0312	0.0533	0.0424
	Repeats	0.0075	0.0145	0.0123	0.0116	0.0155	0.0136
	Filled pauses	0.0463	0.0326	0.0370	0.0235	0.0306	0.0271

[a]From Beattie, 1978.

CONCLUSIONS

We have discussed only briefly a few results from a continuing program of studies of cognitive and social aspects of conversational behavior. The notion of "cognitive rhythm" has proved itself useful at the theoretical level and has been found to predict the distribution of a number of cognitive and interactional indicators.

We hope we have resolved certain controversies in the interpretation of pause time distribution. In our sample, 84% of pauses can be assigned to one or more of the following three functions: semantic planning, lexical choice, and clause boundary marking. (A comparison with Boomer's [1965] clause–by–clause account is instructive. By his own estimate, he can only assign functions to 22% of pauses, and he leaves the status of juncture pauses problematic.)

Our theoretical approach on pause time distribution was supported by the analysis of the gestural activity accompanying speech and by Beattie's observations on the distribution of gaze across rhythms. Additionally, of course, we have tried to show that interactional aspects of speaker behavior adapt to the patterning of cognitive demands revealed by this rhythm.

Nevertheless, we would be the first to admit that we have only scratched the surface. We know, for example, very little about the form of the Idea and only the barest delineation of the processes of its transmutation into speech. Our corpus has, naturally, been confined to samples clearly showing the temporal concomitants of cognitive rhythm and then only for certain (rather competitive) kinds of academic conversations. We would like to know how planning processes might operate when temporal structure does not reflect a cognitive rhythm. Are cognitively less demanding conversational tasks—i.e., those requiring less novelty and semantic complexity of output—organized in a quite different way?

And we would like to know more about listener behavior when the ideational structure of the speech is not reflected in the temporal structure. Will the pattern of speaker switching be different? There is a further class of questions that strike us as especially interesting. Do listeners adapt their comprehension processes to take advantage of the regular recurrence of periods of relative silence, and is comprehension indeed facilitated by the temporal patterning?

REFERENCES

Argyle, M., & Cook, M. *Gaze and mutual gaze.* Cambridge: Cambridge University Press, 1976.

Beattie, G. The dynamics of interruption and the filled pause. *British Journal of Social and Clinical Psychology,* 1977, *16,* 238–284.

Beattie, G. W. Sequential temporal patterns of speech and gaze in dialogue. *Semiotica,* 1978, *23,* 29–52.

Boomer, D. Hesitation and grammatical encoding. *Language and Speech,* 1965, *8,* 215–220.

Boomer, D., & Laver, J. D. M. Slips of the tongue. *British Journal of Disorders of Communication,* 1968, *3,* 2–11.

Butterworth, B. L. *Semantic analyses of the phasing of fluency in spontaneous speech.* Unpublished Ph.D. thesis, University of London, 1972.

Butterworth, B. L. Hesitation and semantic planning in speech. *Journal of Psycholinguistic Research,* 1975, *4,* 75–87.

Butterworth, B. *Semantic planning, lexical choice and syntactic organisation in spontaneous speech.* (Internal report). Psychological Laboratory, Cambridge, 1976.

Butterworth, B. L., & Beattie, G. *Gesture and silence as indicators of planning in speech.* Paper to the Conference on the Psychology of Language, Stirling, June 1976. (To appear in the *Proceedings,* P. T. Smith & R. Campbell, Eds.)

Critchley, M. *The language of gesture.* London: Arnold, 1939.

Cook, M., & Lalljee, M. G. Verbal substitutes for visual signals. *Semiotica,* 1972, *6,* 212–221.

Dittmann, A. T. The body movement–speech rhythm relationship as a cue to speech encoding. In A. W. Siegman & B. Pope (Eds.), *Studies in dyadic communication.* New York: Pergamon, 1972.

Duncan, S. Some signals and rules for taking speaking turns in conversations. *Journal of Personality and Social Psychology,* 1972, *23,* 283–292.

Duncan, S. Toward a grammar for dyadic conversation. *Semiotica,* 1973, *9,* 29–47.

Efron, D. *Gesture and environment.* New York: King's Crown Press, 1941.

Fodor, J., Bever, T., & Garrett, M. *The psychology of language.* New York: McGraw-Hill, 1974.

Fromkin, V. Speculations of performance models. *Journal of Linguistics,* 1968, *4,* 47–68.

Fromkin, V. The nonanomalous nature of anomalous utterances. *Language,* 1971, *47,* 27–52.

Goldman-Eisler, F. Speech production and the predictability of words in context. *Quarterly Journal of Experimental Psychology,* 1958, *10,* 96–106.

Goldman-Eisler, F. A comparative study of two hesitation phenomena. *Language and Speech,* 1961, *4,* 18–26.

Goldman-Eisler, F. Sequential temporal patterns and cognitive processes. *Language and Speech,* 1967, *10,* 122–132.

Goldman-Eisler, F. *Psycholinguistics: Experiments in spontaneous speech.* London: Academic Press, 1968.

Henderson, A., Goldman-Eisler, F., & Skarbek, A. Sequential temporal patterns in spontaneous speech. *Language and Speech,* 1966, *9,* 207–216.

Jaffe, J., Breskin, S., & Gerstman, L. J. Random generation of apparent speech rhythms. *Language and Speech,* 1972, *15,* 68–71.

James, W. *Principles of psychology* (Vol. I). London: Macmillan & Co., 1890.

Jonckheere, A. Discussion. In J. Lyons & R. J. Wales (Eds.), *Psycholinguistics papers.* Edinburgh: University of Edinburgh Press, 1966.

Kendon, A. Some functions of gaze direction in social interaction. *Acta Psychologica,* 1967, *26,* 22–63.

Maclay, H., & Osgood, C. E. Hesitation phenomena in spontaneous speech. *Word,* 1959, *15,* 19–44.

Miller, G. A., Galanter, E., & Pribram, K. H. *Plans and the structure of behavior.* New York: Holt, Rinehart & Winston, Inc., 1960.

Schiavetti, N., & Burke, J. P. Comparison of methods of estimating transitional probability in speech. *Language and Speech,* 1974, *17,* 347–352.

Sokal, R. R., & Rohlf, F. J. *Introduction to biostatistics.* San Francisco: W. H. Freeman, 1973.

Wundt, W. The psychology of the sentence, 1912. In A. L. Blumenthal (Ed.), *Language and psychology.* New York: Wiley, 1970.

Author Index

Numbers in italics indicate the pages on which complete references appear.

Subject Index

TEXAS A&M UNIVERSITY-TEXARKANA